DRAWN TO SEE

DRAWN TO SEE

Drawing as an Ethnographic Method

Andrew Causey

UNIVERSITY OF TORONTO PRESS

www.utppublishing.com

Library and Archives Canada Cataloguing in Publication

Causey Andrew, 1957–, author
Drawn to see : drawing as an ethnographic method/Andrew Causey.

Includes bibliographical references and index.
Issued in print and electronic formats.
ISBN 978-1-4426-3666-8 (hardback).—ISBN 978-1-4426-3665-1 (paperback).
—ISBN 978-1-4426-3667-5 (pdf).—ISBN 978-1-4426-3668-2 (html).

1. Anthropological illustration. 2. Anthropology—Methodology. I. Title.

GN34.3.F53C38 2016 301.072'3 C2016-902633-7
C2016-902634-5

We welcome comments and suggestions regarding any aspect of our publications—please feel free to contact us at news@utphighereducation.com or visit our Internet site at www.utppublishing.com.

North America
5201 Dufferin Street
North York, Ontario, Canada, M3H 5T8

2250 Military Road
Tonawanda, New York, USA, 14150

ORDERS PHONE: 1-800-565-9523
ORDERS FAX: 1-800-221-9985
ORDERS E-MAIL: utpbooks@utpress.utoronto.ca

UK, Ireland, and continental Europe
NBN International
Estover Road, Plymouth, PL6 7PY, UK
ORDERS PHONE: 44 (0) 1752 202301
ORDERS FAX: 44 (0) 1752 202333
ORDERS E-MAIL: enquiries@nbninternational.com

Every effort has been made to contact copyright holders; in the event of an error or omission, please notify the publisher.

This book is printed on paper containing 100% post-consumer fibre.

The University of Toronto Press acknowledges the financial support for its publishing activities of the Government of Canada through the Canada Book Fund.

Printed in the United States of America.

To My Partner in Life, Michael D. Arnold

In Memoriam: Op. Sabrina Doli Marpaung and
Op. Sabrina boru br. Sinaga, my friends "Partoho" and "Ito."

CONTENTS

FIGURES

CHAPTER 4

CHAPTER 5

CHAPTER 6

CHAPTER 7

ETUDES

CHAPTER 2

CHAPTER 3

CHAPTER 4

CHAPTER 5

CHAPTER 6

CHAPTER 7

ACKNOWLEDGMENTS

I'm cheered to think that it's finally time to acknowledge all who've helped me think up and write this book. Top of the list are all my Visual Anthropology students at Columbia College Chicago who, over the past eight years, have helped me to craft the drawing "Etudes" found here. With their thoughtful participation, I was able to discover ways to help them see their world ethnographically.

Four colleagues from Columbia College Chicago—Joan Erdman, Teresa Prados-Torreira, Rami Gabriel, and Steve Asma—helped me with theoretical and practical issues over the years, often offering me insights into academic fields far from my own. Thank you. I have great gratitude for the three anonymous readers whose generosity in sharing ideas and comments (as well as insightful criticisms) helped me better structure the work. I would like to thank Stacy Pigg for her thoughtful and timely suggestions, but this book would not have come to fruition without the support and help of Executive Editor Anne Brackenbury and Editorial Assistant Julia Cadney at the University of Toronto Press, and freelance copy editor Eileen Eckert; thanks to you all.

Great thanks go to my artist-anthropologist colleagues—several of whom I met while writing this book—who have offered their critiques, ideas, edits, and especially permission to use their drawings, and in doing so helpfully supported my research: Carol Hendrickson, a smart and dependable friend who has been a mentor to me, and Rudi Colloredo-Mansfeld, Christine Eber, Zoe Bray, Gillian Crowther, Manuel Joao Ramos, and Troy Lovata. Thank you for all your help.

Betty Edwards really got me started on all this, for I received her book as a college graduation gift back in 1979. It helped me access my own artistic abilities, and inspired me again when it resurfaced on my desk in 2005. When I reached out to her via email for extra assistance, it started a lively conversation that continues today. I want to thank her for her sage advice and strong support of this project.

Kirin Narayan and Ken George are the ones who prodded me to do what I kept *saying* I wanted to do, and I thank them for their persistent encouragement all these years.

I think I'd have nothing to write about if I didn't refer back to my experiences with Batak friends on Samosir Island who gave so generously of their time when I was doing my research. I can't even begin to thank a most dazzling person, Kathleen Adams, who has been my friend and colleague for over 40 years, since we were undergraduates together at the University of California, Santa Cruz. I hope you know how much you've helped me over the years.

I want to give thanks to my deceased parents for providing me with four delightful, funny, intelligent, and loving siblings who helped raise me, form me, and challenge me all these years; I appreciate all that you do. Lastly, I want to thank my life partner, Michael Arnold, who read and edited every page of this book, patiently identifying dis-clarities and marking missing verbs: you've supported me with love all the way through.

CHAPTER 1

INTRODUCTION

Drawn to See

As if doing ethnography wasn't already enough of a challenge, what if I started this slim book by suggesting that you might not be able to see very well?

Ethnographers already have a challenging job to do without me criticizing the ability to see: we try to understand something about social lives and cultural worlds despite using dialects and languages imperfectly, by investigating actions and motivations using methods that are often intrusive and interruptive, by asking lots of questions that are often difficult to answer. And we do this through various forms of transcribing, translating, transliterating, and interpreting into written words such things as personal narratives, folktales, actions, reactions, gossip, history, and artful lies, and by stitching all of this into a final, permanent document that communicates what may end up being a lasting assessment about a single group at a single moment in time from a single perspective. To understand how ethnographers do our work is to conclude that it is a project beyond "complex" and "exacting," beyond "difficult" or "confusing" or "exhausting" or "exhilarating" . . . it is a project that is nearly—yet delightfully—impossible.

There is no way to capture entire cultural worlds[1] in their abundance and in a timely scope, even when they are investigated and experienced daily and

1 My use of the term "cultural worlds" is an attempt to conjure up an image of how most lives, in my experience, are actually lived. We each are drenched in particular social expectations and relations, unavoidable traditions, unexamined assumptions, and object entanglements. At the same time we are all able (in some way or other) to devise extraction strategies, innovative avoidances, reasoned rebuttals, and physical responses. Some features of our social-material matrix are known to us and are part of our everyday chat, whether accepted or resisted. But other features we may be unable to identify or name, much less articulate rationally or emotionally. Perhaps the closest reference to what I am trying to describe here is characterized by Kathleen Stewart's use of the term "worlding":

persistently for an entire year or more, even when it is a collaborative effort;[2] every ethnographer knows this, deep down. Lived experience with others, when the intent is to understand such things as social interactions, can only expose an individual to a modest glimpse of those lives, and only a flicker of that glimpse can be recorded—whether in words, film, sound, or drawing—as documents. Those documents will later be unavoidably partitioned, edited, selected, ignored, forgotten, or lost. And from what remains, the ethnographer will piece together a kind of quilt of what was lived through, hoping that the final product has some truth, some accuracy, some honesty . . . or that it (at the very least) evokes those qualities.[3]

So, knowing that the ethnographic project is "nearly impossible" and yet also recognizing that it is a worthwhile effort, here I am starting a book by saying you might not see very clearly. You might resist me, saying, "The whole thing, this ethnographic experience, is based on the basic senses! You are telling me that I can't see well?!" Yes. That's what this book is about. It is an exploration about how our senses of sight may be failing us, but how we can learn and practice to see more deeply, to not only enrich our ethnographic work, but to enrich our everyday lives. Not everyone will agree with me that we all have impediments to seeing as clearly as we might, and that's okay. Even those people will probably find something of interest or use here, so I urge you to

the acknowledgment we each make, overtly, distractedly, or feverishly, that we are "in" something. She says, "Anything can feel like something you're in, fully or partially, comfortably or aspirationally, for good or not for long. A condition, a pacing, a scene of absorption, a dream, a being abandoned by the world, a serial immersion in some little world you never knew was there until you got cancer, a dog, a child, a hankering . . . and then the next thing—another little world is suddenly there and possible. Everything depends on the dense entanglement of affect, attention, the senses, and matter" (Stewart 2010, 6). We sense our worlds surrounding us and we sometimes tune in, partially aware; other times, "the ordinary hums with the background noise of obstinacies and promises, ruts and disorientations, intensities and resting points. It sediments, rinds up like the skin of an orange, registers invisible airs as public feelings that waver and pulse. It weighs. It demands a tuning in" (ibid.). She refers to these acknowledgments we make as "atmospheric attunements" to what we are "in"; I am using the term "cultural worlds" to refer to her notion of "what we are 'in.'"

2 Ethnographic work is not an extractive process of locating bounded, discernable "social facts" (Durkheim 1982, 52), of course. It rather more resembles a mutually developed process, "a dialogue where interlocutors actively negotiate a shared vision of reality" (Clifford 1988, 43) where that dialogue is understood to be an open-ended, creative act which is struggled over by insiders, outsiders, subcultures, and factions (ibid., 46). "Ethnography, a hybrid activity, thus appears as writing, as collecting, as modernist collage, as imperial power, as subversive critique," (ibid., 13) and documenting the "improvised" character of lived worlds is actually the production of a "serious fiction" (ibid., 10).

3 When the term "culture" was first used in anthropology, it conflated community, identity, language, shared practices, and place, giving the impression that cultures existed as clearly bounded entities. Cathrine Hasse contests the idea that culture is a practiced place that can be studied and interpreted, suggesting instead that the ethnographer's job is to experience how and where people practice cultural activities in (sometimes disruptive or frictive) conversation with objects and words: "Cultural analysis may be an interpretive science in search of meaning, but it is first of all a process of cultural learning wayfaring in geometrical space, which gradually transforms into a dust bunny of practiced place with no beginning or end but increasingly felt frictions. Being a newcomer to this practiced place is to be ignorant of what engages others. And learning engagement implies learning about frictions" (Hasse 2015, 65).

use the ideas and drawing exercises (or as I am referring to them, *Etudes*) here as an entrance to new visual experiences. I don't have all the answers, and I haven't read all the books on the topic.[4] This book is an invitation for you to explore visuality with more curiosity and to allow yourself to play with notions and experiments freely, with me nearby encouraging you and telling stories that might get you motivated.

How did I come to this subject? My own ethnographic research took place over 15 months in 1994 and 1995 at Lake Toba in North Sumatra, Indonesia. My topic concerned the ways that the local Toba Batak people on Samosir Island interacted with Western backpack travelers, particularly during their negotiations in the souvenir marketplace (Causey 2003). Because I was interested in the wood carvers' perspective, I found a master carver who was willing to talk with me about his life and work, then teach me the rudiments of carving. As it turns out, my ethnographic work was as much about creativity and art as it was about tourism and tourists, and because of that I soon realized that my research methodologies would have to include visual documentation, not just the usual ways of getting information such as taking notes via participant observation, mapping, interviewing, and surveying. Photography seemed to be the logical choice for capturing the visual, but photography was not enough, I soon found out.

Those were pre-digital days, so depending on a camera and film to capture events and actions meant waiting weeks before the pictures were developed. I realized I had to have methods at hand that were direct, instantaneous, and unobtrusive: sketching, line drawing, watercolor. Knowing that many times I would have to depend on my drawing skills to record information at any moment meant that my small pocket book would be filled with as many pictorial sketches as verbal ones. As the research unfolded, I discovered ways to keep the two—visual and verbal—in balance with each other, practicing methods that brought out the best of each. There are some things one can capture in words to convey information, some others best photographed, yet other experiences are best drawn. This is one of the reasons I present the ideas in this book: to give you another set of options for collecting, recording, and presenting ethnographic information.

Now, let's have a story.

4 I have had to be very selective in my inclusion of citations and footnotes, despite the fact that there are hundreds of fascinating and deeply interesting works on this and affiliated topics. Trying to limit my temptation to let references proliferate, I decided that this criterion was of paramount concern: each reference must enhance readers' understanding of the specific issue being addressed, either by giving them more details to consider (to help awaken their curiosity) or guiding them to a book or article I think will assist their learning about drawing as an ethnographic method.

"The Marketplace"

When the weekly market on the mainland is over and the vegetable vendors have tossed the rotting remains of tomatoes, peppers, and beans into the overflowing open-weave bamboo trash baskets, and the fruit sellers have packed up the bunches and branches of tropical sweets in sheets of plastic and fabric webbing, and the chicken and fish sellers have washed their hands and knives of blood and intestines, the town cleaners come through. These dour men—first the ones whose long witches' brooms push blackening leaves and split bags before them and then the ones wearing large dark gloves to carry buckets of milky disinfectant to splash the cobblestone pavement as they slowly trudge down the slope to the lake—are the living signs that the marketplace tasks are done. The smell of completion is at once sharply bright, like soda and bleach, and revoltingly sour; one smell never overtakes the other, they simply overlap each other as the breeze happens to change direction.

The cursory cleaning of the market plaza is really done as a gesture to public sanitation, I think, because everyone knows that the afternoon downpour will come in an hour or so and truly wash the cobbles clean, pushing all the rubbish and husks . . . all the skins, feathers, stems, peels, branches, torn bags, broken flip-flops, fallen seeds, spilled rice, piths, and pits . . . pushing everything down to the enormous calm lake that is lapping at the dock. The market's end (this perfunctory cleaning done at about three in the afternoon) often feels like a curtain sweeping across the stage at the end of a performance. Everyone knows how the play will end, but still, the final movements of the cleaners indicate that the show is over until next week.

I'm sitting on the short concrete wall near the dock waiting for the boat to return me to Samosir Island, where I live and do research, so I have leisure time to watch the workers cleaning the plaza in their own slow rhythm. Even so, it's not very hard to imagine how vibrant the marketplace was just a few hours earlier.

Every Saturday, the gray cobbled courtyard of the marketplace—*Tiga Raja*, "The King's Market"—becomes the venue for hundreds of human public enactments. Before the sun lights up the horizon's clouds, wooden boats line up at the concrete dock unloading huge baskets covered in bright blue tarps, racks of emptied bottles, squawking chickens whose legs are tied together, and gunny sacks filled with rice or *kemiri* nuts.[5] Also disembarking are the masses of locals who have come to the market to buy their weekly supplies or to sell their produce. People from the mainland arrive in endless streams of small

5 This is a kind of oil-rich tree nut used in traditional cooking recipes, but is also sold to outsiders to render into "tung" oil for furniture.

buses, each of which honks and threads past another down a narrow street or alley. Vendors vie for the best spots in the courtyard, arguing with a neighbor about an encroaching tarp or woven mat, then unstitching the plastic canvases that cover their baskets of vegetables, of chickens, of fruits, then opening up their huge sacks of grains and their small sacks of spices, then adjusting their buckets of lake fish. Buyers haggle for the best meat and the freshest bananas while the sellers attempt to array their offerings in a visibly pleasing way. Older women, lips stained deep vermilion from betel-nut chewing, push past outsiders like me with determination and unusual strength, while polite younger men in ragged t-shirts make their deliveries as they shimmy past everyone with supple twists, saying "*Sattabi, sattabi*" ("excuse me, excuse me") but without actually touching anyone.

By eight, the market is throbbing with action. There are hundreds of characters and thousands of small gestures in every direction. There are movements that are large and encompassing and that involve large swings of the arms joined by loud voices, and there are other movements that are tender, small, and dainty, the ones that are seen accompanying a raised eyebrow, a puckered lip, a brief flicker of smile as coins are deposited in bras or wallets or pockets. The place vibrates and undulates. Looking around, you can see sales being made: small plastic bags are filled with oil or juice and tied up tight, eggs are wrapped in straw, an extra snake-fruit is given to a regular shopper in appreciation, decapitated chickens are tossed into a loud jangling machine that defeathers them. Everywhere are men, but mostly women, handling their purchases. Bunches of *rambutan* fruit[6] are hidden away from prying eyes, corn meal is eyed suspiciously because it smells of insecticide, a bag of ground coffee is sifted through the fingers to indicate that it has not been cut with rice flour. There are thousands of small details serving as the backdrop to all these thousands of actions: golden tumblers remain on a tall table after thirsty patrons have departed, additional bottles of beer are arranged on a wooden box when three are sold, the candy vendor jiggles his small packets of sweets to attract passing children, a stout woman passes by unaware that a packet of laundry soap has fallen out of her plastic-strap shopping basket. The market is a whirl of subtle actions and movements that are further enlivened by sunlight dappled by passing clouds. Everything is unfolding at once in every direction and there's no way to take it all in—much less record it—even though I've come here for a year of Saturdays. How can I tell you everything I saw?

Now that the market is over and the cleaning men have left, the two overpowering odors waft over, and I have to turn away. I look at the edge of the

6 Rambutan ("hairy") has a bright red skin with long, hairy filaments all over it and a pearly white, very sweet, grape-like flesh inside. It is considered by many to be a delicacy.

lake's water and think of a giant catfish I once saw in a pond back home. Its broad gray-green head came up to the surface of the water and it gaped at me briefly, as if waiting for a crust of bread to be thrown in. I had nothing to offer back then, so we two simply surveyed one another quietly, me staring, it mouthing water in and out and seeming to look at me. I noticed that the pond water didn't really separate from its skin or mouth: they all seemed to be of one substance. After a moment, the catfish slipped back down into the cloudy water and disappeared. That's exactly how the giant lake looks to me now: like an alive thing that might at any moment materialize at the water's edge in the form of a wide-eyed face quietly gaping at me as I gape at it.

Dark clouds were forming over the foothills behind the market plaza now, and the horn of the boat prompted me to stand up and hop on board. The captain didn't wait too long to push off, and we began our ride across the lake, the calm surface at the shore soon turning into choppy waves beyond the small bay. On the jolting ride back to the island, I closed my eyes and tried to remember as many things about the marketplace as I could. I couldn't write because of the jerking movements of the boat across whitecaps, so I pictured it all in my mind and tried to memorize it. Once home, I put away all my fresh food, but then pulled out my drawing pad and tried to draw what I had memorized. I concentrated, with utmost care, on the details of the place, recalling medieval book of hours manuscripts as my model. It took me many Saturday afternoon twilight hours to complete my drawing and then to paint it in watercolors (Figure 1.1). Once done, I was satisfied and had the urge to show it to my Batak friends, Partoho (my carving teacher) and his wife, Ito.

Except for the soft sparking and snapping of his *kretek* cigarette, Partoho was silent as he looked at this picture. Ito was sitting next to him and asked one of the kids to get her glasses off the table so she could see it, too. She was slowly working a splinter of pinewood in between each of her teeth, but other than that, she also sat quietly peering at the image. After a moment or two, Ito said, "That's the school-teacher's sister, the one in the purple *kebaya* there, I recognize her." I told her that this was not really a portrait of any particular person, but rather just an "ordinary" picture. "Well, that's her. I can see it, and that's just how she looks," she replied. "But this one . . ," she said, pointing to the adjacent figure, "you've got the head fabric just sitting on top; that's wrong, they are wrapped behind the head. And this one in yellow, too: it's wrong. Those sarongs would fall right off if they had them like that. Why did you make it wrong like that?" I told her I would fix it next time, since it was too late to correct this painting.

I saw my picture as a kind of mnemonic documentation, a sketch of an ideal place and moment, but Ito saw something different. In addition to minor inaccuracies, she also saw potentiality: pointing to the table in the

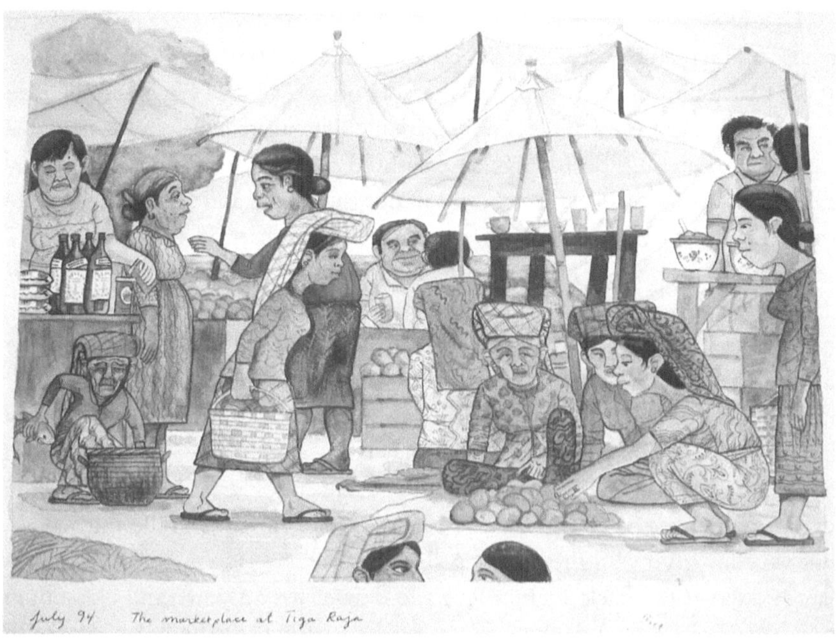

FIGURE 1.1: Drawing of the marketplace at Tiga Raja.

background, where I had painted the three partially finished glasses of tea, she wove a plausible story. "Over here," she said, "this part is good. This is where three people had been talking, and the child they held up to the high table had a bowl of noodle soup. And after they told stories of the day, they left, each going their own way . . . That part is very good, and I like it." She was smiling at the picture but talking to me. I asked my carving teacher what he thought of my imagined re-creation of the Saturday market scene, and all he said was, "*Pasti pasar Tiga Raja. Itulah*" ("It's the Tiga Raja market. That's all").

I Know I Can See More Than I Saw

I came to depend on drawing as an auxiliary ethnographic method the day I became certain that I *could* see more than I *had* seen, more than was recorded in my notes, and more than was documented in my photographs. If the story I just told you has any richness or evocative imagery, it is because drawing the scene enlivened my ability to write about it. But the process of allowing myself to draw ethnographically was more complex than I'm telling it.

I painted that picture of Toba Bataks at the Saturday market in Parapat to record and remember details of the place: Lake Toba, North Sumatra, Indonesia, 1994. I have photographs of the market, of course (e.g., see Figure 1.2), but in those the characteristics of the moment are undifferentiated: the photos are visual stews of competing specificities, all weighted the same, visually and semantically. In the painting, I was able to think out the shapes and forms to re-create them—to *see* them—and to concentrate on those that most honestly represented my experience of the place, without translating the moment to words.

Sometimes, as an artist, I draw and paint what I *hope* I see in order to see it more deeply. Similarly, as an ethnographer, I sometimes draw, paint, or write down what I think I see in order to see it more accurately. It took me several months before I began to see that using drawing as an integral part of my fieldwork was helping my written notes become more perceptive (cf. Stafford 2007, 167). Most of the pictures presented in this book are ones I made while doing my field research on Samosir Island, North Sumatra, in the mid-1990s, but very few of my anthropology colleagues have ever seen them. They have lain hidden at the back of my office file drawer for 20 years, and explaining why they have stayed in the dark is an essential part of the book. As you'll see, there's really nothing to hide here: there's nothing shocking or shameful shown. In fact, what these pictures attempt to depict are scenes of some of the most mundane movements and most ordinary characters that made up

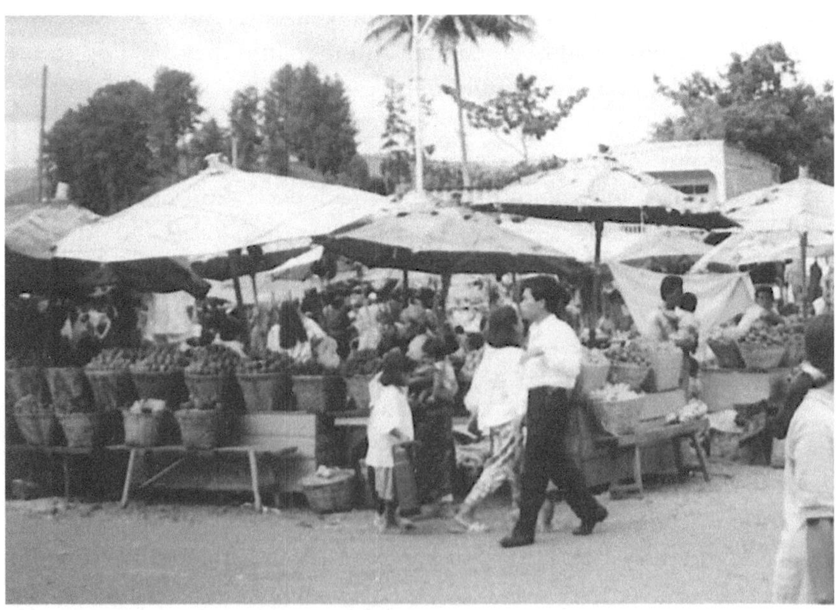

FIGURE 1.2: Fieldwork photograph of the marketplace at Tiga Raja.

the everyday life I saw while living on Samosir Island those decades ago. I hope to show you that what made me put them aside was more about form than content, and that what I was working against were fairly arbitrary institutional and disciplinary boundaries that claimed that "art" was appreciably different from "anthropology."

Now, I grew up in a bright, funny family where intellect was cultivated, so it seemed odd to me in those days—considering that several siblings and I were adept at drawing—that we received scant encouragement for making our own art. As long as the English essays were finished and the math problems completed, I was free to use my spare time drawing cartoons. It was clear, however, that the visual arts were extracurricular: hobbies. My elementary and secondary schools had similar priorities: art was an "elective" or "after school." It came as no surprise, then, that this same hierarchy was in place when I entered college, enforced by even my most avant garde and daring professors.[7]

While I may have acquiesced to the situation, I did not agree with it. My class notes (perhaps like those of some readers here) were filled with as many caricatures of classmates and invented scenes as they were with written terms and ideas (see Figure 1.3). I never really understood the distinct difference between the two forms of note taking (and it's only now that I'm brave enough to say so), and I showed my notes only to a few friends, for fear of getting "caught." I even invented a *nom de brosse* in college, thinking it would allow me the freedom to draw and paint, but this was not sufficient when I entered graduate school. One of my professors discovered that my cartoons were being published in the student paper, and admonished me: "The time spent with those *drawings* would be better spent understanding Marx!" Because my artwork tended to be seen by professors as frivolous (perhaps they were in fact the very froth of the superstructure!), I think it was hard for the handful who

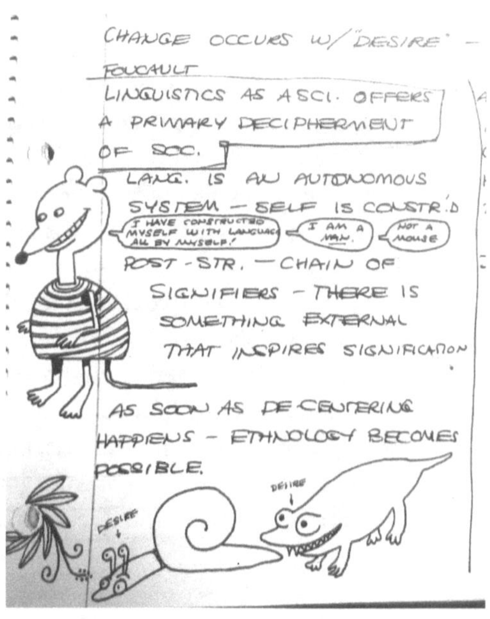

FIGURE 1.3: An example of my college class notes from the 1980s.

7 Rudolf Arnheim mentions this, too, and also describes why he thinks the arts are often disdained in the West (1969, 1–12).

supported my interdisciplinarity to make the case that scarce university grants and anthropology scholarships would be well invested in me. I never stopped making art, but I did try to hide it better.[8]

The Fulbright funding I eventually received to carry out my fieldwork contained no restrictions, of course, against drawing while doing research; nevertheless I carried with me a solid, well-formed inhibition against spending too much time doing so. I considered the drawings and paintings made in the field to be personal explorations, not part of my formal investigations, and didn't intend to show them as a serious part of my ethnographic research—not to the people I was working with, certainly not to my colleagues at home. But things don't always go as planned, and as I have written elsewhere, showing such pictures has diverted the direction of my research.[9]

As noted, in those days (perhaps even still), "Art" and "Anthropology" were distinct disciplines with little or no seepage from one to the other, but the situation may finally be changing (Schneider and Wright 2013, 4). The connection between creativity/art and fieldwork has been the topic of several recent publications (Colloredo-Mansfeld 1999, 49–56; Hallam and Ingold 2007; Grimshaw 2005; Ingold 2007, 2011; Schneider and Wright 2010; Taussig 2011; to a lesser extent Wolcott 1995), and some anthropologists, such as ethnographers Shelly Errington (2014), Sally Campbell Galman (2013), Sally Price (Price and Price 1992), and archaeologist Troy Lavata (2005, 2007) have used line drawing as a primary mode of communication. A few artist-anthropologists, such as Gillian Crowther (1990), Rudolf Colloredo-Mansfeld (1993), Carol Hendrickson (2008), Karina Kuschnir (2014), and Zoe Bray (2015), have even promoted drawing/painting as a legitimate ethnographic method. All of these works have helped me to feel more secure in my own position as an artist-anthropologist and have encouraged me to add to the conversation because I have realized that ethnography and what some call "art" are not so different. Depicting human life and behavior in either written or visual form is an intense, sensual project based on careful perceptions; this book provides an ideal venue for talking about what so-called art and anthropology share, and for keeping alive the discussion about what "Visual Anthropology" is.[10]

8 The images being published were not directly affiliated with my anthropological work, but were rather comics with humorous intent. I suspect the professors thought I was neglecting my academic work, and that the cartoons were a distraction. In addition, because these cartoons were entirely subjective and sometimes opinionated, the professors may have felt the drawings were contradictory to the then-prevailing idea that an anthropologist should always aim to be observationally objective.

9 See Causey 2012.

10 Several works over the years have questioned and investigated what the boundaries of this subfield might be, including Marcus Banks and Howard Morphy's *Rethinking Visual Anthropology* (1999), Anna Grimshaw's *The Ethnographer's Eye* (2001), editor Tim Ingold's *Redrawing Anthropology* (2011), and Rupert Cox and Christopher Wright's "Blurred Visions" (2012), to name a few.

The work of social-cultural anthropology, of ethnography,[11] is founded on the research and study of human social behaviors based on the method called participant-observation. As others have noted (e.g., Ingold 2013, 4), *participating* in the life of a culture at the same time you are *observing* it might seem to be a paradox, for "it requires of the researcher to be both 'inside' and 'outside' the field of inquiry at one and the same time." That is, to use this method effectively, you must be engaged and alive, enacting the behaviors suited to the cultural context at the same time you are partially reserved and focused on watching the proceedings happening to and around you. When actually practiced—and by now there have been scores of anthropologists over many decades who have tried this method (experimenting, inventing, guessing . . . sometimes blundering)—it seems to work, albeit imperfectly. Hundreds upon hundreds of ethnographic monographs have been written and published since the method was first proposed in the 1890s, and the use or accuracy of each can only really be understood when perceived as being a single fragment of a much longer and broader story, that of trying to explain something about the human condition. Some anthropologists end up observing more than they participate, and others do the opposite; because of the imprecise nature of the method there's no telling which is more effective or honest or useful (see Chapter Two for more on this topic). For my purposes here, I will assume that you will try to balance the two. Participation—being active, alive, vital—is as essential as observation—using your reserve, focus, and concentration. The two of them will, I hope, come together in what I am calling "seeing-drawing."

The drawing pedagogue Kimon Nicolaides recognized that any new observation is, in fact, based on previous ones, and that the most effective (perhaps even honest) depictions or documentations are those that strive for "equilibrium, the proper balance between the subjective and objective impulse" (Nicolaides 1969, 210). He also realized that drawing is a process of trying to have "correct observation," that is, having physical contact with the world through *all* the senses, and that it must "utilize as many of the senses as can reach through the eye at one time" (207). He stated that "drawings . . . may be thought of as a way of expressing certain of our ideas about objects, which have been formed by means of visual experience, without being necessarily a literal recording of that experience" (212), and this is because "the subconscious mind has a logic of its own that often transcends the logic of the conscious mind" (211). For Nicolaides, then, the act of drawing itself was a path to the goal—to see—not the other way around.

11 For the purposes of this book, I will not enter into the discussion about whether there is a philosophical difference in the intent or motivations that might exist between "anthropology" and "ethnography," as Ingold does (2013, 2–4). Because I believe that to be an advanced discussion that examines fine distinctions, it does not have a place in a work aimed at those who are being introduced to the field. I will, no doubt, use the words interchangeably throughout this work.

Likewise, Betty Edwards, who has spent much of her teaching life trying to help her readers to draw-to-see, says: "in learning how to draw, I believe you will learn how to 'see differently.' And that, in turn, will enhance . . . powers of creative thought" (Edwards 1986, xiii). The process of drawing, she says, is one where the investigator/drawer researches a problem up to its known limits, purposefully looks at this data from new perspectives, searching for analogic insights, seeks out connections and patterns in the shapes and spaces that comprise the problem, envisions parts of the problem that lay deep in shadows by extrapolating from the parts that are sufficiently lighted to be seen, and finally examines the whole to find the structure of unity. It is that last part—what she calls the incubation period, the time needed to allow the mind to analyze and synthesize what has come before—that ends (sometimes suddenly) with the "Ah-ha!" moment, which is the essence of the illumination of the problem, and ends up being its resolution (1986, 126–231).

In traditions, such as ours in the West, where the focus tends to be on final outcomes (products), such talk of *process* as the goal might appear selfish or idiosyncratic, but on continued reflection the logic of this turnabout becomes clear: if the focus of our actions is not on the honesty and accuracy[12] of our observations, we risk perceiving only what we know or assume to be (i.e., we will be *looking*) rather than being mindful and open to the unfolding presence of that which is perceived (i.e., we will be *seeing*). Can we be content to preserve our thoughts and memories in writing alone, to document and save what we perceive in mechanically mediated film?

Learning to See by Drawing to See

I teach anthropology at an arts college, and something that has become clear to me over the years is that "looking" and "seeing" are vastly different acts: for me, looking is a kind of scanning and tends to be passive, while seeing is a kind of scrutiny and tends to be active.[13] In teaching, I find that students often have

12 My use of the terms "honesty" and "accuracy" here are not meant to imply that I embrace a positivist view of human behavior as a realm in which there is only *one* accurate interpretation. Rather, I am trying to stress that each ethnographer must internally verify that what s/he records (in whatever medium) is an honest and accurate representation of what s/he perceives or experiences.

13 This is in accordance with John Berger, who says, "We only see what we look at. To look is an act of choice. As a result of this act, what we see is brought within our reach" (1977, 8). Arnheim does not use these exact terms, but makes reference to passive and active perception (1969, 14). James J. Gibson similarly does not use the terms see or look, but discusses a dichotomy between what he calls "viewing" and "perceiving" (2015 [1979]). It is important to state here that I am using these terms in a way diametrically opposed to both James Elkins's notion of seeing (passive and unthinking) and "just looking" (something like hunting and more like dreaming [1996, 20]) and David MacDougall's configuration (based on Gregory Bateson's notions), where he says "if seeing implies a passive form of vision that scans a subject or preserves it in some impersonal sense, looking implies a more selective, intentional activity, a search for or an investment of meaning" (2006, 243).

difficulty appreciating and understanding unfamiliar material objects, perhaps because they have not been taught how to scrutinize, depending instead on unencumbered scanning. Much about the contemporary world encourages all of us to merely glimpse our own social environment,[14] allowing us to subdue attention, so it's no surprise that we might feel satisfied that a glance at a carved mask or painted pot is enough. Add to this the fact that Western culture tends to define "art" in very specific terms, often directly referencing such notions as "talent," "genius," or "inspiration" (which may precondition our assumptions and expectations), and also the fact that even academic writings seem unsure whether "non-Western" aesthetic or creative output is art or craft, and it becomes clearer why many of us might tend to undervalue unfamiliar creative works at the same time we seem to mis-perceive what is before their eyes. This book aims to address this problem in a direct and precise way: by teaching you to "see" via line drawing.

Guided by the works of several visual researchers, I have come to the understanding that in *looking*, our vision floats across the visual terrain without directed engagement,[15] while *seeing* interpretively illuminates the visible, in many ways bringing it into being. The more challenging of the two, of course, is seeing—*really* seeing. In my own academic explorations, but also in my efforts to teach students how to understand and appreciate unfamiliar things in the world, I have recently recognized that the struggle to see cannot be performed by the attentive yet passive eye alone. To *see* in order to document an ethnographic experience requires active visual engagement. When that active engagement is made manifest by the hand's creation of permanent marks such as drawn lines that document what the eyes are perceiving, the seeing will be more discerning and more attentive to detail. That's because the marks made with the hand become the actual evidence of visual perception, proof that there is some concurrence between perception and representation. The scene (what is perceived) and the image (the interpretation of the scene) are recorded by the hand, whose subtle and searching movements are constantly checked and corrected by the seeing eyes, to create the picture (the actual document of marks and lines) that represents, to the best of a person's ability, a product that is an honest and accurate document of what was seen. This kind of "drawing-enhanced seeing" is clearly a balanced interaction

14 Collier and Collier note, "Generally, the fragmentation of modern life makes it difficult to respond to the whole view . . . We have drifted out of an embracing relationship with our surroundings, usually dealing only with portions of our environment" (1986, 5).

15 Keith A. Smith refers to this as "simulated vision," where the eyes glimpse something and the mind immediately intercedes. He says, "The danger of simulation is that we are not consciously aware that we are not seeing. The advantage is instantaneous comprehension, a valuable tool for survival. The disadvantage is that simulated vision has as its source only what has been programmed into our (mind) computer: past knowledge" (1992, 16).

between eye and hand, as well as the complex interplay of mind and body: cerebral and muscular, questioning and documenting. It is the active integration of drawing and perceiving that makes this method so valuable for those wishing to see more deeply.

I suspect that because the world around us is increasingly saturated with pictures, messages, and objects (real and virtual), many of us have learned to simply shut them out. As we learn to choose which visual stimuli we must attend to, we inadvertently edit out much of what surrounds us, either by seeing with inattention or by becoming blind to all but the most pressing cues. In the process, we may be losing the ability to see what we want, so pressured are we to see what we must, or see what we should. I think many of us have lost the knack of seeing, with clarity and curiosity, the expected and the ordinary aspects of our surroundings. Now, in the interest of enriching ethnographic research, we need to reawaken our visual curiosity.[16]

As the discipline of anthropology grows and evolves, it becomes evident that our methodologies of observation and analysis must keep pace. Many ethnographers, it seems, continue to collect cultural "data" primarily by means of written notes (whether handwritten or digitally composed) and, when they do use visual means to record information, tend to rely on photographic technologies (both analog and digital). As a natural outcome of this, the majority of ethnographic publications are presented in textual form, with imagery being used secondarily, to illustrate what is written.[17] This book will engage with what Tim Ingold (2011) has recently dubbed "graphic anthropology," that is, an anthropology that embraces all forms of line-making, from handwriting to the drawn sketch, to understand the material world not as being composed of completed objects but rather as part of an unfolding cultural process interwoven with articulating behaviors and actions.[18] It will do this by encouraging you to draw what you see, to enhance your "visual literacy" (Armstrong 2007; Elkins 2008), and perhaps even use your drawings to convey primary information (see, for example, Taussig 2011). The book artist Keith A. Smith may have said it most succinctly: "When I say, 'I see . . . ,' it is not a passing exclamation, but a statement of triumph" (1992, 17).

16 As Peter Dallow notes, visual literacy has become part of the essential 21st-century skills that are "needed to negotiate the changing social complexities of contemporary life" (2008, 98).

17 Even in this era of great changes to publication technology, publishers continue to resist inclusion of images, claiming that they increase final costs.

18 Chris Ballard (2013) investigates the drawings of early 20th-century anthropologist Nikolai Miklouho-Maclay, who worked with varied Papuan groups throughout Melanesia. Influenced by the work of Mikhail Bakhtin, Ballard explores how the act of drawing ethnographically engages with the visual world in a particularly vital form of dialogism.

Who Is This Book For?

While this book is aimed at social science practitioners who desire to expand their understanding of the visual environment, I hope it is also of interest to researchers in other fields who need to see clearly and deeply.[19] It might be used by readers trying to teach themselves how to see-draw, or it might be used as an auxiliary textbook in a classroom; it might be read all at once, or sampled over several months. However it is used, and whoever uses it, readers should understand that the book is more about processes than final products. The information presented here, I hope, is enjoyable to consider and ponder, and the exercises offered are suggestions for ways to practice seeing and drawing, not assignments to be completed, checked off, and left behind.

This book is for readers who are willing to take seriously the following goals: slow down; concentrate and focus; put aside frustration and judgment; remember how to feel joy; embrace playfulness; practice constantly. Sound too dreamy? Well, my experience is that each of these goals is absolutely essential if you are to engage meaningfully with the purpose of this book. This is the time to resist rushing, skimming, browsing, and multitasking. This book is for readers who are willing to accept the challenge to practice doing one thing: to draw in order to see.

Some readers may find familiar ideas and exercises here, and I fully admit and embrace the notion that this book is a mixture of my own thoughts as well as being a compilation of other people's explorations and research; I apologize in advance if I've missed pertinent or allied works. In some ways, however, this book is much more about encouraging and supporting you to engage with the topic (through prompts and enticements) than it is about presenting any novel concepts. This book itself is an exploration not only of how to nudge you to do something different as part of your fieldwork information collection, but to try to show you how to do it. I hope it is effective. I keep these things in mind to keep me going: sometimes, we just need to be *invited* to learn something new rather than be told we must learn it; we need to feel that we have a safe environment to test new skills without being judged.

19 Two recently published books indicate that the medical profession is embracing line drawing as a legitimate method (please see Ian Williams's *The Bad Doctor* [2015] and MK Czerwiec et al.'s *Graphic Medicine Manifesto* [2015]). Nick Sousanis's ground-breaking interdisciplinary graphic monograph *Unflattening* (2015) shows that philosophy, pedagogy, and perhaps even quantum mechanics can also benefit by using drawing as a way of expressing complex ideas.

What Does This Book Cover?

To be clear, this is not a book on "How to Do Ethnography," and it's not a book on "How to Draw." It *is* a book to help you teach yourself to see better and to create line drawings that might help you understand what you saw. No one can really tell you how to do ethnography because it is an effort that is so provisional and dependent, so contextual, that any instructions you get may be useful or may derail you. The only pieces of advice I got on leaving for Sumatra were "Write everything down," and "Tell us a good story when you get back." Each person's ethnographic experience is particular and individual. You must have all your wits with you and all your varied methods available to be supple, agile, and nimble enough to know what to do when. Ethnography is a practice, a process, not an accomplish-able or complete-able thing; it travels on its own path and there's usually not much you can do to control it. That's why it's so important to have all your methodological tools available. Drawing will help you see more deeply, and seeing deeply will help you write evocatively and engagingly to convince your readers of the clarity of what you witnessed; the drawings you produce are primary documents of your research, as well.

The book is a balanced amalgam: partly theoretical (sometimes philosophical), partly ethnographic, partly instructional (how-to). At its very essence, this book is about *why* and *how* drawing can be used in ethnographic research. Several recent works calling for a renewed attention to images and drawings focus on the reception and interpretation—rather than the production—of them (such as Stafford 2007 and Mitchell 1994). Other works promote the use of line drawing as a legitimate ethnographic method (e.g., Grimshaw 2005; Ingold 2011; Rakic and Chambers 2012, 5; Taussig 2011)—in effect telling you *why* drawing can assist your research—but they stop short of showing you *how* to draw ethnographically. There are very few works by anthropologists that suggest you try drawing as a method of better knowing the world (e.g., Manghani 2013), but even fewer that tell you specific ways to put pencil to paper as part of your fieldwork (Kuschnir 2014).

That is the purpose of this book: to reiterate why drawing is integral to seeing, to give you contexts for considering drawing as a legitimate ethnographic method, and then to show you *how* to do it. The drawing exercises, the Etudes, in this book are integral to its scope, and are what set it apart. The intent of the Etudes is to first help you accept the notion that you *can* draw, and later to convince you to use drawing not only as an additional method for doing anthropological research, but to assist you in better perceiving (and understanding) the world around you. But I have to be honest at the outset: because everyone's ethnographic project is different and because each of us comes to our projects with varied sets of skills and expectations, I am unable to instruct you on how to precisely apply what you learn here. It's not as though any one Etude fits exactly with any one method. My intention is, rather, to present you with a set that will assist you in perceiving more deeply, and that will in turn help to make the information you gather (using whichever method) more encompassing and richer. Nevertheless, recognizing that many readers would like more guidance on how to implement the Etudes, I have done two things. First, throughout the book I include sections called "Ethnographic Application" when I think there is a direct connection between the Etudes and specific ethnographic fieldwork situations. Second, I have put together a scheme that tries to tie some of them with certain methods (see Appendix).

I begin by discussing why anthropologists may be perceptually constrained, taking into consideration not only issues of how we've been taught to engage with documenting the visual, but also exploring social structures that perpetuate the idea that only a few among us are "artists" (Rudolf Arnheim 1969; Betty Edwards 1979, 1986; John Willats 1997). I continue by discussing how the act of drawing can help us see. Recognizing that many people are content with simply looking at surfaces, I will give examples from several different authors and artists (James Elkins 1996, Tim Ingold 2011, Michael Taussig 2011, and Lambros Malafouris 2013, to name a few) who help support my contention that deep "seeing" can be taught and learned. Ethnographic examples from my own research in North Sumatra (Causey 2003, 2012, 2015), as well as that from other anthropologists, support my exploration of the philosophical issues about what "seeing" means, and selected examples of "non-Western art" are discussed to assist the reader in understanding the vast diversity of ways of seeing among cultural worlds. I try not to overwhelm the "showing how" with the "explaining about," but even so, lots of words are needed for me to help you see and draw. I need to be clear how I am using three terms: *view* is used to refer to that portion of reality you perceive with your eyes at a given time, *image* refers to your interpretation of that particular view, and *picture* is the visual object you create, whether it is a photograph or drawing (or some other art-like thing). I hope the pictures presented here provide a good balance to the many words.[20]

Central to the purpose of the book are the carefully calibrated drawing Etudes interspersed throughout the work. These are intended to help you bolster your security in drawing, to help you with practical strategies for delineating what you see, to give you encouragement to expand your abilities, and perhaps most importantly, to provide you with a system for developing your capacity to see more deeply as you conduct your field research (in this way, the

20 My use of these terms resonates with W.J.T. Mitchell's (1987, 10), and although his exploration of the words complicates their definitions and uses in fascinating ways, I prefer to keep it simple here, using the terms in their most mundane and colloquial forms.

Etudes here are similar to the writing exercises found in Kirin Narayan's (2012) book *Alive in the Writing*). The Etudes are not necessarily novel or unique, but rather are revised or newly devised expressly for ethnographers to assist you in facing situations common in the practice of anthropological research. As an artist as well as anthropologist, I understand many people's shyness about drawing, and I hope you find these Etudes nonthreatening.

They have varied purposes: some of them are revelatory (letting you show yourself that you can see-draw), others are exploratory (probing the forms, techniques, and limits of depicting your world), some are playful (to help you discover some joy in drawing), others are meant to help you maintain your abilities (practice, practice!), while still others are instrumental (tied directly to a particular ethnographic method). They are introduced in a certain order in the hopes that each will build on the previous ones, and you are encouraged to go back and practice earlier ones when you feel the urge. Not all Etudes will resonate with you, and some may seem positively childish.[21] Still, I hope that you allow yourself to find the time to do all of them, leaving yourself open to discover something of interest or use in each of them.

Notes on Practice

You only need the simplest of materials for the drawing Etudes: sheets of unlined paper (ordinary white paper) and an old-fashioned (i.e., not mechanical) pencil with a sharpened lead. The reason I suggest an old-fashioned pencil is fourfold: it is easily obtainable around the world; its lead tends to be stronger because it is supported by the surrounding wood; it can be sharpened even in the most harsh conditions (rubbing on a flat stone or concrete floor); and the width of the lead allows for more variety in shape of line. For similar reasons, I suggest you use the most ordinary paper at hand: it's easy to obtain; you are familiar with its size, weight, and texture; it is inexpensive; and it can serve many purposes. Some people prefer to draw on precut index cards (making it easy to store the drawings), while others prefer to use a formal bound artist's book; choose whatever suits you. If you want, of course, you can use one of the soft artist pencils (2B or 3B) and loose artist paper (smooth or medium surface, or Bristol board), but I suggest not using a pen until you feel comfortable making art-like lines on paper; ink can be very unforgiving.

21 A thought to consider, from Peter Jenny: "A child's curiosity, awkwardness, experimentation, mimicry, and unbiased attitude are all characteristic of the abundance of his or her imagination. Adults are quick to belittle such childish behaviors, but one thing is for certain: children ask more questions about the world, while adults tend to make declarations" (2012, 27).

Several Etudes ask that you draw a freehand frame (i.e., do not use a straight-edge to make the lines) centered inside the paper, leaving a 1–2 inch margin of white paper. This is done for two reasons: first, because sometimes a wobbling or uneven frame line allows you to draw more freely,[22] and second, because this gives you room to write notes about the drawing if you need to (now or at some point in the future).

In general, my suggestion is to hold the pencil in your ordinary hand as if you are writing a letter to someone you love and miss (with the same grip: no harder, no lighter). There are other ways to hold the pencil, but I think it's wise to move forward with the most familiar circumstances. When you make drawing lines, I think it is best to make deliberate, solid marks, rather than "sketchy" (shaky or light zigzags) or faint lines. Draw your marks as if you are writing a note to your neighbors in block letters—"Lost Dog!"—with boldness and confidence. Such lines are made neither quickly nor slowly, just intentionally.

Each Etude gives you a suggestion on how long to take to make the drawing. Timing will depend on each person, of course, so if you want to take longer, do so. My suggestion is not to take less time, however, because then you may just be performing a task rather than actually seeing.

In drawing-seeing, you will usually be seated at a desk, but some of the Etudes may ask you to take your paper and pencil outside, to draw standing up or on your lap. Don't let these situations undermine your work; accept the limitations and learn from them. What if you sprain your wrist? Can you write with your "other" hand? You'll try doing just that in one of the upcoming Etudes to give you practice and confidence in approaching your work even in dire conditions. Doing ethnographic work sometimes means you must draw or take notes while riding a bus, or even walking along a road, so practice now learning how to overcome obstacles!

In addition to asking you to do the Etudes in order, I also want to guide you with some practical instructions on an effective way to do them. This is not about me imposing my will on you, but is rather me offering you some advice based on my own experiences making drawings as well as my experience as a teacher showing people how to see. To make it easier to remember, I'll write my suggestions as an annotated bullet list.

Suggestions to Start Drawing to See:

- *Relax*. Locate a calm place to do the Etudes—someplace that is not surrounded by noise or commotion—because you will need to focus

22 Cf. Jenny 2012, 53.

and concentrate with as few distractions as possible. Calm yourself, too. It may seem corny, but taking a deep breath in and letting it out slowly will assist you in letting tensions dissipate. It is much harder to draw when your hand is pinching the pencil and pressing down very hard, so allow your hand to feel its natural flexibility.[23]

- *Focus.* The Etudes are meant to show you how to draw to see more deeply. That means you must practice focusing your eyes (and for those Etudes that use your "mind's eye," to focus your mind). What I'm talking about here has nothing to do with whether you wear glasses or not. No, what I'm asking you to do is *attend* to your seeing, something many of us have gotten out of practice doing since we spend so much time looking at our technology screens. Having said that, remember that line drawing is an embodied act, so be sure that you attend to your whole body. As you draw, you will tend to focus on your eyes' seeing, but now also feel yourself in the ethnographic context: the character of the light, the temperature of the day and time, the feeling of *being where you are.* Know what you see, and be fully cognizant of it throughout your body.
- *Concentrate.* Well, what can I say? We are all overbooked, overstimulated, and multitasking heroes! We are encouraged from all directions to be mentally agile and new-project accommodating, and we drive ourselves to be nimble and attentive leaders who can, in a flash, also be striving and well-read team members! What I ask here is for you to put aside your other commitments and enjoyments: turn off the music, leave the social media for later, close the door. Concentrate all your energies on doing the Etude before you.[24]
- *Slow Down.*[25] As you can see, there is a pattern forming here. The world most of us live in requires that we push ourselves to do things faster and more efficiently. We often have as our aim to *finish* a project, but rarely do we get to take the time to discover or take interest in the process of our work. Because the Etudes have no completion goal, you are asked to pay attention to the unfolding of your actions (i.e., the process of your seeing-drawing).
- *Be Accepting.* Likewise, our lives are surrounded by, and impregnated with, judgments of all kinds. It's nearly impossible to avoid "10 Best" lists, "thumbs-up" reviews, A–F grades, "on a scale of 1 to 10" surveys in all media forms, and I think we've gotten so used to them that we've forgotten it's possible to simply experience the world, ratings-free. It

23 See Peter London (1989, 27) for more support in this area.
24 The famous drawing teacher Kimon Nicolaides offers the same suggestion (1969, 2).
25 The only time I will contradict this statement is in Chapter 6's Etude for Gesture Drawing, where I ask you to draw FAST!

is extremely important when doing these Etudes not to judge.[26] Most important is not to judge yourself, but while you're at it, don't judge anyone else. No grades, no assessments, no comparisons. Free yourself of criticisms here; your understanding of how drawing emerges in its own way is your goal.[27]

- *Be Interested, Be Curious.* If you have no reason to do the Etudes, it will be very difficult to attend to them. If you are not attracted to a particular Etude (or, in fact, if you are not attracted to my style of writing, or this book), that's okay. But don't stop. Discover a way to pull yourself into the project: figure out what would be a more interesting way to do it. Relocate your curiosity.[28] We are often trained to do things because we have to, but I'm asking you to do these Etudes because you *want* to see what happens. Let all your senses draw you in.[29]
- *Just Draw What You See.* Draw what you *actually* see, not what you *think* you see, not what you *accept* as known. Partly because we are enveloped by a swarm of images, from Internet pop-ups to holiday wrapping paper, we are nearly unable to free ourselves from representations devised by others. It becomes very difficult to see the world as *you* want to see it. Want to draw a tree? Make a circle balanced on a stick . . . or is that a balloon? The symbols created by others for us are invaluable for communication, of course, but before accepting any of these predigested images, take the time to actually see what they refer to. Draw a hand by carefully examining it; don't just draw what you know as "hand." See first, and interpret what you see into lines, but try to avoid, when you can, passive use of hackneyed images.[30]
- *Lose Your Ego.* Stop thinking about yourself when you draw to see. Many of us become hyper-aware of ourselves when we try something new, saying in our mind's voice, "Okay, here I am: a person drawing . . ." Try to block that introspection when doing the Etudes because it is distracting you from the concentration you need to see. If you are thinking about yourself to pass judgment, just stop. Quit caring what "they" think and you'll find that there are no mistakes, just explorations.

26 Lynda Barry says, "Liking and not liking can make us blind to what's there" (2014, 23; underlining in original).

27 Product designer Kevin Henry uses the term "fidelity" to address an image's mode of realism: a photograph would be "high fidelity" and a quick sketch "low fidelity." He is careful to use these terms uncritically, recognizing that all modes have their place in conveying information (2012, 11–12, 36). Keeping this in mind when you draw/see will help you accept—without criticism—all of the images you produce.

28 See London (1989, 29–34) for a wonderful invitation to "get lost" in order to expand your experiences.

29 Nicolaides said this, as well (1969, 5).

30 Please see Etude Thirteen in Chapter Three for an important variation of this suggestion.

- *Practice.* Here, practice is a kind of engaged repetition. There is no right way to do any of these Etudes, so practicing them is not done to develop some kind of perfection. Instead, practice here means doing something over and over, each time being attentive to whether the process and product are expanding your understanding of what you see. No one can know that but you. Try to take joy in each repetition, for its own sake.

Overview of the Book

Even though I've written the book to flow from start to finish, and have created the Etudes to build on one another sequentially, it is possible to read the chapters out of order or to read them selectively. Those interested in finding Etudes that assist with particular research methods might look at the Appendix for my suggestions.

Chapter Two starts the conversation about the place of line drawing as a legitimate method in the ethnographer's toolkit. I start with a short exploration of the notion of reality and our strong beliefs in how to record what we sense. I then provide a brief historical overview of the uncertain position of drawing as an objective and useful way to document anthropological information, with a specific interest in its connection with photography. Because photography (still and moving) has such an important place in ethnographic research, I think it is important to consider its limitations as well as its benefits in documenting the visual world. With this as a foundation, I begin to make the case for drawing as an integral part of the researcher's repertoire. I introduce the first Etudes in this chapter, mostly to help you get comfortable working with a pencil (or pen) and paper, and with your first forays into *seeing*.

Chapter Three is meant to encourage you to understand drawing as a form of seeing, and to let go of old fears about whether you can, in fact, draw. I explain how I expanded my understanding of drawing as a way to perceive by means of my contact with Batak friends on Samosir Island, North Sumatra, Indonesia. I learned to move past my self-criticisms and judgments to let the drawings I made tell their own stories. Many of the Etudes in this section are exploratory and playful, and are meant to attract you into opening your mind to this research method. Because drawing is a subjective form of documenting the visual world, I briefly describe here why serious consideration of the ethics of representation is so important. In addition, this chapter opens a door into some of the philosophical questions related to perception and notions of reality, later grounding such lofty thinking by considering ways to reduce the complexity of the visual world by creating simple visual "glyphs" of meaning.

Chapter Four considers what it means to see the edges of the visual world and to convey the complexity of our surroundings by focusing on boundaries. Often called "contours," the edges of things around us seem to be certain, but as soon as we start to try drawing them, we realize that we make tremendous assumptions about where one thing starts and the other thing begins. The Etudes in this chapter are more challenging to engage with, but I remind you that the purpose of drawing is more often to *see* than it is to produce a finished artwork. Some of the work here is to see edges in new ways, and to open your mind as to what a "line" is. This chapter also introduces you to ways you might use drawing as a way to elicit information from the people you work with, for sometimes all that's needed to start a useful ethnographic conversation is something that can spark a connection: in this case, a drawing. Because line-making is not easy, nor is it "natural" to know how to make the kinds of lines that will successfully depict what you see, I encourage you to begin collecting different kinds of lines to have at hand when you take notes.

When I feel you are confident in making lines to convey your visual thoughts, I introduce you to ways to see the insides of things. Chapter Five tries to help you see the weight, posture, pose, and structure of the world around you, and gives you a variety of ways to try to draw these characteristics. The chapter also discusses how important it is to see surfaces: decorations and designs, but also textures and features. Making reference to the work of various other artist-anthropologists, I help you see ways you can examine surfaces carefully and then ways to document what you've seen with care, not accepting your assumptions and not ignoring the small details.

Chapter Six deals with seeing and depicting something that is very difficult even for professional artists to convey: movement. The Etudes in this chapter are peculiar, and I admit that, but they are meant to help you find your own ways to give your drawings life. I try to encourage you to see drawings as moving lines and to prod you to let them tell a story that no other recording system can do as well. Sometimes, this means you have to get up and move! That's the only way to know what movement means, to experience it yourself. Other times, it means that you should become aware of other technologies (such as moving film) as the basis for understanding how you can document the actions you see. Essential to this chapter are the Etudes that ask you to free your drawing arm, from shoulder to hand, to let your own movement find its way to the paper. Because movement drawings can convey much more than static ones, I take the opportunity here to reiterate the importance in considering the ethics of making drawings.

Chapter Seven is about seeing what's no longer there. There are many times in our lives when we see something that quickly disappears, either through physical loss or from simple cessation. Because visual absence is such an intrinsic part of the ethnographic project, I think it is vital to discuss it and engage with it as a way of communicating to you how important it is to keep your sharp, visual mind active at all times. Memories of an event can often be as useful as notes taken on site, and the Etudes in this chapter try to help you *see* in ways than may not necessarily use only your present-attentive eyes.

With luck, this book will help you perceive your own world much more vividly, and by enhancing that level of seeing, you will be able to engage in your ethnographic fieldwork with more confidence and curiosity.

CHAPTER 2

CAN'T SEE?

What Is Reality and How Do You Know You've Seen It?

Before we can really talk about seeing deeply or using drawing to assist that kind of scrutinous observation, I want to give a very brief overview about what may underlie our notion of reality (ontology), and then—again very briefly—discuss how we know what we know (epistemology). Because these are huge philosophical ideas, I will only explore them a little here . . . just enough to reveal how complicated it truly is to say something as simple as "I see."

I said earlier that I started to use drawings in my ethnographic fieldwork when I realized that there was more to see than what I was writing down and photographing. This happened, I think, because I was living among the Toba Bataks, who had a moderately different way of conceiving what reality is. After several months of living with them, it began to make sense that the wind could cause illness and it began to seem possible that spirit entities live among us (Causey 2003, 43, 60), and when my sense of "what is real" began to change, my sense of how I was going to document it also began to change.

Most of us trot happily through our lives with an idea that we know what is real, an idea that is shared by others around us: it is taught to us by our friends, families, and those we share our towns with, is confirmed by the media, by scientists and our teachers, and often verified by the clergy; we continue to learn what our society says is real as we age. Many of us become fairly certain of our ontological perspective as we move through life and soon begin to feel content that our learned perspectives are "natural," and thus shared by all humans. Ethnographic works show us, however, that this is not true. Our own ontological notions form but one of the thousands of ways to define human existence, to enable us to get along in the earthly environment that surrounds us, and to explain all the seemingly unknowable features of natural and spiritual worlds. If you really want to test the veracity of your group's ontology, go live a little while with those whose perspectives are vastly different from yours. Soon you might see that your explanations and definitions don't really cover all the situations you are experiencing there.[1]

If you are an introspective or exploring person, you might have already sensed that things are not as they were explained to you. We grow up with the idea that there are five senses, but at some point you might have wondered if, for example, a "sense of urgency" is connected to premonitions, if a "sense of fear" is related to extrasensory perceptions, or if a "sense of direction" has to do with the effects of the earth's magnetic poles on your body. You might have wondered why, so often, if you stare at someone they suddenly turn and catch you eye to eye, or you might have wondered why your dreams sometimes blend easily into your awake life. James Elkins suggests that we may have more senses than our culture tells us (1996, 136).[2] Perhaps some of these can be scientifically tested but others are just quietly recognized (consciously or not) by a lot of us.

We often verify our notions of the real by testing them with accepted ways of knowing. In Western culture, which since the Enlightenment has tended to legitimate the concept of "the real" with scientific experimentation and proof and with rational (logical cognitive) approaches to questions, we usually distinguish between "I believe" and "I know" based on what information supports them. Epistemologically, "I believe" is based on ways of knowing that are personal, idiosyncratic, emotion- or faith-based, while "I think" is based on ways of knowing that are factual, evidence-based, and based on reason. Thinking about this distinction leads to one of the most interesting questions raised in ethnographic research: How do we know *how we know* what we know? It sounds like a nonsensical thing to say, doesn't it? Well, it's a question that's been asked many times before in dozens of different ways, but let me put it this way and maybe you'll see why it's so interesting to think about. You know what you know (for instance, where you were born, your cousin's name, your favorite band), and you also know what you don't know (e.g., the use of a Roman bulla, what grosgrain means, how electricity works), but you *don't* know what you don't know.[3]

1 Barbara Maria Stafford states that to understand the world around us we draw on predeveloped visual mental representations (2007, 167), and these, we will see later in this chapter, are conditioned not just by our bodies and minds but the culture within which we are raised.

2 He specifically adds the senses of feeling temperature, feeling gravity, and knowing where the body is in space (proprioception), noting that there might be others.

3 Donald Rumsfeld, Secretary of Defense during George W. Bush's administration, famously used a similar idea when trying to defend the US invasion of Iraq (Rumsfeld 2011), but a more cogent use of the concept appears in Nassim Taleb's *The Black Swan* (2007) in reference to the way unknown unknowns can engender social change because they force us to rethink our notions of what is improbable or unpredictable. That's because we usually "have a natural tendency to look for instances that confirm our story and our vision of the world" (which is called confirmation bias; Taleb 2007, 55), and when something truly unexpected happens we must then concoct an explanation so that our ontology continues to make sense.

That is, if you are unaware that something actually exists, then it can't be a specific part of your ontology, and there will be no way for you to investigate it by any of your familiar epistemological means. How will you be able to identify it, much less document it, if you don't know it's there?

Well, this is one of the reasons ethnographic research is so fascinating: it can expand your understanding of what "reality" can encompass. When you work with (or read about) people from a different cultural world, you are exposed to their notions of what's really real—you'll begin to understand their ontology—and often you'll be introduced to the ways that those new aspects of reality are verified—you'll learn something about their epistemology. I honestly never thought I'd seriously consider that ghosts or spirits inhabited the world around me until I lived in Indonesia. From Sumatra, to Java and Bali, to Lombok, however, I met several people who (no matter what their religion) believed as a matter of fact that the animate world was found in both visible and invisible forms. After months of living on Samosir Island and listening to the stories told, I began plucking a tender green leaf to hold it between my lips if I had to walk home in the dark because it repelled malevolent ghosts. In those days, such small acts made perfect sense to me.

In visual documentation, we are making a picture of an image, where "image" refers to a kind of cogitation (or interpretation) of that which we've delimited from all available visual stimuli (i.e., our view of reality): the 3-D visible world is translated to 2-D visible code.[4] This notion of image (i.e., the idea that we always define what we see meaningfully) refers to the idea that people don't usually perceive their surroundings "in general." Instead, all our visual behavior is engaged, situated, context-bound, and interpreted, whether we are consciously aware of it or not.[5] Even "looking," which I noted in the last chapter is a kind of passive perception, uses the brain's cognitive processes that are translating and decoding the present-seen in comparison with the past-seen. George Lakoff and Mark Johnson say that because the brain is necessarily housed in the body, the work it does in understanding the world around *must* be framed within that physicality (2003, 217, 255). That is to say, the mind interprets our surroundings *in terms of* our bodies. This notion of the "embodied mind" suggests that humans are unable to make truly "objective" or "unaffected" observations.[6] We don't ever perceive generally, but always within the

4 If you are interested in understanding more about how the eye sees and how the brain conceptualizes sight, I refer you to Wade and Swanston's *Visual Perception: An Introduction* (2001).

5 See William Washabaugh (2008) for a discussion of how vision is also gendered and racialized, and masculinist (see also Berger 1977, 45–64).

6 For a more theoretical and philosophical examination of this topic, please refer to Keyan Tomaselli (1996, 51–69), where he untangles the notion of the photographic "real" in terms of Peircean semiotics, and discusses "reality" as the "struggle for the sign" (44).

boundaries of a body-self,[7] and that varies from person to person, and from culture to culture. Now, it's true that we can have direct experiences that we need not translate to language (a sudden electrical shock, for example), but to understand those direct experiences, we usually revert to the structure of language, often analogy, to help us out (Stafford 2001). The potential problem here is that "language is double-edged: through words a fuller view of reality emerges, but words can also serve to fragment reality" (John-Steiner 1985, 29).[8] When we articulate the interpretations of what we perceive *using language*, we must do so by using linguistic metaphors (Lakoff and Johnson 2003, 4). So, our understandings of experiences are filtered through comparisons to what we already know.

Some would say that "if you can't say it, you can't see it," but I suspect we've all had experiences when we've come upon something that we are astounded by, something that makes us blurt out "What IS that?!" It may take us a long time to put it in a category (awful, amazing, revolting, beautiful, disturbing, sublime), but in the meantime, we are, in fact, perceiving it. This kind of pure perception, which might happen for only a single jagged gasp, is our experience of seeing without words. Interestingly, when we do categorize what we've seen, either by finding the word for it or putting it into a verbal metaphor, we might then discard it by ignoring or dismissing it, by looking away in disgust, or by rationalizing it as something ordinary. In some cases (especially with the easy access of camera apps on phones), we might cherish it and take a quick photo or even make a drawing of it, but usually, as ethnographers, we do the academically appropriate thing: we write about it.[9]

". . . Words, and Words and Words . . ."

The ethnographic project recognizes that human cultural existence is an amalgam of interactions between humans, nature, animals, and objects (cf. Schiffer

7 Stafford (2008) provides a thorough discussion of this concept. In addition, Margaret Wilson makes a strong case for further distinguishing the ways that the body is integrated with the environment in cognition (2002). Of particular interest for this book is her suggestion that humans "symbolically off-load" cognitive work onto the environment in order to better comprehend and utilize it; this would help explain how visual imagery created in the process of ethnographic research becomes useful as a record in, and of, particular moments of the emergent experience of the surrounding environment (natural and social) (p. 629).

8 Vera John-Steiner continues on about language, quoting the British literary critic Christopher Caldwell: "But in language reality is symbolized in unchanging words, which give a false stability and permanence to the object they represent. Thus they instantaneously photograph reality rather than reflect it" (1985, 30).

9 Michael Taussig speaks at length about the need to document the suddenly experienced event or thing, so a curious reader should seek out and read his book *I Swear I Saw This* (2011) to fully understand the importance of such moments in ethnographic research.

2009), a bluster of mundane tactics, crafted intentions, and incoherent affects swirling around us, all of them ever-emergent (cf. Hasse 2015, 6). Life is, in the words of Phillip Vannini, "a viscous becoming in time-space," and is "marked by an instinctive intentionality . . . that transcends consciousness, and by an effervescent energy unharnessed and unprogrammed by thought" (2015, 3). Ethnographers try to communicate something about this: we try to devise some semblance of order for our experiences, ordinarily using written words—our field notes—to document what is evoked in our varied senses. Writing one's experiences is so deeply ingrained in the discipline that Clifford Geertz was moved to state, "The ethnographer 'inscribes' social discourse; *he writes it down*. In so doing, he turns it from a passing event, which exists only in its own moment of occurrence, into an account, which exists in its inscriptions and can be reconsulted" (Geertz 1973, 19; italics in original). It is also, in fact, Geertz who proposed for anthropologists a paradigm where we interpretively "read" culture as a text (Hasse 2015, 68), a development that gained footing in the 1980s as part of the reflexive anthropology movement that focused attention on "writing culture" (which was also the title of James Clifford and George E. Marcus's seminal 1986 book; see also Clifford 1988, 37–46).[10]

> While it's true that the common gloss for "ethnography" is writing about culture, in fact the more general definition is "the scientific description of nations or races of (people), and their customs, habits, and points of difference" (Murray 1971, 314), where "-graphy" is defined as "denot(ing) processes or styles of writing, *drawing, or graphic representation*" (361; italics added), which is something important, for the purposes of this book, to ponder. Whether or not "ethnography" contains in its very essence the possibility of documenting cultures via visual methods such as drawing, the truth is that writing remains the foundation of the field.

What's interesting here is that much ethnographic fieldwork hinges on visual perceptions that must be "translated" from an ocular to a verbal code. Some might say that such a translation happens so naturally, so quickly, and so thoroughly that it's a bit silly to even raise this topic (Lakoff and Johnson 2003, 246). As an artist, however, I would say that a more *direct* documentation (still interpreted, but less translated) of the ocular stimulus might be via one of the visual codes, that is, film or drawing.[11] To imagine that this translation

10 Those interested in a probing review of the theoretical transformations happening in the social sciences and history at this time should refer to V. E. Bonnell and L. Hunt (1999).

11 This is a point also made by the artist-anthropologist Carol Hendrickson, who uses C.S. Peirce's notions of index and icon to describe how her Yucatan drawings "accurately conveyed some sense of the world that I witnessed" (2008, 123).

(visual to verbal) is of no consequence is to miss the very point of this book: that drawing provides a method of recording experiences that is categorically different from writing.[12] In fact, a useful way to ponder this issue is to consider whether listening to a poem being spoken could be effectively documented in a drawing, which is the reverse translation: oration stimulus to visual code.

This is not to claim that one form of documentation or the other is better, simply that one or the other might be more direct, depending on the stimulus. In the visual documentation, as I noted above, we are making a picture of an image, where "image" refers to a kind of cogitated, conceived, or constructed entity chosen (delimited) from all available visual stimuli: the 3-D visible world is translated to 2-D visible code.[13] In language-based documentation, we perceive the same "image" mentioned above, but we make two translations: (a) the 3-D visible world into a 2-D code (writing), and (b) visible imagery to conceptual words. Despite the fact that writing doubly interprets our visual perceptions, as Lakoff and Johnson and others have suggested, our human minds seem to have developed with a language-like code readily available, and indeed this capacity to think through language is immediate, physiologic, and genetic (e.g., Chomsky 1968; Lakoff and Johnson 2003; Werker and Gervain 2010). This helps us understand why verbal codes are so often used to express visual stimuli: they are embedded in the human way of thinking.

But ethnographic research is not about slavishly following our "natural" proclivities! It is about trying to best document and communicate social and cultural experiences we have had with others. To allow ourselves to do this in the most honest and accurate way, we need as many appropriate methods as possible. You'd think, then, that if we were going to document our visual experiences, we'd teach ourselves how to enlist visual systems, knowing that the more similar the coding (translation) system, the more representative the documentation would probably be (cf. Bouquet 2012, 95; Collier and Collier 1986, 10; Hendrickson 2008). This is not how things turned out in cultural anthropology (cf. MacDougall 2006, 230).

The friction between writing and visual methods as appropriate forms of documentation in ethnography is not new. Because written ethnographic field notes are considered to be "primary documents" in our research, most

12 J.J. Gibson says, "The image makers can arouse in us an awareness of what they have seen . . . and they do so *without converting the information into a different mode*" (2015, 250; italics in original).

13 I am extending James Elkins's discussion about the relationship between image and picture, hopefully not too far (2008, 17–18). Elkins says that an image is the visual remembrance that a viewer has of something like a photograph that is lost, inferring that the image's stimulus is depicted in some material object (thus, he says, an "impression of a fossil in stone" is an image of the original creature). However, because humans perceive their surrounds meaningfully, I am suggesting that an "image" can also be the mental or cognitive interpretation of what is seen, which is then reproduced as a "picture."

of our conclusions will be drawn directly from them, so they must be exacting. Margaret Mead (in 1975) suggested that because earlier anthropologists had to depend on informants telling them about recently abandoned cultural ways, "ethnographic inquiries came to depend upon words, and words and words ... (so) anthropology became a science of words, and those who relied on words have been very unwilling to let their pupils use the new tools (i.e., visual means such as photography and film)." (1995, 5)

So much is riding on our research being seen as "honest," "accurate," and "useful" that many ethnographers think fieldwork documentation *must* give writing precedence: even recognizing that such documentation is partial and imperfect, it is still felt to be the most precise communicative code. It's true that several anthropologists have called for more varied approaches to ethnographic documentation over the years (see, for example, Grimshaw 2005; Grimshaw and Ravetz 2005; Vannini 2015), but visual forms still tend not to be given as much credence as writing. This is slightly ironic since one of the very founders of the field, Bronislaw Malinowski, promoted the importance of vision in fieldwork (Grimshaw 2001, 3; Hendrickson 2008, 122). It is not entirely clear why visual documentation continues to be subtly sidelined,[14] but the history of the discipline's formation might give us some clues.

A Brief History of the Visual Depictions in Ethnographic Research

There is a long history of Western scientists devaluing, sometimes distrusting, image making as a way of communicating their research (Asma 2001, 41; Collier and Collier 1986, 8; Geismar 2014; Grimshaw 2001, 6; Topper 1996, 216).[15] In the days before photography, imagery made by hand[16] was the only way to communicate ethnographic or other scientific information. Artists would train to draw "accurately" the real world before them (Smith 2006, 35) (see Figure 2.1), and what they produced was considered to be an honest representation. But the West's attitudes about the "truthfulness" of hand-drawn imagery (in particular those forms referred

14 There are, for certain, anthropologists who call for the discipline's communication to become more affectively encompassing, and who are doing what they can to transform the way by example: see, for example, Phillip Vannini's edited volume *Non-Representational Methodologies* (2015), and also the "Ethnographic Terminalia" group, a "curatorial collective" interested in "demonstrat(ing) how contemporary artists, anthropologists, and institutions are engaging with ethnographic methodologies and art" (see http://ethnographicterminalia.org/about).

15 For a more thorough exploration of how perceptual (image) systems have been divorced from conceptual models of human cognition and how they can be productively reconnected, see Barsalou 1999.

16 This includes all forms of creative depictions from line drawings to etchings and other prints, paintings, and, to a lesser extent, sculptures. The focus of attention here is on hand-drawn imagery rather than paintings or sculptures.

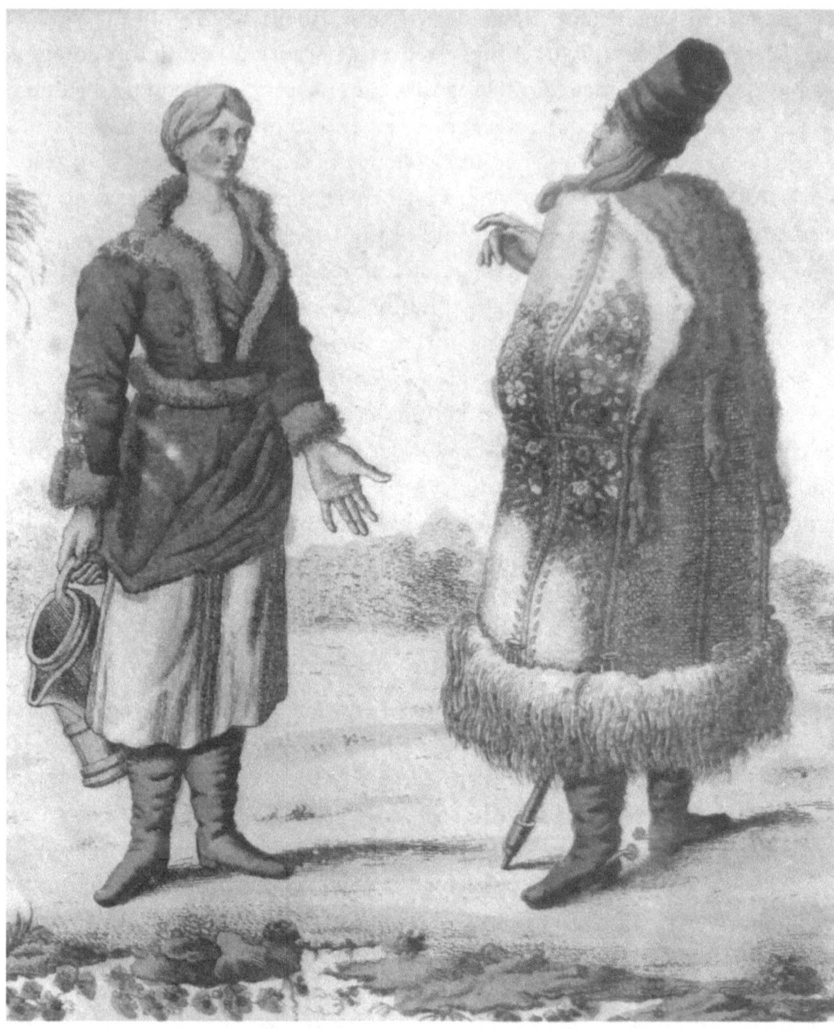

FIGURE 2.1: Nineteenth-century drawing of traditional costumes of Hungary.

to as "non-art"; Bruhn and Dunkel 2008) have been contentious. There have been times and philosophies in which aesthetic, hand-made depictions were considered to be the single best way to perceive reality because they joined heart and mind, and there have been other eras and other systems of belief in which images were believed to be seductive, and able to "overwhelm through dazzlement" (Jay 1999, 24). At issue here is whether Western picture making could ever be sufficiently objective that it could depict others free of bias (Steiner 1995) (see Figure 2.2). Given the West's long history of labelling hand-drawn images of other cultures and ethnicities as being inferior ("savages" or "heathens") (Jahoda 1999; Ramamurthy

2003), it is really no wonder why early anthropologists were suspicious of line drawings as honest documents and why they embraced the new technology of photography with the sense that "for the first time (humans) could see the world as it *really* is" (Collier and Collier 1986, 8; italics in original).[17]

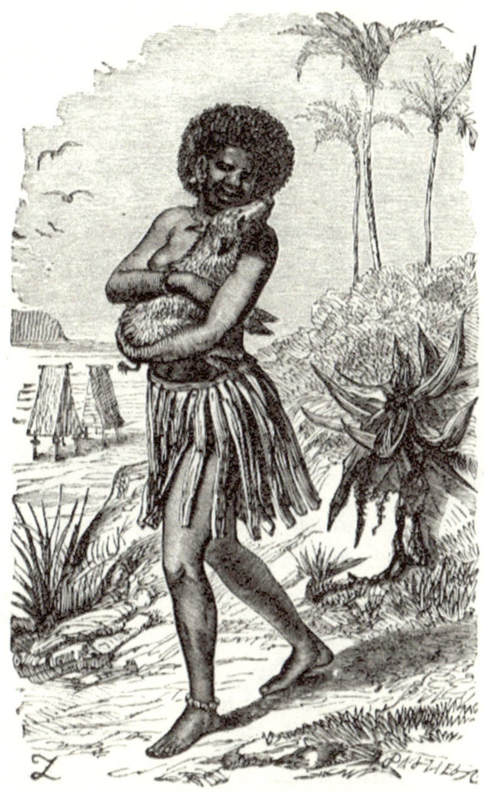

FIGURE 2.2: Image of a New Guinea woman with pet pig, from Rev. J.G. Wood's *The Natural History of Man* (c. 1880, 234).

As Emilie de Brigard (1995) tells it, anthropology and photography have always been intertwined—you might say they evolved together. In the 1890s, ethnographers were among the first academics to incorporate this technology into their research work (El Guindi 2004, 2), and photographic documentation was considered a godsend for preserving "reliable data for future generations. These photochemical records of human behavior were regarded as superior engines of description because they were believed to be objective—unimpeachable evidence" (Ruby 2000, 44). Maybe the early practitioners (anthropologists as well as professional photographers) were too eager to accept without question the promises this new invention offered, however. Because there was rarely any introspection about how and what the photographic images might communicate to viewers, decades of so-called documentary photos tended to perpetuate the Western colonial project and to support notions of racial superiority (Maxwell 1999, 38–72; Webb 1995).[18] This was why, after the 1930s, there began to be a reticence about actually engaging

17 Alison Griffiths notes that not all anthropologists embraced the new technology of cinematic documentation because of its connections to films intended for popular entertainment (1996, 18–19).

18 In the case of the US magazine *National Geographic*, it was not so much racial superiority that was being communicated in photographs of diverse people. Rather, they tended to support "the comforting feel of 'commonsense' realities captured on film" (Lutz and Collins 1993, 30). On the other hand, certain researchers, Edward S. Curtis as an example, had a great sympathy with those they photographed, yet still participated in small falsehoods (such as manipulating their images) in order to better communicate to their audiences (Slemmons 1989).

with photography as an unequivocal data-recording system (MacDougall 2006, 216). Even as seminal ethnographers were promoting observation as the foundation of ethnographic research, as noted above, there was, in general, a move away from using visual technologies in fieldwork documentation (Grimshaw 2001, 6), partly because of moving film's transformation into an "expressive" medium (MacDougall 2006, 229) that was increasingly associated with entertainment.

Recognizing the Promise and Limits of Photography

Even though anthropologists still tend to marginalize visual documentation of culture, and writing continues to be the foundation of the ethnographic project (and, in fact, the main avenue for career advancement in the field), surely we should still be able to find *complementary* ways to document complex and enigmatic social lives *visually*, right?[19] As noted above, film (still and moving photography) remains the most reliable visual recording tool for most of us.[20] Recent technological advancements have allowed us to create pictorial documents of great subtlety and detail; we can now even make plausible ethnographic films without much training, a feat that in previous decades would have been left to the experts.

We should realize, however, that the amazing photographic technologies made available to us over the decades might be deceptive, for the advantages and deficiencies of film as a documentary medium really haven't changed very much since the early 20th century. Yes, we were given portable cameras (1888), commercially available color film (1935), zoom lenses (1959), and synchronized sound for our motion pictures (1960s). More recently, we have been presented with digitally rendered pictures, storage devices that can hold thousands of images, software that can manipulate images in dozens of ways, and home color printers that can produce detailed photographs on specialized paper. Still, many of the essential limitations of the medium have remained.

What we admire about photography as a documentation system is also what limits it: as a mechanical process it allows limited interpretive input by an untrained individual at the moment the image is being made. The ethnographer controls the camera, but the camera is creating the picture. The very same act of composing and constructing a film shot, eliminating all but what appears in front of the lens, is also an act of recording thousands of visual

19 While it's true that writing is a visible means of documentation, I use the word here more in keeping with the points made by Carol Hendrickson (2008, 123) and others that drawing (and by extension photography) creates iconic representations, that is, images that actually resemble what is seen.

20 As Collier and Collier say, "The camera's machinery allows us to see without fatigue; the last exposure is just as detailed as the first" (1986, 9).

elements, many of which are, as yet, beyond our ability to analyze meaningfully (cf. Collier and Collier 1986, 13).

From my perspective, as someone who has used both photography and drawing in fieldwork research, I might even suggest that photography is a kind of "not-seeing" because it can easily become passive scanning, or mere looking—a "meandering gaze." I say this because I suspect many people who take fieldwork photographs do so as a quick shortcut for careful observation in the belief that once the image has been made, careful examination can occur later. Ethnographers may take hundreds, or even thousands, of photographs in the field, but I wonder how many of them go back with care and precision to investigate the specifics they preserve. Of course they serve the purpose of documenting a moment in time, but if this is the limit of their use, then they truly are illustrative, not deeply instructive. Reflecting on my own photos decades later, I now forget what details in the image I should be attentive to and I can't recall what those details meant in the context of the life I documented. Without reference to the particularity of behaviors in their cultural context (either through separate written descriptions of them, or notes taken directly on them), these photographic images—which seemed to hold so much promise—may have actually permitted me not to see.

For all the technological advances, ethnographers must accept that an ordinary photographic image is but a cultural interpretation, a glimpse of cultural life as seen (and heard, if sync-sound or digital technologies are used), not as fully experienced. We have to admit that it records only what is in front of the camera-eye (naturally editing out any connection to what's going on behind or beyond us and lacking simultaneous reference to parallel existences on each side).[21] We must recognize that the image is simply a depiction, a representation, that is temporal and tied to the moment that is fixed on film, and that the vision documented implies a linear and sequential reference to subsequent images made, whether they do or not. The photograph's "accuracy" is always contingent. Even though it may seem strange to say, we also have to acknowledge that photographic images can only document what is visible (the unknown, the subatomic, and the numinous worlds are unavailable to this technology).[22] Most importantly, we have to remember that a photograph is an unapologetic reduction of reality from three dimensions to two.

But I'd like to make another point here about the very practical limitations of photography as a way to document lived culture visually. Many of us have experienced the frustration of trying to "take" a photograph and being

21 This is often referred to as the *pro-filmic*, a term that tries to address the fact that there is a real referent in front of the camera at the same time we are recording our representative slice of it.

22 James Elkins explores the many things we "don't see" in our daily lives, including things that don't correspond to our desires, things that are useless, things that are too familiar, and things that are camouflaged, to name a few (1996, 51–63).

thwarted in one way or another: subjects of our attention suddenly look away or hide; the camera apparatus fails us; we drop the camera; the batteries are dead; we lose our camera roll or memory disk.[23] The wonder of the camera is its technological prowess, but that is also its weakness, because when we depend on it and it fails us, we are at a complete loss.

Eyes, Mind, Hand, Paper, Pencil, Line

Recognizing the limitations of the photographic medium might make us wonder in what additional ways we can document the complexities and richness of life visually. That's where drawing by hand comes in. Now, while drawing has never been completely left behind by ethnographers and others seriously interested in documenting culture (see, for example, Colwell-Chanthaphonh 2011 and Geismar 2014), historically it has been devalued if not outright ignored. I have to admit that drawing has some of the same limitations found in photography noted above (e.g., it can only be a glimpse of a moment in time; it is an interpretive depiction—a translation; and it reduces three dimensions to two), yet as a method of documentation it can offer capabilities that surpass it: the drawn image can be added to and subtracted from, it can be made over a period of time, it can slip in details not currently in the "frame," it can stretch and compress real views, it can depict such ephemeral things as dreams and feelings and "events (that) bring forth drama and conflict" (Vannini 2015, 7), and it can incorporate a variety of coding systems beyond the pictorial such as words, numerals, punctuation marks, and familiar symbols like arrows and motion lines (see Figure 2.3).[24] When an event or image remains alive in our minds, even as a fragment, we can reconstruct it in drawing—no matter how we perceive our own abilities or skills in this act—from any perspective we can imagine and as many times and ways as are required. Line drawing, as an ethnographic method, not only supplements the didactic preciseness of writing but also complements photography's ability to visually document cultural-social life, adding a distinctly human touch when it is needed.

In this "visual thinking,"[25] the ethnographer is using an attentive, active, and intelligent eye, and is "engaged in streamlining, accentuating, and categorizing

23 In 2003, I returned to Samosir Island to see what changes had occurred. I had my trusty Pentax camera with me at all times and used a 36-shot roll to document the loss of tourism. Because I was depending on the camera doing my work, I was not really paying attention to details. When I lost the roll getting on a moving bus, I could not later reproduce in drawing what I had seen, because, as noted above, I had not *seen* what I perceived.

24 See both Carol Hendrickson's article "Visual Field Notes" (2008, 121) and Karina Kuschnir's article "Teaching Anthropologists to Draw" (2014) for other ways and reasons to consider using drawings in ethnographic research situations.

25 See Rudolf Arnheim's book *Visual Thinking* (1969), but also refer to John-Steiner's chapter of the same title in her book *Notebooks of the Mind* (1985) for more discussion on this concept.

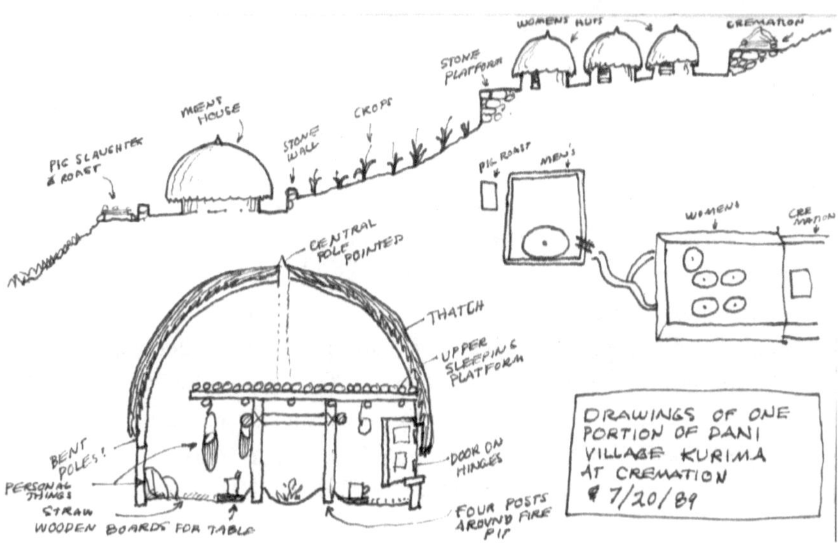

FIGURE 2.3: My field excursion drawing of houses in Kurima Village, Papua Province, Indonesia.

impressions that are then crystallized into larger entities. These acts of knowing are both individual and social in nature because categorizing is rooted in and influenced by the cultural framework of experience" (John-Steiner 1985, 108). Drawing to see is a way to allow your ethnographic mind to incorporate varied ways of knowing at a single moment.[26] Because you will be translating the visual world into a visual code (rather than into a verbal code),[27] you might find that the data you record will have stronger resonances to the "real" (people, objects, practices, relationships, performances), and may perhaps be more honest and perhaps more accurate.[28]

There are other reasons for considering drawing to be a way to help document ethnographic observations, too. For one, both anecdotal evidence and careful academic research seem to indicate that taking notes by hand, and by extension making visual notes via drawing, engages the brain in a way that increases cognitive processes and memory (Edwards 1986, 40; Mueller and Oppenheimer 2014; Schifrin 2008; Stafford 2007, 11, 154), particularly

26 In speaking of creative arts therapy research, Shaun McNiff notes a similar effect: "Art-based research comprises both introspective and empirical inquiry. Art is by definition a combination of the two. The artist-researcher initiates a series of artistic expressions as a means of personal introspection and the process of inquiry generates empirical data which are systematically reviewed" (2000, 57).

27 This is keeping in mind that symbolic writing systems, particularly those from the Near East, are deeply intertwined with representational pictorial systems (Schmandt-Besserat 2007).

28 Lucien Taylor notes that this is the case with ethnographic film as well, saying that (moving) film "captures something of the lyricism of the lived experience" and suggests that if it does have a resemblance to any literary form, it might resemble poetry rather than prose (1996, 88).

analogic thinking—the ability to connect different domains of perception and thought (Kantrowitz 2012b, 11). Unlike the possibility of passive scanning mentioned above, active scrutiny of the observed world through a coordinated behavior like the act of drawing can allow the viewer to perceive *more*, or see more *deeply*.[29] Gregory Curtis describes how important it was to make copies of the ancient cave paintings of Europe because "it is impossible to see the art merely by looking at the wall. The intense concentration copying requires reveals signs and images that were invisible before" (2007, 203). In my own ethnographic research in North Sumatra, Indonesia, I found that I gained appreciation of the entomological world around me by collecting and then drawing moths I found, something I considered to be a hobby. However, upon seeing these drawings, my carving teacher introduced me to aspects of Batak culture that I would never have discovered otherwise—from local conceptions about drug-taking tourists to traditional notions of "filth" (Causey 2012).

"Okay, great," you might say, "you are telling me that I should learn to draw because it'll make my ethnographic observations stronger or more perceptive. What if I tell you I *can't* draw? Then what?"

Well, here's my answer: I'm pretty sure you can draw (somehow) because, unless your vision is seriously impaired, I know you can see (somehow). Perhaps what you need is encouragement to draw in order to see. Perhaps that's all you need . . . that, and an interest in drawing, a conviction you can do it, and regular practice. Perhaps what you need is to give yourself the permission to enjoy exploring line-work without judgment. If you are willing to give it a try, I'll introduce you to some strategies to start and some introductory practical Etudes. But first, here's another bullet list:

Basic Strategies for Drawing to See

- *Remember That Attentive Seeing Is Not "Natural" and That Drawing Is Not Easy*. Seeing-drawing as an ethnographic method is not a genetic inheritance, it is a system for perceiving the world. It is a code, very much like language, and must be learned and practiced to be of any use.

29 Art educators Andrea Kantrowitz (2012a) and Terry Rosenberg (2008) both give strong evidence to show that the practice of drawing enables unique kinds of discovery. Similarly, Barbara Maria Stafford explores in depth how the physical brain perceives the spaces surrounding us, addressing the question, "How does our unconscious internal spatial map become conscious as an actualization of presentation: that is, as a concrete image or extra-personal place to which we are attached?" (2007, 105).

It may be true that some people are more adept or quick in learning how to see and draw. Okay, that's fine: some other people have beautiful voices and yet others have graceful movements. Nevertheless, singing and athletics must be taught to them and they must practice what they have learned. Similarly, you will teach yourself to see by means of drawing exercises. It's really that simple.

- *You Are Allowed to Be "Mindless."* I noted above that our culture (particularly via language) provides us with ways of defining, naming, and interpreting the incredibly complex world around us. Language gives a set of concept-utterances that allow our minds to conceive of a given situation within seconds so we can interact with it effectively. I stressed above that we take the language-based system for granted and that we usually use it without thinking, noting that this can either mollify or divert our perceptions. What I'm asking you to do here is practice seeing the world *without* words.[30] This kind of documentation may take more time, and that is why you must relax and focus.
- *Reduce Complexity in Order to See.* Instead of seeing the world as a string of nouns and verbs, try to see your visible surroundings as a single collage of simple shapes and forms. Remember what it was like to be a child drawing the world. Temporarily reduce the world to familiar shapes and find the edges that seem to separate them (from their constituent parts but also from things near or around them). Make a line where you perceive an edge. Focus on form, not meaning (and remember that visual details can be added later).
- *See the Whole Before the Parts.* As you are reducing the complexity of what you see, try to perceive the entire view within your scope before you distinguish each of the elements. Try to see what's before you as an entire composition, looking for the balances between lights, darks, colors, textures, between still and moving objects, and between inanimate things and vibrant life forms. Sometimes if you blur your vision you will see the whole more easily.
- *Abandon Caution.* Seeing-drawing can be a rash or transgressive act: you are making energized dashes and lines on paper that claim to stop the onslaught of the unfolding real in an effort to capture one glimpse of it.[31] It is, in some ways, a reiteration of the original act of creation (see

30 Similarly, the writer William Burroughs once said, "When you start thinking in images, without words, you're on your way" (John-Steiner 1985, 29).

31 Drawing, and the arts in general, express the intentions and perceptions of creators in a way that is said to be "sovereign" (that is, it cannot be sublimated into other rational codes; it is its own autonomous system and it "cannot be recognized without being reduced," Menke 1998, 253–54), and because of that it may clash with (or subvert) non-aesthetic rational codes (231–34).

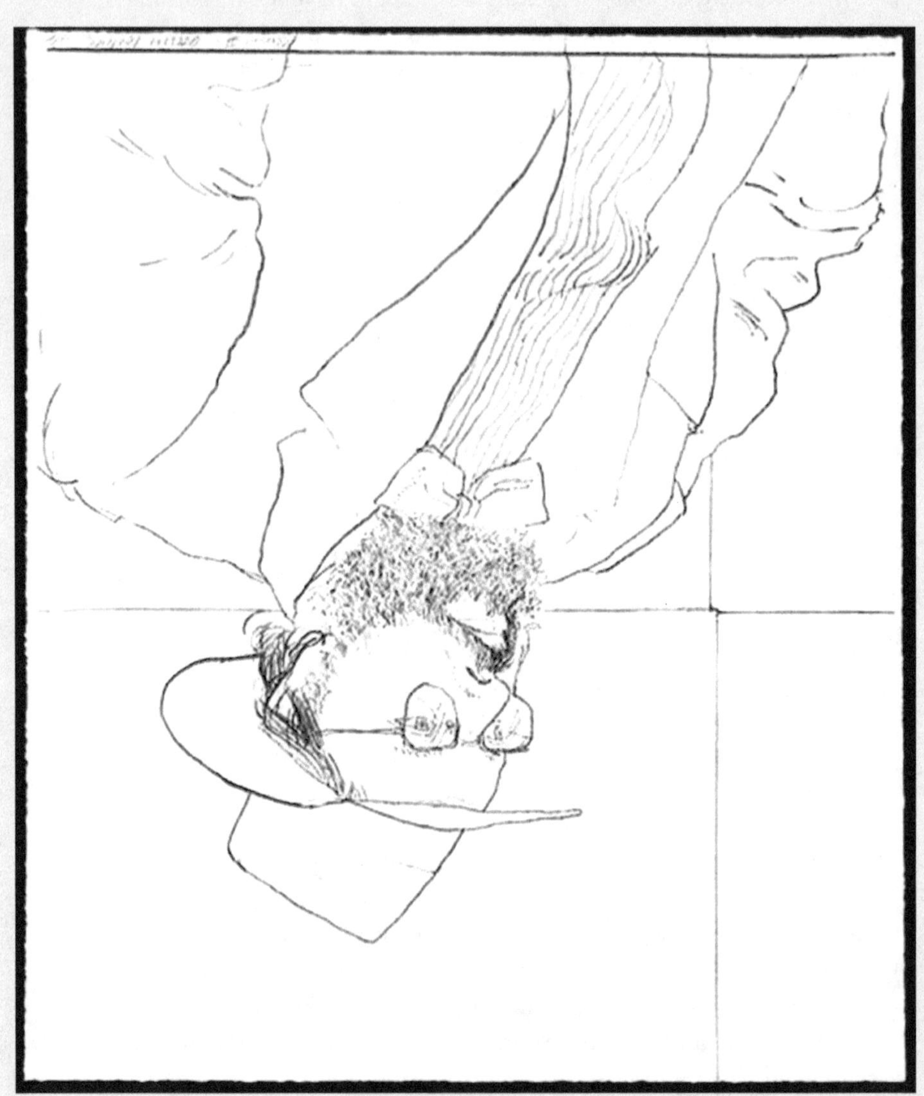

FIGURE 2.4: Upside-down drawing (David Hockney, "Henry Geldzahler with Hat" 1976, Lithograph, Edition of 96, 14 1/4 x 12 1/8", © David Hockney / Gemini G.E.L.).

ETUDE ONE, Upside-Down Drawing (5-6 minutes): This first exercise is very straightforward: copy the lines of the David Hockney drawing you see in Figure 2.4. Don't turn the drawing around, but rather draw exactly what you see, line for line. Try not to "interpret" what you see, and certainly don't make your mind do a mental flip of it (so that you are drawing right-side up to what you are seeing upside-down). Just start anywhere in the drawing and copy precisely what you see. (This exercise was adapted with permission from Betty Edwards's *Drawing on the Right Side of the Brain*, 1979.)

Chapter Three). Seeing-drawing is also like the utterance of any performative word (e.g., "I promise," that becomes true when it is uttered) in that the line *becomes* the perceived. Because of this, you must be brave and abandon all caution and fear.[32] But rather than becoming stern and serious, you will try to remain playful and curious. Remember the world is never complete—no scene or object is complete—so your rendition can only be a version of how things seem to you at THIS moment in time. Your drawings are merely "notes" on what you've seen.[33]

- *Take Charge.* Take charge of your Etudes—with gusto—and just allow the lines you make to unfold before you. Accept what you are given. If all you have when you are working in the field is a stubby pencil, or a piece of torn paper, if it starts to rain when you need to put your lines down, or if your eyes are straining in the darkness, continue on. Use all of your circumstances to your advantage and integrate whatever situation you are in as part of the data you are recording (see Chapter Three).
- *Draw to See, Not the Other Way Around.* You are drawing to see, not seeing to draw. Seeing is the product, the line is the process to get there.

First Etudes

As noted in Chapter One, what you need for most of the exploratory Etudes are sheets of unlined paper (ordinary white paper) and an old-fashioned (i.e., not mechanical) pencil with a sharpened lead. Sit comfortably at a well-lit table, without fear or tension. Now, follow the directions.

32 See also Weir 1998, 87, for more encouragement in this area.

33 The notion of drawn lines as simply imprecise marks that attempt to capture a person's perceived image is perhaps comparable to Theodor Adorno's concept of written notation trying to capture music: "Musical notation is an aide-memoire. It does not carry the whole, (which) is much, much too undifferentiated, and this is something fundamental that still remains—and possibly even increases—the more refined one's notation becomes" (2006, 93; for a more thorough discussion, see 52–53).

Etude One is an exercise I adapted (with generous permission) from Betty Edwards's book *Drawing on the Right Side of the Brain* (1979). One of the reasons that copying a master drawing upside-down works is because you are freed from doing something you think has to be "right." Once you turn the drawing around and see how well your drawing resonates with the one given—even though it is not an exact copy, it does convey visual information that is content-rich—you begin to see what you are able to do.

Copying, whether right-side-up or upside-down, is not cheating. Copying the work of others is an essential way for all of us to see the world around us in a different way. Accept that the other drawer might have solved a problem of visual translation, and learn that solution. We may have been taught that so-called Good Drawings are "original" and that they spring from some special place called "creativity." But the truth is that while all drawings are unique, they are often inspired by—and thus derivative of—the work of others. There is nothing wrong with that. Knowing so should relieve you if your fear is that you must create something "new" when you make a picture. Recognizing that each image you make (whether depicting the real world, or copying the work of others) is a response to images already made, and that you are "in dialog" with them,[34] will give you confidence that there is no impossible standard by which you will be judged. Claiming your confidence is the struggle half won!

For those who want to understand much more about the process of drawing, and for even more explanation on how the process of drawing helps you see, I strongly suggest finding and reading a copy of Edwards's book *Drawing on the Artist Within* (1986). It was this book that changed my perceptions about what drawing could be and that opened my eyes to *see*.

In this book, Edwards talks about how our educational systems might actually be telling us we can't draw (1986, 5–6) and leading many of us to believe that we have no "talent" for drawing. When you think back, some of you might remember that the last happy time you experienced drawing was when you were about 7 or 8 years of age. After that, teachers began to notice the so-called good drawers and held their work up for all to see, ignoring or perhaps belittling those whose drawings didn't fit the preconceived notion of "good."[35] As you might guess, that kind of subjective judgment can crush the aspirations of people whose works do not fit the criteria, so they stop. This is a preposterous situation. As Edwards notes, "In my work with groups

34 This idea resonates with Mikhail Bakhtin's notion that every utterance is a response to another that has gone before (for which he used the term *dialogism*), suggesting that all of our "original" works—spoken and written—are simply part of an ongoing human conversation (1990, 276, and 1994, 68–69).

35 I was one of those whose work my teachers held up, but I was never proud of it, knowing even at that age that the criterion being used was nothing but opinion. When a teacher's back was turned, I was busy copying classmates whose work I thought had more life or energy.

of artistically untrained people, I have discovered that any person of sound mind can learn to draw; the probability is the same as for learning to read . . . I claim that anyone can learn enough seeing skills to draw a good likeness of something seen 'out there' in the real world" (1986, p. 7).

Ethnographic Application: This exercise is not a parlor trick to show you how much better you can draw than you might think you can! It is a serious, cognitive activity. It allows you to free yourself from interpreting and translating what you see and encourages you to simply see (and draw what you see). In terms of ethnographic research, this Etude is useful when you are attempting to understand shape relationships or object distances. If you need to carefully depict a person's facial expression or a detail of their costume, or perhaps need to draw exactly how a carver holds his knife (as I did), take a photo, turn it upside-down, and practice this Etude by simply copying down exactly what you see, not what you think you see. In drawing the carver at work, I began to appreciate the tension of his hand's firm grip as well as to notice where the energy of the scene was: the point of the knife in the wood. Drawing this can convey more than a photograph is able to do.

Now that you may be feeling more comfortable with imagining yourself as a "good drawer," let's move on to the next Etude.

ETUDE TWO, Simple Tracing (2–3 minutes): Find a photograph with high contrasts between lights and darks (portraits from the newspaper business section or sports page will work, or you might consider using an image of your prospective field site). Hold the image securely (or tape it to the desk), and with an ordinary pencil (for this Etude, a felt-tip pen would also work) trace what you consider to be the *basic outlines* of the main subjects. Don't fuss with the details—just discover the edges that separate one entity from another (e.g., hair from head, arm from torso, body from background).

What seems like a simple, even childish, project is actually encouraging you to see that complex images are composed of uncomplicated shapes. *Tracing is not cheating.* Tracing is a legitimate way to see some of the essence of life. Drawing on top of the newsprint photograph is important here because the photo has already performed one of the most difficult tasks of making a picture: translating the three-dimensional world into a two-dimensional one. Trying to figure out distances between objects or people, trying to judge sizes of what's in the foreground and what's in the background, and trying to conjure up the proportions of a face . . . are all solved by the camera. Now that it's done, you can concentrate on imagining how to render the image in very simple forms (geometric, linear, amoeba-like, angular; you decide). Remember: a drawing (even a tracing) is simply a rendition—an interpreted depiction—of the visual world. There is no "right" or "perfect" rendition, so there's no reason to think that your lines must look any particular way. As long as you are concentrating on seeing basic forms, you are learning how to translate the complex visual world into simple lines.

Reducing the complexity of the visual world is one of the most useful skills you can develop. As I've noted, we tend to see the world around us as a seamless whole, much of it preconceived for us into discrete entities that we can name and that we can then take for granted. When trying to really concentrate and see that same world, we may become distracted by textures, colors, and natural movements, all of which our eyes and mind tell us are distinct and meaningful. The photograph helps us immensely by mechanically freezing a single moment so we can focus not on details, but on the composition—the fundamental shapes integrated together. It is best to do this Etude several times on a variety of different kinds of images: portraits, action shots, landscape views, crowd scenes, still lives.

Come back to this Etude whenever you feel that you might be forgetting how to see basic physical forms and practice finding the essential shapes you are familiar with.

Ethnographic Application: This kind of drawing has immediate use in your ethnographic research, for you can use this technique on your own photographs to re-examine a familiar locale or scene, to better understand a complex design, or to discover subject interactions you may have overlooked. By making a tracing of a photographic image, you are at once teaching yourself how to both see and draw basic edge boundaries while also examining the image with great care. As you make the general outlines, your mind and eyes will be registering details that might not appear on first look. This is how my professor Linda Schele taught me to investigate the subtleties of ancient Maya inscriptions to allow the intricate elements to "pop" into view (Causey 2015).

Other Familiar Shapes

You've practiced seeing simple forms in a complex picture, so now you are going to practice adding to your repertoire of forms. Like Etude Two, this one might seem like I'm sending you back to primary school. That's okay, right? Shrug your shoulders high, hold them there . . . then drop them suddenly. Loosen up and have a little fun. Now, practice Etude Three.

Copying the letter and number shapes reminds you that you already have facility in holding and controlling the pencil. When you realize that they are simple shapes that can be turned and manipulated (stretched, bent, made huge or small), you'll see how you can begin to take them out of their ordinary coded context and join them in novel ways, whether joined side by side or stacked.

ETUDE THREE, Numbers and Letters (5-7 minutes): With broad, certain strokes, draw the elements you see in Figures 2.5 and 2.6. Try to replicate *just* the shapes you see rather than writing "letters and numbers" because then you'll see that these familiar forms (forms you have vast experience making) are simple and direct. Work diligently and attentively, but don't take too long to copy each letter or number shape. Please see Figures 2.5 and 2.6.

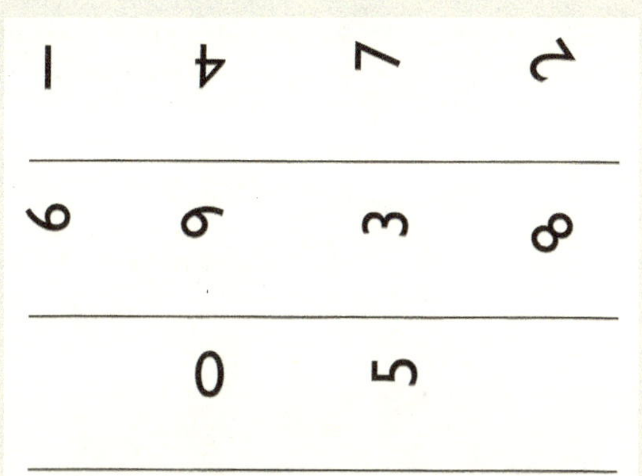

FIGURE 2.5: Numbers.

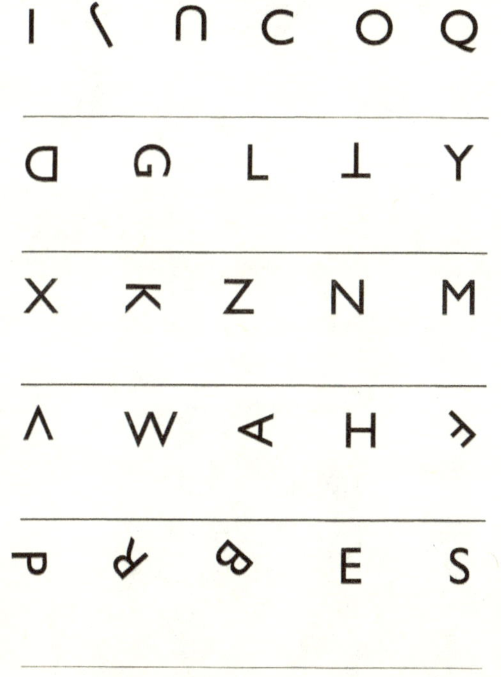

FIGURE 2.6: Letters.

Using letters and numbers in this way is not cheating. Each of us has already been taught (at some time or another) how to make the letters and numbers, so why not apply this visual knowledge in a new way, if it enables you to better document what you are seeing? Every computer-literate person knows how to

ETUDE FOUR, Finding Numbers and Letters (5–7 minutes): *Part A*: Joining what you've learned in Etudes Two and Three, find another printed image and trace its essential structure with your pencil using the form of letters and numbers. Look for the edges (where one thing is distinct from another) and draw the shapes you see (please see Figure 2.7). *Part B*: Once you feel comfortable with finding letter-number shapes in an image, find another picture and copy freehand the familiar shapes you see there on a blank piece of paper. Try to copy the composition of the picture as closely as possible, without going into too much detail (please see Figure 2.8).

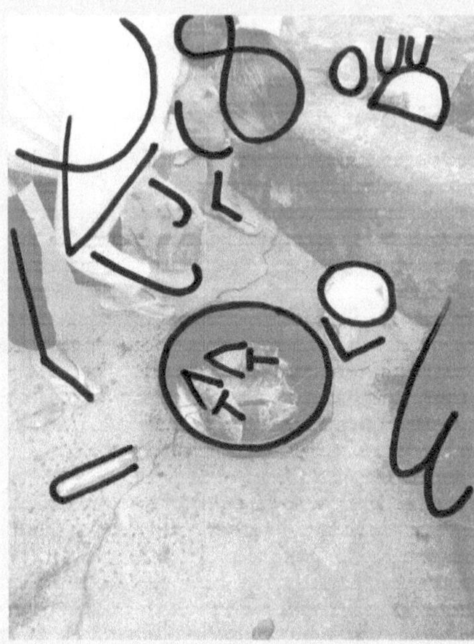

FIGURE 2.7: Finding number-letter shapes in a photograph.

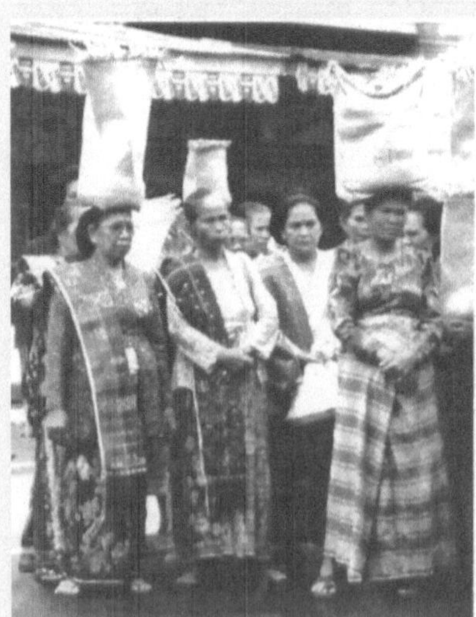

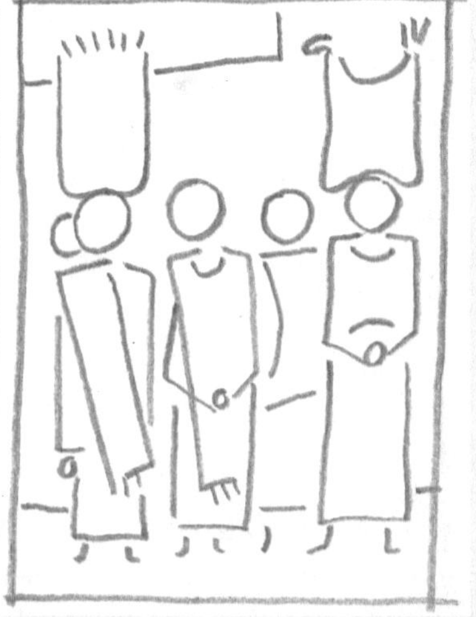

FIGURE 2.8: Drawing number-letter shapes freehand on blank paper.

use or invent emoticons using the keyboard symbols, right? Well, using letters and numbers to recreate the basic structure of an image in picture form is just an expansion of that notion and is much more flexible.

Here, try it: make a horizon line anywhere on your paper; make four strong capital H's one after the other standing on the horizon line, left to right; balance four capital A's on top of the H's. There! You have a row of gabled houses. Make a slanted, elongated H touching one of your houses and put several more cross-lines in it. Now you have a ladder leaning on it. You have begun to tell a visual story. Please move on to Etude Four.

When you practice seeing your surroundings intently, it is sometimes difficult to translate the visual complexity into lines. With practice, you will soon be able to reduce the complexity of what you see into simple forms to draw the structure of the view you are seeing. Once you have this structure, the composition, and the spatial relationships between the things, you can then focus on adding necessary details using other kinds of lines (see Chapter Three). For now, you are honing your fundamental skills using familiar systems (here, letters and numbers) as *visual codes*, not connected to verbal or mathematical processes. Later, you will develop a more nuanced set of techniques using the Etudes in coming chapters to help document your seeing via drawing with greater accuracy and confidence.

Ethnographic Application: When doing participant-observation in the field, it is often not appropriate to bring out your drawing pad to carefully draw what you are seeing. Instead, you might only be able to jot a few lines to remind you of a view or action. If your mind wastes time fumbling for a way to translate the vision, you may have lost your chance to draw what you saw. Once, when I was walking on a rural road outside Ubud, Bali, I happened upon a small knot of people making preparations for a cremation. I wanted to document as much as I could without intruding on the rituals happening nearby and, because I always carry a small notebook in my pocket, was able to make a few rapid drawings before my presence became too obvious (Figure 2.9).

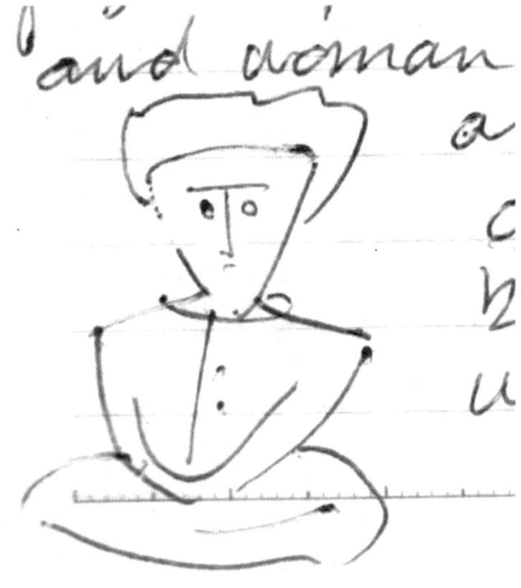

FIGURE 2.9: Quick drawing of a Balinese seated figure.

As you can see, my drawing of a seated figure is a quick reduction of all the intricate details to basic letter forms: V for face, T for eyebrows and nose, O's for eyes, nested U's for arms, T and a colon for the shirt, parentheses

ETUDE FIVE, Doodling While the Mind Wanders (7–10 minutes): This Etude is partly for fun, but it also lets you practice using your hand-pencil dexterously. It's simple: turn on the radio or television to a foreign language station, only listening and not paying too much attention. Let your mind wander while the voices speak and then begin to doodle on plain paper. (For some reason, it often helps to tear off one or two edges of the page so it is irregularly shaped.) Just play with shapes, trying out spirals, concentric circles, rows and columns of straight lines, zigzags, grids, squares, and so on. Let your mind wander to some calm place and think about things you like. You can admire your doodles while you are making them, or you can just let your eyes fall into a blur while you do this. It's a different kind of doodling than you might have done before (while chatting on the phone or listening to some dull talk or lecture), so give yourself to the exploration of making shapes, feeling the pencil, trying out different textures of lines. Resist writing words, but you can also play with variations on the shapes (numbers, letters) in Etude Three.

for the thighs, two dashes to indicate legs. It's enough to help remind me what I saw, documenting only the most essential aspects. Expanding your visual system to include such code systems as letters, numbers, and even musical notation—and feeling confident in using them—will increase the speed at which you are able to draw what you see and will provide you with an additional way of documenting the fast-moving visual world around you.

An important part of drawing to see is becoming more familiar with your hand's ability to manipulate a pencil or pen. As we move further into the digital world we may have less chance to work in this analog medium. Doodling while you listen is a way to reacquaint yourself with how to move your hand and fingers to make different kinds of lines, to practice your dexterity skills, and also to explore what it feels like to simply play with lines on paper.

Last Words

I think you have a good sense of how drawing may help you see better, particularly when you are doing your ethnographic research but perhaps also in your own daily life. Relaxing into these first Etudes will allow you to see that drawing, when the focus is actually seeing more carefully and fully, is less daunting than you might have thought it was . . . it might even seem to be a little bit fun. But there's more to it. It's time to move forward. It's time to take some big risks.

CHAPTER 3

DARE TO SEE AND DARE TO DRAW

A Fascinating Risk

I got some very good advice once. I was taking a course called "Masculinities" with Professor Bob Fernea and was trotting down the hall beside him after class, offering some ideas for my final paper. He listened to each, making a funny "Mmmmm?" after each idea until I ran out of topics. We walked a little further and he said, "Well, you could do any one of those, really, or . . . you could take a risk. I say: take a *risk*!" He clapped me heartily on the shoulder, raised his smiling eyebrows very high, and returned to his office.

Since then, anytime I question whether I should follow a predictable path or try something new, that advice sings in my ear. So I pass that thought on to you. It doesn't mean to do dangerous and thoughtless things, or to pounce on a project with half-baked assumptions. What it means is that when you are feeling comfortable and safe and are wondering what is next, you might consider taking an inspired and logical jump into the unknown—that is, take a calculated risk. In trying to draw to see, you are doing just that. You are, in fact, daring yourself to perceive the world in a new way when doing your ethnographic research, and in taking that small risk you might find out something unexpected, remarkable, or even revolutionary.

When you use pencil and paper to help you see, you are claiming the fundamental right to represent the world around you imagistically. Your act is a direct statement to yourself and others that "This is how I see it." There is no backing down, and no apologies are needed or expected, no matter what others might tell you. It is your right to document your interpreted rendition of the unfolding, emergent world—your fraction of it—and as long as you can stand behind what you create (ethically, morally, intellectually), your work is as much an unassailable statement as any other document you make. It is a fascinating risk, a real dare, to commit the three-dimensional space-time reality to two dimensions using your own unmediated rendition of a visual code because it is unarguable and irreducible.[1] You are indicating both that you choose to depict your surroundings through pictures and that you have permitted yourself to do so.[2] Your interpretation via drawing is not purporting to be the real (how could it be?), but is rather an admission that this is your best effort at depicting in drawn form what you witnessed: to say, in Michael Taussig's words, *"I swear I saw this!"* (2011, 1; italics in original).

Daring to Draw

One of the most difficult tasks of my fieldwork, which focused on tourism, was to make photographic images of the actual tourists about whom I was trying to write (Causey 2003, 18). For this reason, I began to make drawings of tourists from life, thinking that I would not be perceived as invading their vacation space if it appeared that I was writing in a journal. My prying eyes betrayed me nonetheless, and I was almost always "caught": the subjects of my sketch would pick up and leave, scowling at me as they passed by. It was for this reason that I began to memorize tourist features and styles that I would re-create in line and paint at home.

In trying to remember what I saw over a period of days, I'd amalgamate several individuals into one and in this way create a kind of visual Weberian "ideal type" (Weber 1969, 109–12). Making these composite character studies helped me "see," in my mind, details of Western tourist attire and pose, features that I would go back and refine until I was content that I had created an accurate sort of stereotype. I made two kinds of representation: "type" drawings of individuals out of context, and "genre" scenes with the types interacting. Each of these pictures took many months of intermittent work to complete, and it was with interest that I saw my style changing as they progressed. Several of the composite examples exist in pencil sketch or ink form only, a sign that I had not fully embraced that particular type.

1 I say "unmediated" in reference to similar image-making acts that use such machines or instruments like a camera. I mention "visual code" to further define this act as daring because such a thing could also be said of writing, which is a much more expectable act.

2 Barbara Maria Stafford discusses the value in understanding that the viewer (or artist) is "emblazoned" by what is perceived, and that the act of perceiving is a "variegated experience (that) becomes personal for us, revealing how we catch ourselves in the intimate act of feeling and seeing" (2007, 139).

Working with my carving teacher, Partoho, at his carving table most days, I saw tourists' behavior up close. At first, I tried to depict what I saw in a documentary style. But I'll be honest with you: there came a point in my research when I began to feel first annoyed and then disgusted by tourists' petty desires and childish ways. I began to see the tourist type drawings change from attempts at accurate (albeit cartoonish) portrayals to exercises in pure self-indulgence. I even wrote a memo to myself in my field notes that I should be careful not to let my flights of fancy—which actually felt like naughty acts of revenge since tourists had been so difficult to interview—to take grip on me, forcing me to lose my sense of ethnographic neutrality.

. . . But I didn't stop. I allowed myself to develop everyday genre scenes of the tourists, just as I had for the Bataks (see Chapter One), except in these I freed myself from restrictions and any pretense of "objectivity." I still wanted the pictures to convey an amalgamation of events and actions, and I still focused on *accurate* portrayals, but now I gave in to a wicked humor, too.

It was fairly late in my fieldwork when I finished the genre scene of the souvenir marketplace (Figure 3.1), and because I had developed a good relationship with Partoho and Ito, I showed it and the tourist "type" paintings to them (Figure 3.2). They examined them in the same quiet, thoughtful way they

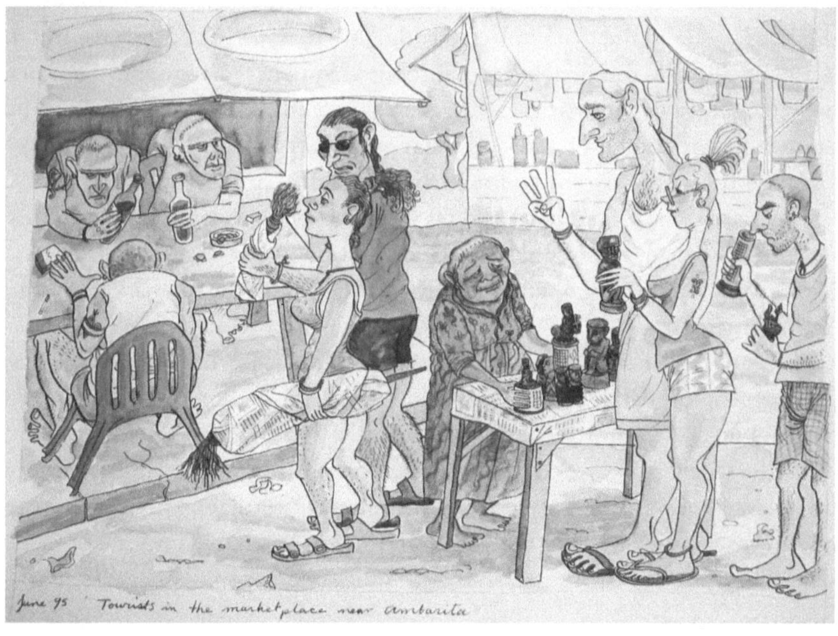

FIGURE 3.1: Genre scene of the souvenir marketplace at Siallagan.

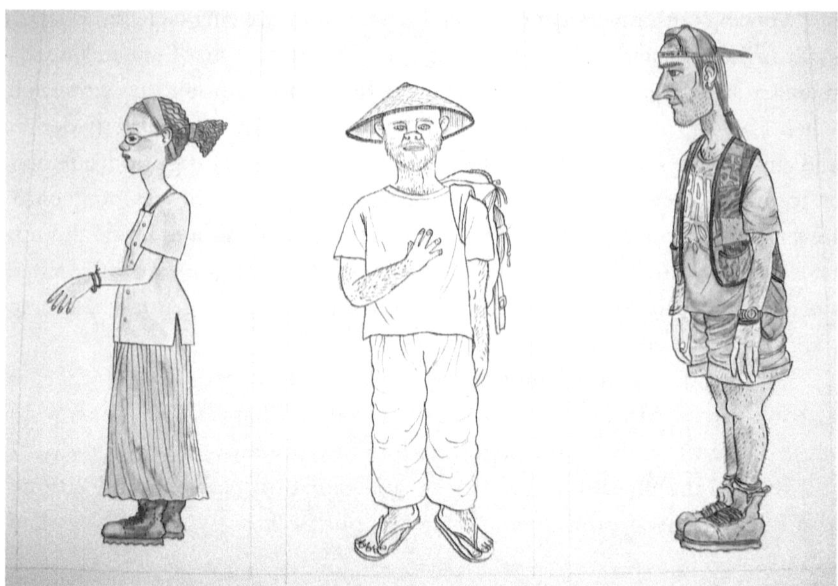

FIGURE 3.2: Tourist "type" drawings.

had looked at the market scene many months earlier. Ito pointed out what she saw as "mistakes," such as the great difference between the focal tourist and the Batak seller in the marketplace (saying, "We're not THAT small, Andru!"), but generally saw the drawing as a factual document. Partoho, on the other hand, having spent more time with me, looked askance when he started to "read" the painting. "It's funny . . . but there's no need for such anger," he said.[3] His wife Ito was intrigued by his remark and said, "Anger? Who's angry?!" I knew Partoho meant me, but I told his wife that the tourists sitting at the back table looked mad; she responded, "Yeah, that's how they are sometimes . . . but you got this wrong: there's no café like that down at the market, Andru. You changed that."

When I returned home to Texas, one of my graduate school friends saw my paintings and urged me to exhibit them in one of the anthropology conference rooms. I got permission to do so, and included many landscapes and still lifes in the mix. The reactions to the Batak genre paintings and the tourist depictions came swiftly: several of my cohort were worried that by juxtaposing the humorous tourist drawings with the more serious narrative ones, all of them would be "read" as caricatures and I would be seen as someone who was at

3 Partoho said, *"Gambar ini lucu! ... Tapi, janganlah begitu marah, ja?"* This last phrase can either mean "don't you be so mad" or "don't make it (the painting or the tourists) so angry."

best cruel and at worst racist. Several people sternly warned me that exhibiting caricatures was tantamount to admitting I lacked any sense of "ethnographic objectivity," a characteristic still valued and defended at that time (although it was being questioned). And so I removed them, keeping only the landscapes and still lifes on view.

I didn't defend my paintings at the time, as I would now, but I do remember wondering how other (non-anthropologist) Westerners might perceive them. I dared myself to represent the world I saw in a way I thought best suited it. My intention in making them was, as noted, a way to visually document a world in a way that film could not, recognizing that some of the paintings were serious and others were humorous. Except for my picture of the tourists in the souvenir marketplace, I did not—and do not—see these drawings as caricatures (a style of drawing that "loads" meaning into a depiction to tease or humiliate), but rather as fitting with the long Western tradition of "genre" paintings (those whose focus is daily life and ordinary people) (Silver 2006, 1), the most familiar of which may be those from medieval marginalia and house-books (Figure 3.3)[4] and from later 16th-century Flanders artists (Pieter Bruegel the Elder's being the most famous). Lately, I see my drawings as, in the words of art historian Larry Silver, a "pictorial laboratory" for viewers (myself included) to measure ourselves (2006, 9), perhaps even including, as did Bruegel, "allegorical figures and moralized landscape spaces" (51). And perhaps this is exactly why they make some anthropologist viewers uncomfortable: they are perceived as objects of unconscious judgment that define "social distinction and hierarchy" (108) and "urban bourgeois disdain" (107).

Even if seen in the light of Bruegel the Elder's more respectful compositions, my paintings might still be perceived to have, as Silver notes, the taint of "condescension without criticism" when looking at the "honest and persevering peasants" (2006, 125). In speaking of the Flanders paintings, Silver echoes James Elkins's fears of inattentive "looking" mentioned earlier. He says, "Each act of vision mingles seeing with not seeing, so that vision can become less a way of gathering information than avoiding it" (201) ... "The paradox of seeing is that the more forcefully (we) try to see, the more blind (we) become" (210).

Silver's words may seem to contradict what I'm saying here—that attentive perception can increase a drawer's access to "seeing" more accurately—but I think a deeper reading of his words shows otherwise. The crucial difference is the intent of the person drawing, for if one simply falls back on pre-existing

4 To see other such images, please refer to Wolfegg 1998.

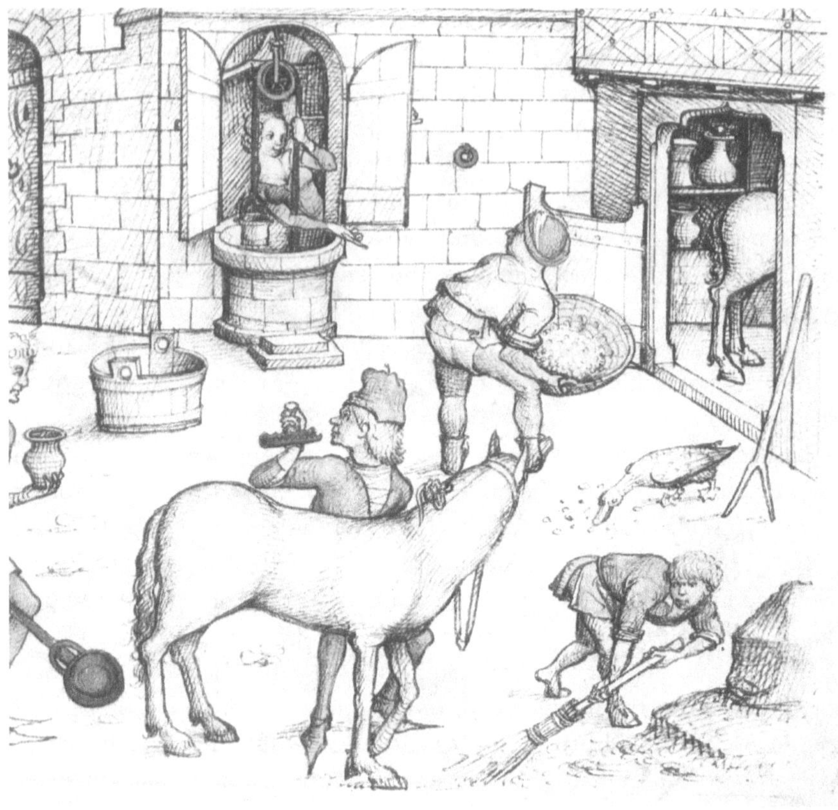

FIGURE 3.3: Image from a medieval house-book (used with permission).

assumptions and prejudices to articulate in pen and paper what comes into sight (as Silver suggests might have happened to the Flanders artists), the resulting drawings will not, of course, be able to open the drawer's eyes to the possibilities that present themselves. The point of drawing to see is precisely *not* to settle for preconceptions but to allow delineation to act as the window into a lived reality.

If drawing can be useful for gathering, assessing, documenting, and understanding cultural behavior, it is clear that the ethnographer-drawer must engage with it attentively and without self-imposed fear, and must analyze the resulting pictures with candor and reflexive honesty. Using drawing as a legitimate ethnographic method will only help us understand what we see *if* we can learn to appreciate the subjective insights it provides, and we can only do this if we approach the act of drawing-seeing with happiness, playfulness, and curiosity.

ETUDE SIX, Blind Ostrich (1 minute): This Etude is adapted from a 1906 book called *Pig Book* (by "A. Pigge"), which is a kind of autograph album where each signer would also have to draw a pig . . . with eyes closed. Like the signers of a century ago, you are going to draw "blind," but not a pig.[5] Please do the following: First, put the tip of your pencil in the middle of the paper. Now close your eyes and see an ostrich in your mind-eye. Focus. Really see the image in your mind. When you have it fixed, keeping your eyes closed (No, I mean it! Keep them closed!), draw the outline of what you "see" in a *single, continuous line*. (It might be easiest to start at the beak and work around from there.) There is no rush to draw your ostrich, but keep your eyes *closed*. Keep concentrating on seeing the animal in your mind as your hand draws it on paper. When you are finished—still keeping your eyes closed—you may lift your pencil and draw the round eye. Now have a look at your work (see Figure 3.4 for one student's drawing of the ostrich).

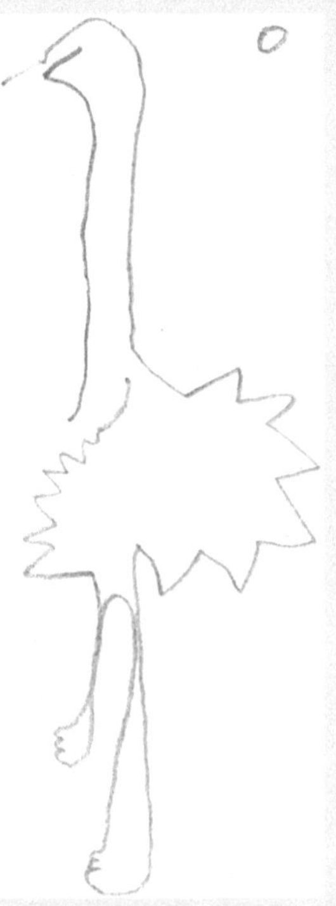

FIGURE 3.4: Student drawing of an imagined ostrich (by Clarissa Salman, used with permission).

What may seem like a party game at first is actually a very potent Etude in using your mind-eye. When you close your eyes and concentrate on an image, you are not "seeing" it through your eyes, but rather think-imagining it, often somewhere that feels like it is above or in front of your forehead. Most of us are not used to perceiving in this way, so it's difficult to get rid of the other images already there: the lines, orbs, halos, and afterglows. When I say "See an ostrich," you may have trouble finding any *part* of an ostrich in your mind, but if you release tension for a few moments and realize you are not

5 I have changed the focal animal because cartoon depictions of pigs are so common that you might draw someone else's construction of "pig" rather than seeing the animal yourself in your mind-eye.

projecting that animal onto the darkness before your eyes, but rather conjuring up a memory of it, you will have an easier time.

Many people find that the assigned image (ostrich, in this case) will come and disappear, sometimes very quickly. Practice is needed to hang on to the image and keep it free of interruptions. I suspect a mind wearies of seeing one single thing for too long, so it sends other interesting signals to entertain us; sometimes the disruptions seem random and contrary, other times you may see your ostrich running or flapping. Try to keep everything but "ostrich" at bay. Calmly focus, concentrate. Let your mind see every detail as you are concentrating on the outline; you'll soon see that you know a lot more about the texture of the bird's skin, the shape of its legs, the color of the feathers than you might think. Each of us has a lot of information stored that we usually have no reason to access, even if we've only seen something fleetingly. This is a challenging Etude.

Ethnographic Application: Your intent, in this and allied Etudes, is to memorize what's around you to draw it later. Remember, you are trying to see a portion of your world, and if you tell yourself that you must draw it later on, you will be more attentive at observing. There are several reasons this Etude will come in handy when you are doing your ethnographic fieldwork. For one, there will be many times when you are in an unfamiliar place where it is inappropriate to draw people, places, activities, just as it would be inappropriate to take photographs; you must memorize what you experience to make a document later. Other times, it might be fine for you to draw in public but you don't have your materials. Again, you must inscribe the image in your mind to later commit it to paper. Yet other times, you only see a scene or image fleetingly. You see something in the shadows, perhaps, or, as happened to me, see something secret, like an animist heirloom brought out from a cupboard for a mere split second. In the case of Michael Taussig, he saw something that made no sense when he quickly passed by it. His only way to understand the view was to draw it immediately: a dead body being sewn into a bag (2011, 1–9). In all these cases, you must use your most attentive mind to capture and fix the momentary perception to draw it later.

It takes a little practice to save such "after drawings" because you need to focus (see deeply), concentrate (*want* to remember), reduce complexity (see shape before details), and save (commit—or burn—to memory). For those who have strong visual memories, looking at a thing or scene with intensity is akin to forming a mental snapshot of it; such people will simply close their eyes later and remember what they saw (see Chapter Seven). Not all of us have that ability, I think, but don't worry. Some people remember numbers and letters better, so if need be, compare what you perceive to the letter-number forms practiced earlier in Chapter Two to help you remember basic shapes. (For an example, consider the ostrich: see it [facing left] as an elongated number 2 that flows into a large squat O from which hang two long L's. Telling yourself "2-O-LL" while closing your eyes and drawing those symbols may be all it takes for you to clearly recall the image.)

Memorizing more complex scenes and groupings is slightly more difficult, but the essential system is the same: focus, concentrate, reduce complexity, save. For now, let's continue our focus on one image.

ETUDE SEVEN, Calligraphic Ostrich (1 minute):[6] Return to your mental image of the ostrich (including, now, your blind drawing of it), but this time keep your eyes open. Using a fresh (i.e., loaded with ink) felt-tip pen, lightly draw a 2-inch square on a poor-quality paper such as a napkin.[7] Stay calm and take charge (get ready to take a risk!): in the square, draw a simplified version of your mental image of the ostrich, seeing it in your mind as you draw it on the paper with your eyes open. You may need to practice this Etude several times to get a feel for how fast the paper and the pen interact, and consequently how light your touch must be (Figure 3.5).

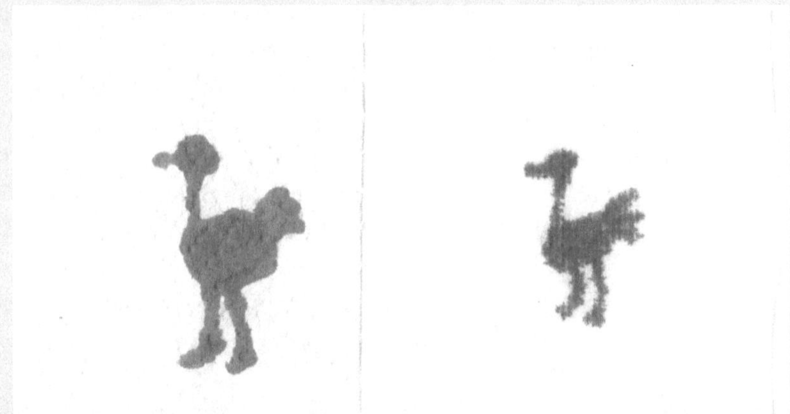

FIGURE 3.5: Calligraphic drawings of an imagined ostrich.

6 Etudes Seven, Eight, and Nine are adapted from Heather C. Williams's excellent drawing primer *Drawing as a Sacred Activity* (2002, 32–46), with permission of the author.

7 You are seeking paper that will soak up the ink quickly.

Here, you are again practicing seeing your mental image, but this time fusing it with what you see being drawn on the paper. The fact that the paper soaks up the ink so quickly will force you to draw what you see in your mind quickly, to attend to form and not details. You are doing what Asian calligraphers often do: concentrating on what is seen in your mind with what is actually seen emerging on the paper. You are combining mind- and eye-images to create a rapid, yet somewhat truthful, image of the subject. Note also that your line here is not an outline (contour) of "ostrich," but *is* ostrich. (That's something important to think about.) We will come back to this notion in Chapter Five.

Depicting as Representing

An issue of great salience to the ethnographic project is the representation of cultural worlds: who has the power (and who will take the responsibility) to depict individuals, their lives, and their possessions, homes, and traditions? What are the consequences for creating such depictions? For decades, Western anthropologists traveled to distant places to study various groups to understand, then document, their behaviors, beliefs, laws, and norms, but it took some time before we began to wonder (often at the urging of the groups being studied!) what it actually means to create a picture (written or otherwise) of a group of people—who are known for only a short while—to tell others (primarily fellow Western others) all about them. We began to rethink our project and deeply consider what a momentous obligation it is to publicly and semi-permanently represent people of another culture. It's not an impossible task, I think, when done with compassion, understanding, honesty, and respect for local feedback. In fact, from my point of view, it's based on one of the most ordinary human endeavors there are: to try to explain how and why people do the things they do. But to *document* that understanding can be a terrifying act, and we can't just shrug our shoulders and say, "Never mind, it's okay!"

To the extent that ethnography can be effective and have some meaning in the world, it needs to be thoughtful and empathetic, and the research we do must always keep in mind the welfare of those we work with.[8] We need to be guided in research by our, and others', ethics, our sense of shared humanity, a genuine and open-minded curiosity, an ability to change our assumptions and expectations, a belief that the more we know about each other the more

8 For those interested, here is the link to the American Anthropological Association's statement on professional ethics: http://ethics.aaanet.org/category/statement/

rich and fascinating our world will be, and a conviction that we owe more to the people we study than we do to the people who enabled us to study with them. It also helps to stop for a moment and think, "Why represent another?"

I won't even try to answer that fundamental question (although you have a hint above that I happen to think it is an aspect of our ordinary human behavior), although it's a very good question to think about. I will rephrase it in a slightly more purposeful way, however, to explore how and why visual depictions in ethnographic research happen: "Why *visually* represent another?" It's a question central to the aim of this book, and one I've already talked about in passing, but here I want to probe an issue that Nigel Spivey brings up: why was the first representation made? What purpose did it serve?

While it may be "ordinary" for humans to examine each other and the world around them and try to communicate, in speech, what we see to our friends and family, it is a different sort of question to ask about why we committed our perceptions to permanent documentary form. To address this topic, Spivey guides us to consider some of the oldest extant human drawings, the cave paintings of Europe. Noting that there is solid evidence to dispel the age-old belief that the animals depicted served some kind of hunting magic, he says there is also evidence that humans "need to have some mental experience or training in order to *recognize* (pictorial) symbols," asking, "how did we ever acquire the ability to *create* them in the first place?" (2005, 31; italics in original). David Lewis-Williams suggests that the ancient cave paintings were made to "fix" fleeting mental images (i.e., hallucinations caused by light deprivation) to prove they had been actually witnessed (2003, 193).[9] It was a way for the ancient people to make a permanent record of something perceived as real, something that appeared and then seemed to disappear.

The desire to identify and record the "thingness" of the emergent or ephemeral world (whether we define it as "real" or "hallucination" or "dream"), and to mark it in lines, may be something we do as children (when given the chance) to make meaning of an otherwise chaotic world, to "'arrest' the dynamic, changing quality of everything we perceive" (Mavers 2011, 74–89). If this helps to explain what we continue to do as adults doing ethnographic research, then we need to make sure that our efforts are not simply selfish explorations to control our world, but rather intensive attempts to render visual reality via simple lines that communicate honestly.

As Betty Edwards (1986) put it, in drawing to see, we must find out "as much as possible about the problem—ideally, a thorough research of the chosen

9 To answer the question "What exactly is a picture a record of?" J.J. Gibson developed this concise answer: "Any picture *preserves what its creator has noticed and considers worth noticing*" (2015, 262; italics in original).

subject. At the same time, one must maintain a 'clean-minded approach to a problem,' to use James Adams's phrase . . . , a state of mind in which one *knows nothing*, so to speak. One must sift, absorb, arrange, and re-arrange incoming new information along with previously known 'old' information without ever drawing conclusions. One must be alert for misinformation or misinterpretation, yet at the same time be willing to risk taking chances" (134; italics in original). I will discuss the ethics of ethnographic representation more in Chapter Six.

Responsibilities of Representing

Representing the world that we know and see carries with it certain responsibilities, too. As noted earlier, we should strive to communicate as honestly and accurately as we can, and to be alert for misinterpretations; if we investigate varied cultural attitudes toward the act of creation, we will see that representing is a solemn endeavor. The wood carvers I worked with on Samosir Island told me that the father of the first earth-born Batak, called Si Tuan Rumauhir, was the first one to carve (Causey 2003, 111),[10] which meant that every subsequent act of carving was a kind of reenactment of his first feat. To reenact the original behaviors of the progenitors is something that must be taken seriously, and it was no doubt because of this that mindless talking, joking, and playing around were disallowed in their workshops. It's not just the Bataks who feel that a sense of focus and formal attention needs to be practiced when creating a rendition or recreation (whether of the "real" or of the spiritual world) as it is perceived.

No, it's not just the Bataks. Many cultures around the world believe that creative behaviors are "extra-ordinary." Ellen Dissanayake (1988) notes that there is a difference between mere markings and those meaningful line-makings that have some kind of extraordinary character (which she refers to as "making special"), saying, "Making special is to be distinguished from 'marking,' because it seeks to shape and embellish reality (or experience) so that it appears otherwise *additionally or alternatively real* . . . reality is converted from its usual unremarkable state . . . to a significant or specially experienced reality in which the components, by their emphasis or combination or juxtaposition, acquire a meta-reality" (95; italics added). Some Australian Aboriginal artists are said to communicate directly with—sometimes become one with—the Eternal Dreamtime beings when creating their works (Anderson 2004, 73–75), while Anang carvers of southeastern Nigeria

10 His name translates loosely to "He, Honorable Carved House."

call on the help of both guardian spirits and magic spirits to ensure success in their work (Messenger 1975, 107). Carvers of Trobriand Kula canoe boards must be in a state of equilibrium to access a free flow of magical knowledge if their work is to be able to attract desired trading partners (Gell 1999, 175–77), and a Kilenge mask carver from Papua New Guinea will retreat to a secret area in the bush because his skilled work is sacred (Dark 2011, 488). Yekuana basket weavers of Venezuela recognize that in creating their works they must perform rituals to realign the natural materials into the ordered worlds of humans (Guss 1989, 95), and artists of the Pacific Northwest must balance the thrust of their own creative desires with the counterthrust of their cultures' strict rules and conventions to create an object "filled with latent energy" (Dark 2011, 490). The Navajos believe that mortals "have the responsibility for sustaining and restor(ing) the world's primal beauty," and that this is "effectively accomplished through the production of art" (Anderson 2004, 123). Turkish artisans believe that their finest works of art are "devices created in devotion and designed to lead the viewer, step by step, to higher understanding . . . the eye draws the mind behind it . . . (and) the mind knows the world and arouses the soul to its beauty. The soul lifts in bliss and fills with love for God" (Glassie 1999, 76).

I don't bring this up to alarm anyone interested in using drawing as an ethnographic way to record their surroundings, but rather to point out that this is not frivolous behavior. To claim the right to depict the world, and to stand behind our work and have it taken seriously, means that we must practice it with honesty, curiosity, respect, and some kind of joy.

Halakhalak

My rental house on Samosir Island was in the fields, far removed from the rest of the village, which was something I valued when it was time to write my field notes in peace. The main room's windows looked out on both *ladang* (dry fields for such things as onions) and *sawah* (flooded fields for rice), and it was beautiful to watch the rice plants change from chartreuse threads only inches high to golden yellow swaths loaded with seeds. When the plants were heavy at the end of the season, they moved in the breezes as if they were one entity, slowly rolling, swaying.

This is a precarious time for the rice plants, not so much because a sharp wind might shake the stalks and loosen the seeds, but because field rats and birds will plunder the crop. Not much can be done about the rats, but the farmers have a chance to scare the birds away using *halakhalak* (scarecrows, literally, "human-like"). Unlike the scarecrows I've seen in the United States, the Batak halakhalak hang from a rope that is attached to a long wand of bamboo that bends over from the weight of the contraption. Even a soft breeze is enough to catch the clothes of the halakhalak, moving it in a jerking fashion that startles the birds waiting nearby.

When I first saw them, there was something charming and friendly about these objects, but after they'd been dangling in the wind for a week or two, I didn't give them another thought. It was only when I began drawing my elegant neighbor hoeing her ladang (see Chapter Six) that I suddenly *saw* them again. I shifted my chair so that the window framed them and began to draw, first in loose pencil lines, and then in tighter pen lines (Figures 3.6 and 3.7). I tried to catch some aspect of their character because otherwise I knew I'd again forget about them; they were not the topic of my research, after all, just a funny footnote to the context of my field site. Now I'm glad I documented them, though the act seemed frivolous at the time. They still charm me, but more importantly, they take me back to the particular time and place. I can still resee that view out my window, can still hear the rustle of the wind in the stalks, and can still hear the sounds of a lively village excited as harvest time approaches. More so than photography, the time and focus required for drawing can etch an entire sensory scene into the ethnographer's mind, enriching her ability to conjure up that scene in subsequent work.

The world around us can seem chaotic and overwhelming, even if we just focus on the visual, and it's often exhausting to decide which of the myriad

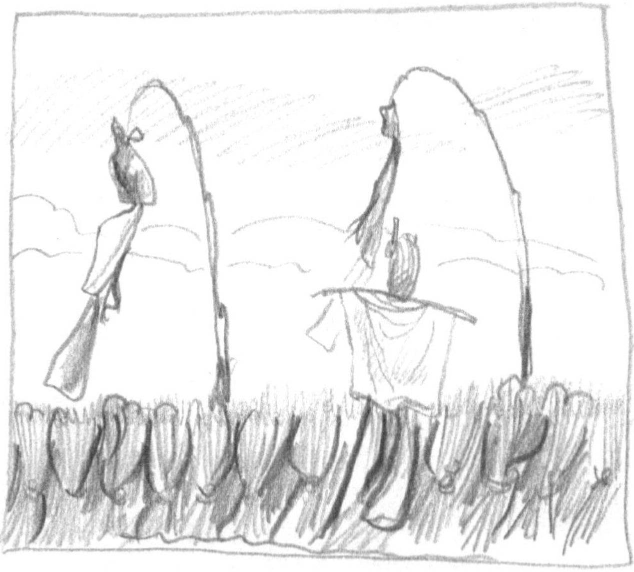

FIGURE 3.6: ***Halakhalak* in looping pencil lines.**

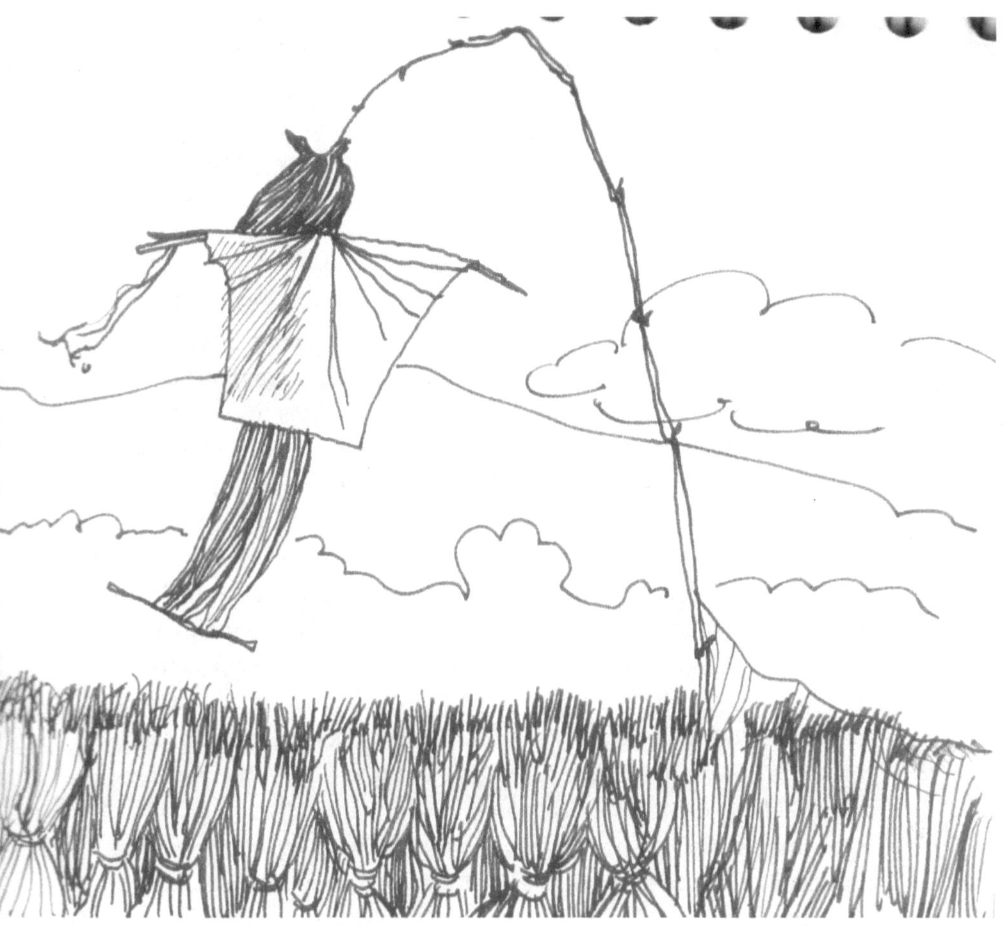

FIGURE 3.7: *Halakhalak* in firm pen lines.

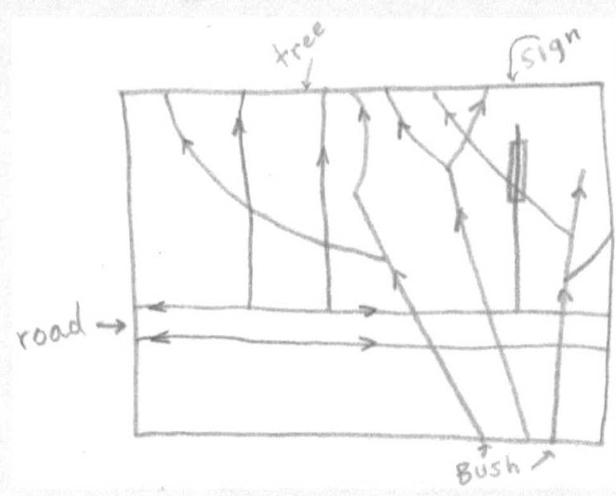

FIGURE 3.8: Drawing basic lines with directional markers.

ETUDE EIGHT, Essential Lines (2 minutes each): Choose any view out a door or window (hint: windows are a little easier). There are two parts to this Etude, but neither should take more than two minutes to complete. First, draw a freehand frame representing the door/window opening centered in the middle of the paper. *Part A*: Spend about 30 seconds seeing the view. Focus, concentrate. What's inside the frame? Now, with your pencil, mark only the essential verticals, horizontals, and diagonals using simple straight lines; try to draw the line slowly and continuously rather than "sketching" it in a zigzag fashion. *Part B*: Turn your paper over. Again, make the freehand window/door frame in the center of the paper, and again make the essential lines with your pencil. This time, using arrow marks, indicate if you think any line feels like it is moving in a particular direction. If the line feels static, just leave it (Figure 3.8).

things that confront us in every direction we should be concentrating on. This Etude allows the window or door to do some of the work for us: cutting out all visual stimuli except those directly in front of the architectural opening. Even then, what we see can appear too complicated. That's why Etude Eight asks you to focus only on four things: verticals, horizontals, diagonals, and their sense of direction. Simplifying the world this way, especially using a continuous (non-sketchy) line, will help you to see basic structures upon which details can later be added. Sensing the direction of the lines will help you understand how to communicate the details of what you see to those who cannot be there to experience it in person.

Ethnographic Application: The Etudes in this chapter are meant to help you become comfortable with the idea that you are drawing to see, which means that they might not be directly transferable to your research. Still, when you are doing ethnographic fieldwork, your surroundings will likely be exponentially more overwhelming than your familiar world because what you'll

ETUDE NINE, Finding Y-Shapes (4 minutes): Choose a different window or door. Make a freehand frame in the center of the paper. Now look at the view, draw the basic lines, and then search for the places where lines intersect. Decide which of these are the most essential in your picture (i.e., which seem to have the most energy), darkening the Y-shape they make, paying attention to which lines are in front and which in back. If you sense that some lines are "stronger" than others, you may want to use even darker lines (Figure 3.9, Y-shapes circled).

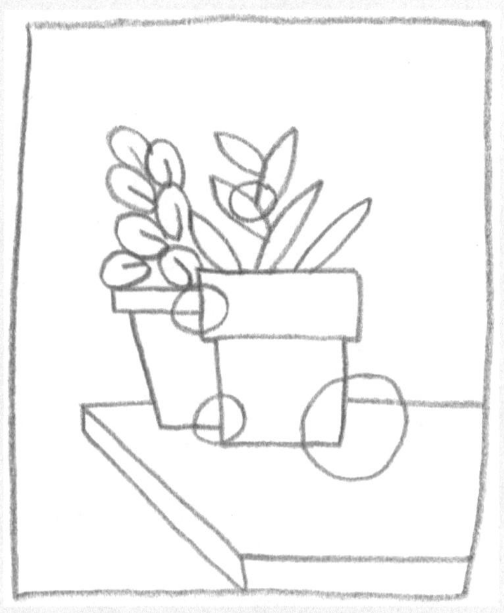

FIGURE 3.9: Drawing the Y-shapes in a view.

see is so new and indefinable. Once you've done these Etudes and can apply what you've learned to your new setting, you'll be better able to gain a sense of control over your perception of your surroundings. "Drawing is a way to sensually connect with the world," says the artist Heather Williams (2002, 40), and having that connection may make your fieldwork experience richer and more comprehensible all the more quickly. The deeper connection will help you cement your memory of the place, pan-sensually, and may even help you to write about it more evocatively. Work on Etude Ten.

Visually, the intersections of lines tend to create a stable composition of a picture because our eyes seem to be drawn to the places where two lines come together. Williams calls such intersections "anchor points" (2002, 41) and notes that in the drawing they often carry its "story." By concentrating on seeing these Y-shapes in the world around you, not only are you teaching yourself to be attentive to foreground and background, but you are also seeing where the real action in the view might be taking place.

Using the knowledge gained in the previous Etudes, you will begin to see how the basic three lines underlie the structure not only of all chairs but

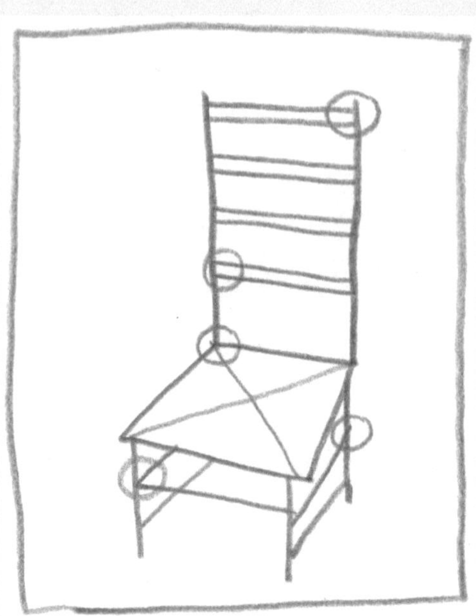

FIGURE 3.10: Drawing a chair, attentive to Y-shapes.

ETUDE TEN, Seeing a Chair (10 minutes): Draw a chair within your freehand frame in the center of the page. Any kind of chair will do, but one built with an exposed structure may be easier than an upholstered one. See and draw the basic lines first. When you are content with your drawing, go back and add substance lines that will help convey the materiality and weight of the chair, keeping your eyes attentive for the intersection of lines (the Y-shapes) that indicate which lines are in front of others (Figure 3.10, Y-shapes circled).

many other kinds of objects around us, both man-made and natural. You will begin to see that when you reduce complexity, focus, and concentrate, you will be able to visually document much of the world. You are not ignoring the fact that there are curved, or sinuous, or spiraling lines, but rather are trying to see their underlying structure for the vital purpose of creating a simplified picture of what you see.

Considering "Firstness"

Maybe now is a good time to talk a little more about the way we conceive of our world. As noted above, there seems to be an innate ability in all of us to perceive the world in an interpretive way: we see things in our surroundings as discrete named entities, as having articulating relationships to other things, and as being meaningful. We assume that words naturally attach to the entities, we see connections between them whether they exist or not, and we make judgments or ratings to understand them. But really, if you think about it, things simply *are* whether we are there to perceive them or not, right?

Charles Saunders Peirce was a great thinker who tried to discuss this paradox (i.e., that there is a "real" out there, with or without us conceiving of it; yet by calling it "real" we've already defined it in our terms). He used the terms "firstness," "secondness," and "thirdness" (Peirce 1998, 267) to help us find our way out. "The First," he says, "is that whose being is simply in itself, not referring to anything nor lying behind anything ... It precedes all synthesis and all differentiation; it has no unity and no parts. It cannot be articulately thought: assert it, and it has already lost its characteristic innocence; for assertion always implies a denial of something else. Stop to think of it, and it has flown!" (Peirce 1998, 248). In short, The First means "just is."

The Second is our identification of The First, that is, our naming it as a category or thing, and The Third is our sense of the connection between the two: the "is" and the name. The Third, in essence, is *us*—as co-interpreters, as interacting mediators, as those who find meaning in the world by using our various codes (primary among them, language) to identify the determinacy (the boundaries, the edges) of all that "is."[11]

Perhaps you can see now why thinking about Peirce's notion of The First is so interesting for us here. In drawing to see, we use one of our human codes (a two-dimensional visual one) to depict how we articulate and define the "is." In line drawing, we are interpreting The First—all "that precedes synthesis and differentiation," all the indeterminate—in a kind of code that makes sense to us, a code that is, admittedly, somewhat self-invented by each of us as we practice. When we recognize that our drawings of what's around us simply use one version of a code with innumerable variations, we are offered visual freedom!

There are no "right" or "better" drawings, and there is no single way to see the "is" around you. Your act of drawing, when done seriously and with focus, is evidence that you saw, and manifested it in *your* form: it is simultaneously a souvenir of your experience, a primary document, an interpretive remembrance, a concocted mnemonic. Oddly, when complete, your drawing-seeing itself becomes one of The Firsts, and so, as Peirce says, "is a being simply in itself."

Some people don't know where to start with this Etude because there are so many possible anchor objects on a well-used desk. My suggestion is to start *anywhere* and move in any direction. If you are more comfortable doing this as if you are writing a sentence of words, then start with the object at the far left of the desk. However, if you see one thing on the desk as being the most

11 See Hendrickson (2008) for more information on Peirce's ideas as applied to ethnographic drawing.

ETUDE ELEVEN, Drawing Your Desk: You are now even freer to use drawing as a way of seeing. So, try this: draw the table/desk in front of you, including all objects on it. See the whole; see the parts. Draw a freehand frame on your paper and decide what will be included inside, choosing an "anchor" object, something you feel dominates the scene, to mark in first. Find your basic lines, and your familiar shapes, looking for line intersections to help you see what is in front and what is in back, and doing your best to judge distances between things. Once you have marked the anchor object, reduce the complexity of the view you see by marking out a simple composition of lines and essential shapes. Later, if you feel like taking a risk, continue your work by filling in the details of the objects.

essential, or the largest, or the most interesting, then start with that, adding things to the right and left, above and below. The point is to see the desk as a composition of order within a frame.

Sometimes, the complexity of the world you experience in ethnographic settings seems overwhelming and incomprehensible. This exercise will help you recognize that you simply need to reduce complexity (by narrowing your view with the delimiting freehand frame first), and by choosing an anchor (the most important subject in a view) around which to work. Carefully seeing the anchor object or person in a scene, and concentrating on it as a starting point, will assist you in figuring out where other objects

ETUDE TWELVE, House Glyphs: This Etude is adapted with permission from Ivan Brunetti's *Cartooning* (2011), and here you are creating a series of pictures of a single thing attending to "minimalism, dynamic drawing, and clear, simple lines" (25). Divide both the front and the back of your paper with lines into four boxes each. Use your "mind-eye" to conjure up your favorite house, then draw it in detail for 2–3 minutes in the first box. Once done, move to the next box and start over, doing it in 1 minute. Then do it in 30 seconds, and then 15 seconds. Turn the paper over: now draw the house in 5 seconds ... next box: again, for 5 seconds . . . 5 seconds again . . . and again. You have reduced the complexity of the house to the point that it has become a refined "glyph," communicating its essence with the fewest lines.

or people belong within the frame. In this way, you can create basic sketches of compelling views that seem to encapsulate your ethnographic field site's character.

The Etudes here ask you to alternate between seeing your real world through your eyes and perceiving that world in your mind's eye. The purpose? To help you practice sharply seeing the real—particularly in an ethnographic setting that is unfamiliar to you—then making it a permanent part of your visual memory. The better access you have to habitual (not to say pat or hackneyed) pictures that you can "download" into your *own* code, the more likely it is that you will be able to draw more *fluently*. While I have stated before that your primary effort is to *see* the world around you precisely and clearly, it does not mean that you must re-envision every single thing you perceive again and *again*. If you were to be an artist by profession, perhaps you would be expected to do that. But here, you are trying to depict what you perceive in your ethnographic field-site honestly, but also easily and quickly. Having familiar symbolic representations, or "glyphs,"[12] to use when you need them most is a visual shortcut to make the process more simple.

ETUDE THIRTEEN, Collecting Comic Glyphs (ongoing): This is an exercise that you can do throughout your day: collect visual shortcuts. These are symbols that can easily convey clear, direct meaning in quick form. First, make yourself a small booklet,[13] something easy to carry in your pocket or bag, and be sure to actually carry it with you when you are out and about. Start by looking at comics wherever you can find them, because here you will find some of the most reduced and clarified elements useful for communicating visually.[14] Look everywhere and draw in your little book all the simple forms you think will be useful to you; make written explanations if a symbol is vague or you think you'll forget its meaning. Comic artists happily share their work with each other, but don't just copy; make the symbols your own.

12 For other ideas on how to create essential "glyphs," please refer to Mike Rohde's *The Sketchnote Handbook* (2015, 31–36).

13 Simply cut ordinary white paper into four even pieces, stack them, fold them, and staple the center line of the fold to make the small book. For a sturdier book, use a postcard or magazine illustration as the cover for the stack of pages; fold and staple as before.

14 See John-Steiner 1985, 90–93 for examples of how cartoon art can assist your efforts.

Ethnographic Application: Part of drawing-seeing is the development of your own visual code. Every artist, of whatever stripe, has their own way of depicting what they want viewers to see. Some might call this an artist's "style," but here I refer to it as their "code" because we are investigating ways to communicate with logic and order. To develop your code, you will add to your existing knowledge of the basic lines (vertical, horizontal, and diagonal) and simple shapes (including letter, number, and punctuation marks) by collecting essential glyphs that will assist you in creating your ethnographic visual documentation. Look everywhere for visual shortcuts that may be useful to you and include them in your small book. Don't restrict yourself to Western cartoon drawings, but look broadly. Examine the ways artists from around the globe have solved problems of depicting the world and make note of what you can use, such as Carol Hendrickson did when making visual depictions in Mexico's Yucatan peninsula, incorporating ancient Maya images in her notes (2008, 125).

Look carefully at the ledger drawings of the Plains Indians,[15] and carefully examine how Japanese woodcuts work.[16] Look at Mithila paintings from India and Nepal,[17] and study the ancient codices of the Mixtec and Maya people.[18] Even without understanding the content of these art forms, each of these visual documentation systems may have elements that you can adjust to your own needs. Choosing such glyphs must be done with care: they must resonate with your own careful perceptions, so don't just copy without being certain they *mean* something to you. Doing this ethically and with respect to the original artists' perceptions is essential.[19]

All of us who have been reading comics since childhood have learned to decipher and interpret their complex symbol system, even being able to adapt our knowledge to make some sense of cartoons from other countries. Their direct, clear presentation of information is what makes them so accessible. But, even though you can read the comics passively, you might need to teach yourself the various symbols' explicit meanings so you can use them actively. A quick search for "comic symbols" online will give you a great start, but for more information on this topic also have a look at books that teach you how

15 A good start is the Plains Indian Ledger Art Project at the University of California, San Diego (https://plainsledgerart.org/ledgers/).

16 There are hundreds of sites online to explore, but a useful start would be to examine the *ehon* books of Masayoshi Kitao (http://digitalcollections.nypl.org/collections/chju-ryakugashiki-how-to-draw-simple-animals?filters[name]=Kitao%2C+Masayoshi+%281764-1824%29&keywords=#/?tab=about).

17 Carolyn Heinz's article "Documenting the Image in Mithila Art" (2006) will help guide interested readers.

18 There are dozens of excellent works on the folded bark books of pre-Columbian cultures. You might start by looking at L.A. County Museum of Art's website for the Foundation for the Advancement of Mesoamerican Studies (http://www.famsi.org/index.html), clicking the link on the home page entitled "writing."

19 Please refer to the excellent inspirational guide *Steal Like an Artist* (2012) by Austin Kleon for further instruction on how to engage with the world creatively.

to draw cartoons (see, for example, Barry 2014; Brunetti 2011; Walker 2000; Abel and Madden 2008, 2012).

Having such glyph-like images "at hand" is not to relinquish your efforts to see deeply. That is, using a formulaic drawing to help you get your perceptions down faster does not mean falling into the trap of using these increasingly familiar shapes *rather than* seeing carefully. Instead, what I am suggesting is that you develop your own quick glyph images to capture some basic or common structures of what you see, giving you time to focus with more concentration on the novel aspects before you. So, using your own version of a stick figure to communicate a cluster of human bodies does not indicate you have stopped seeing; rather, it shows that your main perceptual interest is elsewhere.

Last Words

I'd like to remind you of an instruction I gave previously to "Abandon Caution." Being too careful and restrictive in your work will hinder you. Please move forward with your effort to see-draw with calm abandon. By working with this book, you have tacitly agreed to stop judging yourself (and if you see the work of others, you have also agreed to stop judging them, too), and that's the first step of finding the freedom to use drawing as an ethnographic method. Drawing can be a transgressive act, and the act of recreating means you are taking on an amazing responsibility, whether you see it as being slightly dangerous or intensely playful. For those of you who are (for whatever reason) fearful, I say: remember that the focus here is the process, not the product. For those of you who feel like a crazy door has just been opened, I say: focus on the process and exult over the product!

CHAPTER 4

SEEING EDGES AS LINES

A Line Removed or a Line Exposed?

When I was finally allowed to hold the knife and hammer, rather than just watch, my carving teacher Partoho started me off with a flat piece of wood. With a brown felt-tip pen, he drew a kind of open spiral with "leaves" curling out from it, a version of the intricate surface *gorga* carvings the Toba Bataks make on the planks of their traditional homes (Figure 4.1). He put my piece of wood in the vise to let me figure out how to carve the lines he had drawn. Holding the knife upright and slightly canted, I tapped the water buffalo horn hammer to move the razor-sharp edge through the wood. It was difficult to control the knife, moving past imperfections in the wood and spots of sap, but I managed to get several of the leaves carved by the time he came back to examine my work.

He took the wood back to his workbench where we both sat on a log for my critique. He puffed on his clove cigarette and then announced, "No, this is not Batak carving," continuing to say, "For some reason you've decided to be a Minangkabau[1] carver, to carve the Minang way ..." By now, his three sons had left their benches to see what I'd done and all were leaning over us chuckling and repeating their father, "He's a Minang man ... a Minangkabau carver ..." I shrugged my shoulders to show I didn't understand. He elaborated, "See, the Minang people carve *up* the line, but we Bataks carve it *down*," but I still didn't understand and my frowning eyebrows must have shown it. Did he mean that the curling lines should go up, not down? Perplexed, I started to say, "But I followed your drawing ... " to which he added, "Yes, and you did it wrong!"

1 The Minangkabau people live to the south of the Bataks in Central Sumatra and are Muslims.

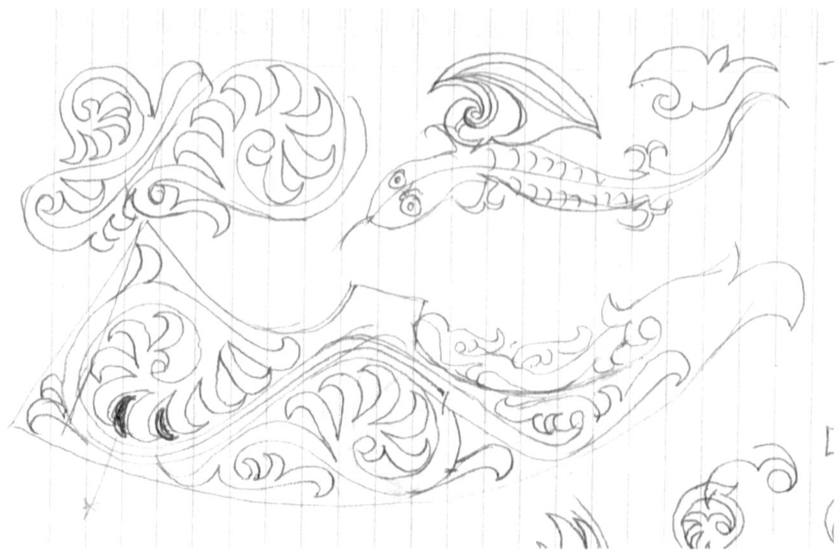

FIGURE 4.1: Partoho's drawing of gorga lines.

He pretended to take offense now, looking sullen and hurt, saying, "If you prefer the Minang way, then you must move there . . . and if that's true, I can't show you how to carve." Feeling like I had to plead to continue our lessons, I told him I just didn't understand: Up? Down? He said, "Okay then, let me say this: the Minang carvers raise the line up while we Bataks carve it *in*." He found a small piece of wood lying nearby, drew an arabesque in brown felt-tip pen lines on it, then put it in his vise. "Look here," he said, and then began removing wood on either side of the line, leaving the pen line exposed. "That's the Minangkabau way" (Figure 4.2). Then he went to the other side of the design and set the knife at the edge of the line.

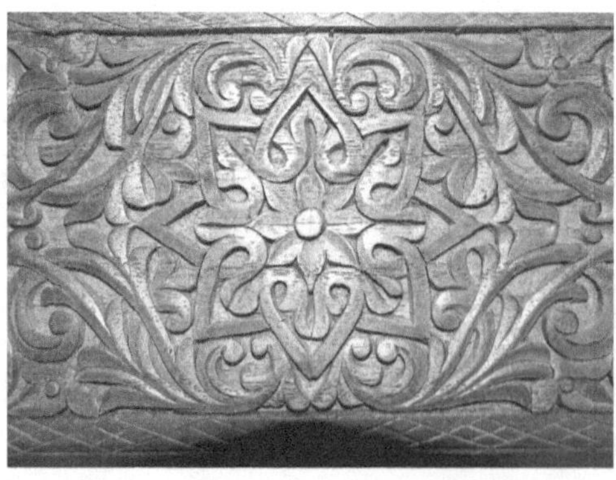

FIGURE 4.2: Photograph of Minangkabau surface carving style.

This time, he carved a V-shaped groove (the knife first going one way, then tipping the other direction and coming back), and the brown ink line was gone, now just a tendril of wood on the ground (Figure 4.3). "That," he announced, "is the *Batak* way to carve, the *right* way to carve. That's what you need to practice, so back to work!" I headed back to my vise, thinking

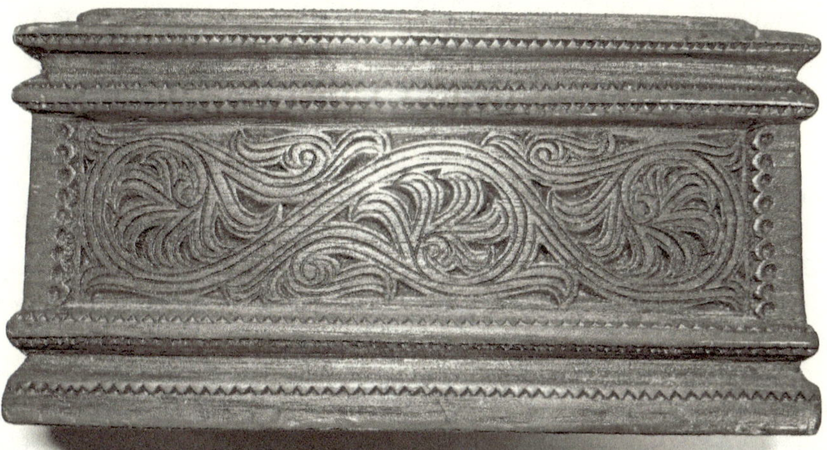

FIGURE 4.3: Photograph of Toba Batak gorga carving style.

about how such a small change can create such a huge difference. A line is not just a line.

Learning to See, then Draw, Edges

As you can see in the ethnographic vignette above, there is no single way to see a line or to distinguish edges. All of our perceptions are conditional and contextual, which means that seeing such a thing as a line and carving it as an edge, or seeing such a thing as an edge and drawing it as a line really depends on your cultural traditions and, of course, what you mean by the terms "line" and "edge." For those growing up in the West, many of us take a lot for granted about edges. We become so used to thinking that the boundaries of things in the material world (where something or someone "ends" and the adjacent thing—whether it is another thing or simply the atmosphere around the thing—begins) are certain and real that we forget to consider if different things might actually meld and become part of each other. A simple thought experiment can help you understand this: if I asked you to draw the edge of a nude model, you would draw the contour or profile of that person's skin; if I asked you to draw a clothed model, you would still draw the contour or profile seen, whether it was bare skin or draped. Where are the person's actual edges when you perceive them?

Consider how you perceive the multiple kinds of edges in the world. Seeing the edge of a leaf or of the side of a desk or the corner of a concrete building, is relatively easy because those things exist with defined perimeters. But what about uncertain surfaces, those that are rounded like an apple, curved like a bowl, or irregularly sinuous like the human body? Deciding where the edges of such things are to create a line drawing can only be made when we are in a fixed position vis-à-vis that thing, and thus able to determine the extent to which our perception of them is limited, either by recognizing where the thing comes in "contact" with its context (e.g., the air around it), or where it disappears from sight when the roll of its surface moves away and behind that which is in the foreground.[2] Betty Edwards makes a very useful dichotomy here, saying that *contours* are "the edges as you perceive them," whereas *edges* are "the places where two things meet" (1979, 83).

Now consider how you perceive textures. When you are standing 100 feet from a rooster, it might be simple to choose a simple shape to depict it with a drawn line (perhaps an inverted scalene triangle?), but if you were to see that same rooster being held by the farmer you were interviewing in the field, how would you draw the contours of its feathers? How much detail would you put down on paper to convey the edges of multiple tail feathers as they cross each other and overlap?

How much detail of the edges is necessary if you are trying to record a craggy opening to a cave, an intricately textured fabric, or a pile of manuscripts stored in a cupboard? Surely basic lines and geometric shapes won't always be enough to preserve the ethnographic details you are hoping to document.

Part of the answer lies in the purpose of the drawing and the context of the objects seen. If one is merely trying to indicate essential relationships of the positions between the things in view, then perhaps geometric shapes and basic lines are enough. Then again, if one is trying to focus on something particular in the view, say a central figure in a sacred setting for example, then the edges of peripheral people or objects need be sketched in only simply. In creating your lines to depict the surrounding world, you are making a series of complex decisions about the nature of the edges and contours and are marking down your best effort to convey honestly what you see.[3]

The point of asking you to ponder how you see edges is really to bring your attention to it: to encourage you to investigate carefully what you may have earlier assumed. To help you think about this, consider the words of Betty Edwards: "By drawing an edge of one thing, you have simultaneously drawn the edge of the adjacent thing" (personal communication).

When you are working with pictures made by the camera, the edges have already been frozen in time and discovering edges is not so difficult. It's very good practice to work with such pictures because it helps you train yourself

2 See Gibson (2015, 69–78) for a more thorough discussion of this topic.

3 See Gibson (2015, 274–8) if you are interested in reading more on this topic.

ETUDE FOURTEEN, Finding Edges (3–5 minutes): This is another version of Etude Two (Simple Tracing), except here you are looking for edges, both defined and uncertain. Like you did before, find a photograph with a clear image, and with your pencil, trace the edges you perceive, making sure to *see* where the outline of one thing (the defined line of a shirt collar, for example) overlaps another (e.g., the uncertain line of the neck). As you move across the picture you are teaching yourself how to see edges and deciding how to recreate them in lines.

to identify where uncertain edges are as they are not moving and their shadows are not changing. When you practice this kind of tracing, you'll also start to see more clearly when edges intersect and when one "occludes" (overlaps, or covers over) another.[4] The sooner you feel comfortable making lines that convey these varied kinds of contours in a photograph, the easier it will be to use drawing as a method to *see* them in real life.

ETUDE FIFTEEN,[5] Contour Drawing (5–7 minutes each): There are three parts to this Etude, and you may want to practice it multiple times to gain drawing-seeing facility.

Part A: "Sighted Contour." Place any object on a table five feet away from you. Put your pencil lead near the center of the paper, then look up and focus on any edge of the object. Let your hand become your eye, and as your eye moves *very slowly* around the edge of the object your hand will make the same line you see. Focus seeing only on the edge and concentrate so your eye does not "slip" by looking inside or nearby. Look at your drawing only when *necessary*, and don't judge what you see. Focus on seeing the edge and on drawing slowly. You won't get very far in the time given, and that's just fine.

Part B: "Glancing Contour." Use the same object (or choose another), and do exactly the same thing as you did above, but this

4 See Gibson (2015, 72–5) for a more complete description of occluding edges.

5 Etudes Fifteen and Sixteen are adapted from Kimon Nicolaides's contour exercises (1969, 9–14; 73–77).

time try not to glance more than once or twice at your drawing as you move slowly around the edge of the object.

Part C: "Blind Contour." Use the same (or a different) object, and do the Etude again, but this time find a large cloth napkin or hand towel to completely cover your drawing hand and the paper. Do not look at your drawing until the time is up.

ETUDE SIXTEEN, Eye-Is-Hand (5–7 minutes): This Etude builds on the previous one. Here, you will choose any one thing in your surroundings to focus on (selecting objects or elements in a landscape that are unmoving will make this exercise easier). Again using the cloth to cover your hand and the paper, make your pencil/hand create lines that mimic the movements your eye makes, allowing your eye to follow its natural flow up and down, back and forth around the thing. Your hand IS your eye. If your eye sees a curved edge for a moment, your hand draws it; if your eye jumps up to the top and then flies back down to the center, let your hand imitate exactly that move. Don't look at your drawing until the time is up, realizing that it may not make logical sense when you see it.

Etudes Fifteen and Sixteen are teaching you to concentrate on an edge to draw a contour line. The interesting thing about such drawings is that when you concentrate so much on just an edge, your mind gets a bit bored and starts "seeing" adjacent areas through peripheral vision. When you are done with your contour drawings, you'll find that you can go back and complete the details (not just the outline) of the subject of your focused gaze from memory. You might be surprised at how much you actually *saw*.

As an ethnographic method this kind of drawing is invaluable. Looking with focused attention at anything and making a slow, calm line that mimics your eye's movement is one of the best ways to truly examine something. In the field, you may need to have a thorough knowledge of an object (a carving, a particular flower, a certain architectural feature, or a special article of clothing), and in my experience this is the best way to perceive it most deeply. Forcing yourself to look at the edge of an object for five to seven minutes means you are attending to it, and only it, with a kind of attention that few things in your life have gotten before.

ETUDE SEVENTEEN, Fast Contours (30 seconds each for the first 4, 15 seconds each for the next 4): Adding to what you have learned above, now choose an object in the world and draw eight Blind Contours drawings in a row. This time, however, you are going to use that same focused gaze to draw the contours very fast, from beginning (wherever you choose to start) to end. Fold a piece of paper into four, using one square for each drawing, front and back. Don't move, and don't change the object; only look at the drawing under the cloth to find the center of the next box. Draw the same object contour with intense concentration and move on to the next.

An Interest in Lines

In this section, you've been practicing seeing edges and interpreting them as lines. But before we go too far, it's important to note that lines are not always depictions of edges. Recent exploratory research has introduced us to the notion that there are all kinds of lines and that only some of them are drawn.

Tim Ingold's book *Lines: A Brief History* (2007) is a seminal work in this field of research, and he shows us, following the work of J.J. Gibson, how most lines can be experienced as "threads" (material filaments that can be entangled, such as yarn or a net) or "traces" (enduring marks either cut into—think scratches on a stone—or marked on top of—think a drawing on paper—a solid surface). These two sorts of lines can be human-made or can be natural, and they exist all around us, but he adds a third kind of line for us to consider: ruptures. These, he says, take the forms of cuts, cracks, and creases, and likewise surround us in the world as *material* realities. But what of those lines we experience that do not have a material form? These he refers to as "ghostly lines."

Ghostly lines might be thought of as abstract or intangible lines, Ingold says, lacking any substance but existing concretely in our conceptual worlds nonetheless. Consider a geometrical line—that is, the idea of a set of straight, contiguous points existing in a single dimension, which has no depth or width—or consider the way we look into the sky and join the stars with invisible connections; think of national boundaries, of the Chinese energy lines called *chi*, or of culturally confirmed (but unmarked) paths that link sacred sites, such as the so-called songlines of the Australian Aboriginal people.

All of these kinds of lines, and more, are embedded in human cultural conceptions and enable us to make sense of the world around us. Recognizing that the drawn contour is but one kind of line may help us open our eyes to other kinds of lines and other ways to portray them.

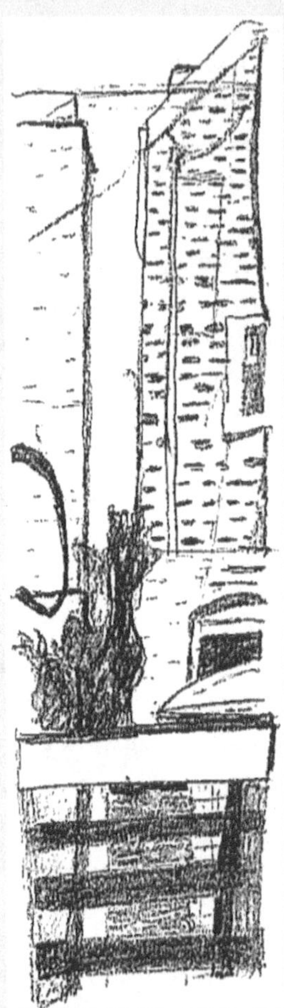

FIGURE 4.4: Student drawing made by seeing in between two buildings (by Cynthia Mercado, used with permission).

ETUDE EIGHTEEN, Seeing in Between (5–7 minutes): Find a place where two buildings come very close together. Move yourself to a position where you can see out between them. Examine the edges of the buildings, but don't actually draw their straight contour lines. Instead, look at what's between them, looking carefully at the edges of trees, cars, and other buildings to draw *their* contour lines. By drawing each of the things seen in the view between the buildings, you will, of course, end up making lines that indicate the edges of the buildings (Figure 4.4).

This is an exercise in seeing "negative" space (focusing not on a subject, but rather where the subject isn't), and trying to see what's in that space. By allowing the occluding edge (the overlapping edge that obscures your view) to frame the view, your attention shifts to all the things that separate the two main objects in the scene (in this Etude, the two buildings close together).

In ethnographic research, sometimes the most interesting things happen in "negative" spaces—the spaces between other, seemingly more important, entities. Sometimes, these spaces are referred to as "marginal" or "in-between," and are easily ignored as being peripheral to our research interests. But think for a moment about a big urban sprawl as an example, and you'll realize that you can learn a lot about the life of a city by looking at its alleys, highway median strips, side yards, and gutters.[6] Focusing on what's *in* these intermediate places will help us see and understand the larger entities that encompass them. This Etude provides you with a way to train yourself to see a more complete and complex world.

ETUDE NINETEEN,[7] 360 Degrees (10 minutes total): Using what you have learned so far about seeing edges, both defined and uncertain, put your paper in your lap (on a book or magazine atop a pillow), and do a Sighted Contour drawing of the edges of the things around you (i.e., in a room, in a park) in one continuous line. Start at the very far left edge of the paper (turned sideways) and move slowly to the right. This will end up being a 360-degree view of the contours of everything from one your starting point and back to it, so you will have to move in your chair as you look around (or sit in a swivel chair); your drawing will continue to the back of the page, and you will try to align the contour line to the place you started (Figure 4.5).

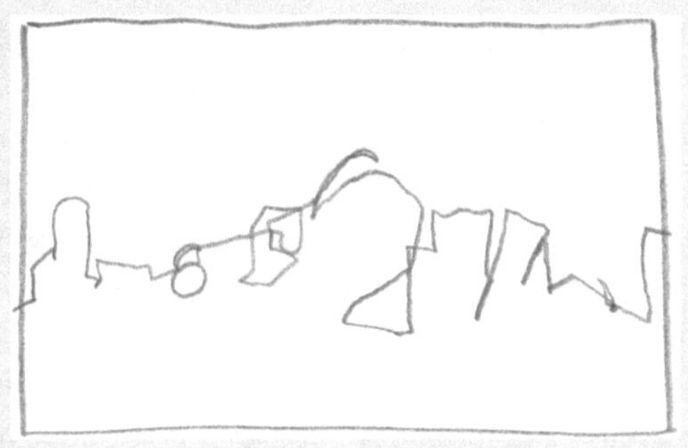

FIGURE 4.5: A 360-degree contour drawing of a room.

This Etude asks you to draw a 360-degree view of a space, whether it is your bedroom, an office, a café, or an outdoor environment. In the end, its purpose is the same: to help you attend to your entire surroundings in a given cultural context. Many times in our everyday lives we tend to think of

6 See Kathleen Stewart (1996, 13–40) for information on what happens "at the side of the road" in rural West Virginia.

7 This Etude is adapted from Maslen and Southern's drawing exercise 17, "Taking a Line for a Walk: The Route of Discovery" (2011, 128–31).

ourselves moving through our material world as if we were on a track, with our focus on whatever is in front of us, rarely considering what's to the sides and behind us. In this way, we tend to sense our lives—our worlds—much like the moving camera does, looking in a single direction with purpose and intention. In fact, as you probably know, biologically our eyes are more like those of other hunting animals (such as lions and coyotes) than of prey animals (like rabbits and antelopes), and help us to focus and perceive distance accurately. Imagine how you might see the world simultaneously in the round, like a prey animal.

Ethnographic research requires that you see and begin to interpret the entire world around you, and although you may not always need to attend to that 360-degree cultural context, knowing your surroundings even partially (such as is shown to you in the drawing Etude above) is essential. Even if you do not always draw your total surroundings, this exercise will help you learn how to take mental note of your surroundings with a somewhat brief examination, will give you insights into what is happening in front of you, and will make your ethnographic experiences much richer.

Ethnographic Application: One of the ways to use simple contour-line-based drawings in ethnographic research is to show your drawings to local people. Now, while it may seem strange to show others your 360-degree drawing, many of the other contour drawings might open interesting dialogs. Eliciting information from the people with whom you work by showing them your pictures (although it is often photographic imagery) is a well-tested way of interacting with them, especially if you are not well known to them.[8] Gillian Crowther used her simple cartoon drawings in this way (Figure 4.6), showing her drawings to Haida people of the Pacific Northwest "as ice breakers when interviewing artists (who) were fascinated to see how I saw Haida culture" (1990, 57).

Similarly, Kathleen Adams used a sketch she made to elicit information a cross-section of all the people living in the village of Ke'te' Kesu in North Toraja Regency (Sulawesi, Indonesia) to better understand their interactions with Western tourists.[9] By showing her drawing (Figure 4.7), which was

8 See William Cannon Hunter's article for an example of using drawing to elicit ethnographic information from local people (2012, 126–50).

9 There are a number of works written about the use of drawing as a way to elicit information from people about their cultural ways or personal attitudes. For more information on researchers using children's and adults' drawings generally, please see Theron, Mitchell, Smith, and Stuart, 2011. To find out about ethnographers using their own line drawings in this way, please see Causey 2012; Colloredo-Mansfeld 1993, 1999, 49–56; and Crowther 1990. For works describing the use of local people's own drawings as a door into understanding their perspectives, please see Dicks 2015, Grant and Dicks 2014, and Suhrbier 2004. For an example of an artist-anthropologist drawing *with* local people, please see Colloredo-Mansfeld 2011.

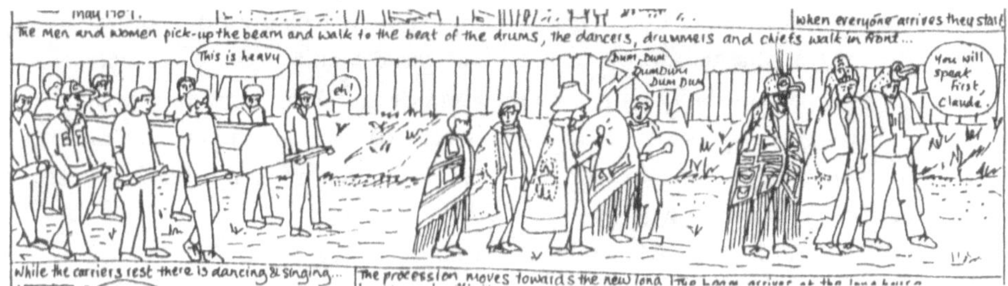

FIGURE 4.6: Gillian Crowther's cartoon drawing of Haida people (used with permission).

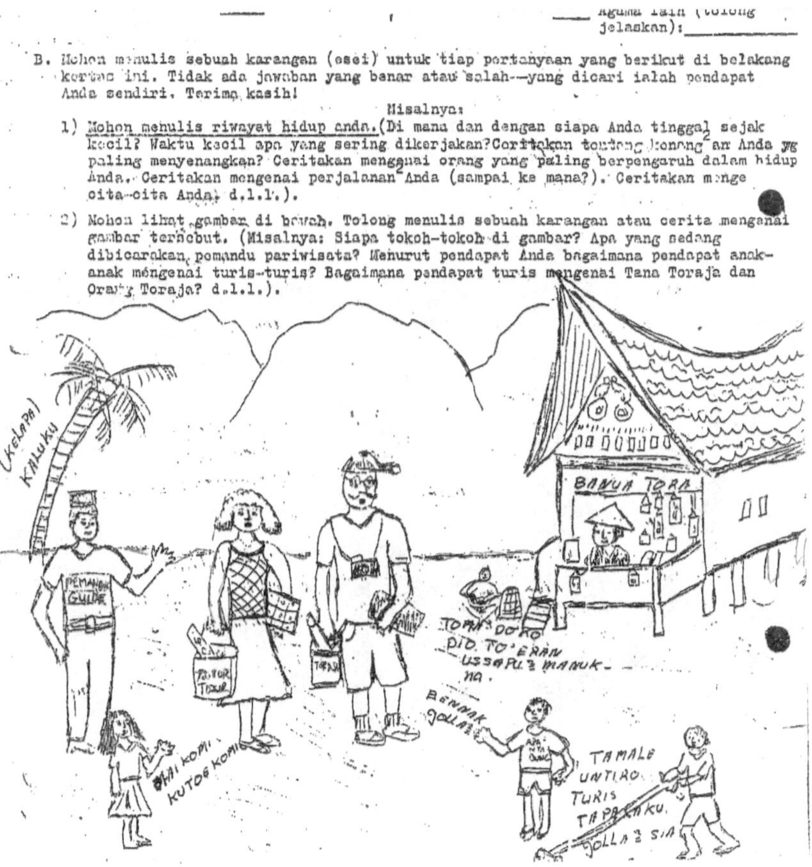

Agama lain (tolong jelaskan): ____________

B. Mohon menulis sebuah karangan (esei) untuk tiap pertanyaan yang berikut di belakang kertas ini. Tidak ada jawaban yang benar atau salah—yang dicari ialah pendapat Anda sendiri. Terima kasih!

Misalnya:

1) Mohon menulis riwayat hidup anda. (Di mana dan dengan siapa Anda tinggal sejak kecil? Waktu kecil apa yang sering dikerjakan? Ceritakan tentang kenangan Anda yg paling menyenangkan? Ceritakan mengenai orang yang paling berpengaruh dalam hidup Anda. Ceritakan mengenai perjalanan Anda (sampai ke mana?). Ceritakan menge cita-cita Anda, d.l.l.).

2) Mohon lihat gambar di bawah. Tolong menulis sebuah karangan atau cerita mengenai gambar tersebut. (Misalnya: Siapa tokoh-tokoh di gambar? Apa yang sedang dibicarakan pemandu pariwisata? Menurut pendapat Anda bagaimana pendapat anak-anak mengenai turis-turis? Bagaimana pendapat turis mengenai Tana Toraja dan Orang Toraja? d.l.l.).

FIGURE 4.7: Kathleen Adams's drawing of Western tourists and Toraja children (used with permission).

deliberately made to be unclear (are the children asking for gifts or waving?), Adams was able to address an issue that was difficult to discuss directly with the parents, and allowed them to interpret the scene however they wished. As she says, "(The drawing) evoked a rich array of attitudes and cultural assumptions that would have been hard to tease out in a normal interview" (2015, personal communication).

Rudi Colloredo-Mansfeld, on the other hand, realized that making his ethnographic line drawings where the local people of Otavalo, Ecuador, could see him "brought about (a) role reversal, with the sketches themselves often prompting the questions about and reactions to my research interests" (1999, 53) (Figure 4.8).

Sometimes, showing people your vision of their world can get them to perceive their ordinary assumptions in new ways. To do this, you must first be sure you are acutely aware of your ethnographic surroundings, not taking anything for granted and not overlooking the banal. Your drawing is your interpretation, of course, but it must be based in clear and precise seeing, even when you can't be overt in your examination of the cultural context. Practice Etude Twenty.

This is another valuable exercise to enhance your ethnographic seeing. Learning how to look straight ahead but actually focusing on the peripheries

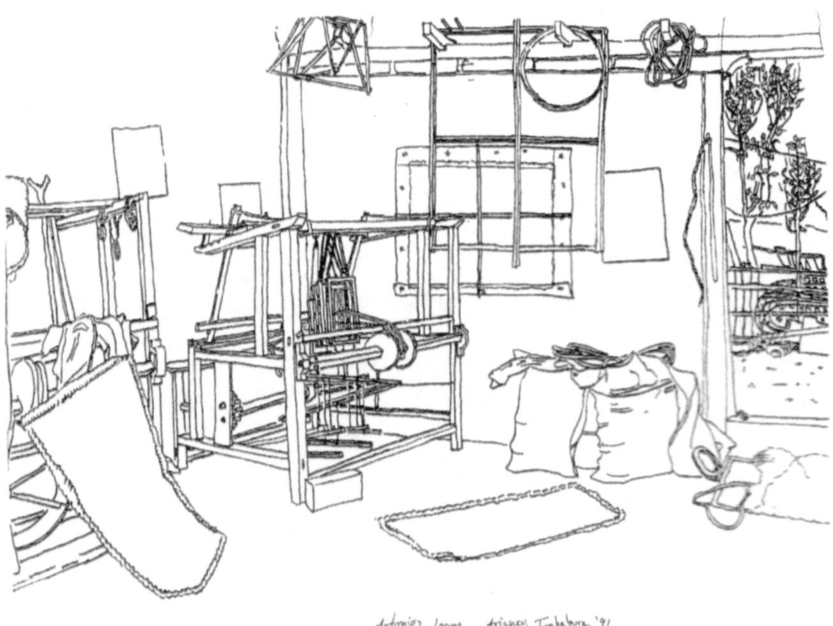

FIGURE 4.8: Rudi Colloredo-Mansfeld's contour drawing of a loom in Otavalo, Ecuador (1999, 128; used with permission).

ETUDE TWENTY, Lighted Peripheral Vision (3–5 minutes): Find a well-lit view (perhaps outside, drawing on your knee or lap?) and draw a freehand frame in the center of your paper. Place your pencil at one of the sides of your frame, left or right, and before you start to draw, *stare* straight ahead at the view, without moving your eyes, for about 30 seconds; concentrate on some aspect of that view that is not near (say, a city block away). Without moving your eyes from the fixed point, start to draw the contours of what you see in your peripheral vision, first one side then the other. Then draw what's in your peripheral vision above and below. When all the peripheries are drawn in as blind contours, you may look down at the paper and fill in what you see in the center (Figure 4.9).

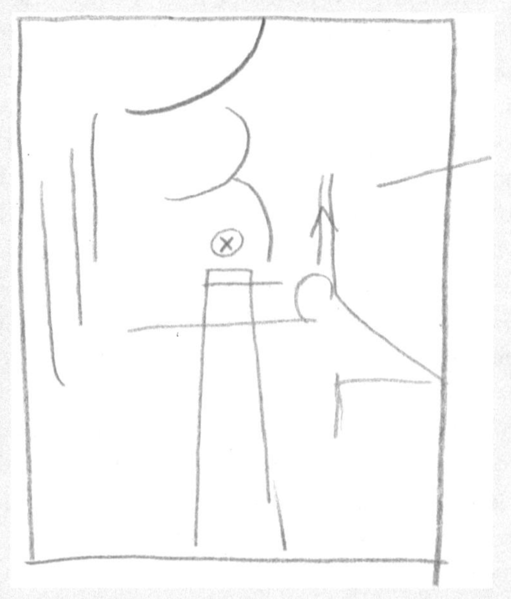

FIGURE 4.9: Lighted Peripheral Vision drawing.

will help you broaden your ordinary seeing but, perhaps more importantly, will assist you in seeing what you may not be encouraged to see.

Ethnographic Application: Consider the following example to see how such seeing may be helpful in understanding your ethnographic field site. The ex-*Camat* (local village mayor) invited me to come interview him about life after World War II and about the advent of tourism in the area. My other friends in the village told me that this was a great honor because he rarely invited people to his home after he left office because of the death of his wife. Their theory was that he had become more and more suspicious of his neighbors' jealousy of all the possessions he had accumulated over the years he served as leader of the village, and they asked me to be sure to remember all the things he displayed on the walls and shelves.

His house was very dark when I entered, and as there was only one teenaged son remaining at home to help him, the refreshments were very modest. I had trouble adjusting my eyes to the darkness, having come in from full afternoon sun, and he made it clear that he had very little time for the interview, so asked me to start right away. I realized I needed to focus on him, which was not physically difficult because he was seated directly in front of me, nearly knee to knee. But this meant I had very little chance to cast my eyes around the room. Any observations of his décor would have to be done through my peripheral vision. I had practiced expanding the scope of my seeing (in part by using this Etude), so I was able to do both things: concentrate on interviewing the ex-Camat while also partially perceiving his home. What I saw was not at all what I'd been led to believe: his home was not grand at all, it was completely disheveled and unkempt. I could see couches and chairs to each side of me completely covered in stacks of books and newspapers interleaved with clothes, fabrics, boxes, and topped with unwashed dishes. Even in the darkness I could peripherally see that there were mounds of unwashed clothes in the background and objects jumbled to the side of the couch I was sitting on.

The interview went well, and I learned a great deal about the war and about tourism. I also learned that my neighbors were wrong about why he no longer invited them to visit him after his wife's death, though I never told any of them what I'd seen.

Finding a Vocabulary of Lines

My carving teacher Partoho and I sat together for many hours, talking about carving and tourists, of course, but also chatting about politics, about global exchange rates, about life in America, and about truly crazy things, like whether the sun shining on us in Sumatra could possibly be the *same* sunshine that shone on people in the West. Partoho had a sharp mind for thinking things out logically and analytically, but he also had a mind that liked to drift off and ponder while looking at his *kretek* cigarette's smoke rising. During those pondering times, I told myself to stay attentive (because I was doing research) even though I wanted to let my mind wander, too. I felt the obligation to remain vigilant when he drifted away, waiting for the moment when he'd return, so I could ask more probing questions.

Sometimes, when he'd come back from what appeared to me to be a reverie, he'd ask for one of my notebooks so he could write or draw what he wanted to communicate to me. One day, when I'd been asking about life in the Batak homeland, I guess he just got tired of talking about it, and wanted to relive it in his mind. Off he drifted, staring into the corner of the soot-stained wooden ceiling. It didn't take too long for him to return to the space we were sharing that evening, his children watching TV with the sound off, and his wife seated dozing in the corner. He gestured for my notebook, and I pulled it out of the bag. He found a corner of plain, unlined paper and used my pen to draw a very small drawing of a man, done in traditional Batak form, standing in front of a fancy old traditional house (Figure 4.10). The man was out of proportion to the house—at least three times as large as he might be in the real world—and the house seemed to lean forward toward him as if in conversation. All the faces, the man's and the architectural figures', were smiling slightly, and the tone of the work was, to me, a happy one. Partoho seemed content with his work, saying "*Itulah*" ("There, that's how it is") as he handed it back to me.

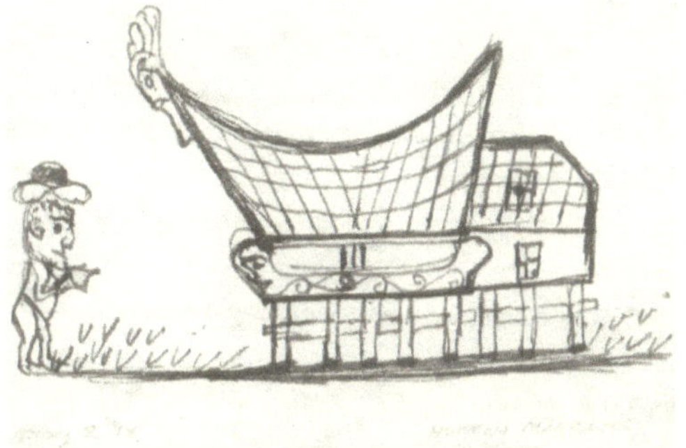

FIGURE 4.10: Partoho's drawing of "Batak Homeland."

I then realized that the evening had ended, and asked permission to return home. Once there, I looked at the drawing he gave me—my first from him—and tried to "figure it out": What meaning might it have? Why was the man larger? Was it him? Was this the past or some nostalgic past? Perhaps a mythic past?! In the end, I figured there was not much to read. It was just exactly what it was: a Batak man standing near his home. What really started to needle me over passing days, however, was the style and character of the lines with which he drew it. Some of the lines were light and positively airy—grass around the house was conveyed by a series of "V's" hovering above the horizon line—and others were drawn hard, back and forth, over and over, to darken them. The thickness and thinness of lines didn't seem to communicate importance, or weight, but something else, something unclear to me, while other lines, like those detailing the animate figures of the house, were loose and free.

I never asked him to explain the drawing because it might show that I totally missed his point, so I merely kept it on my desk to look at, to enjoy, to ponder. It was months later that I looked at the drawing in a new way. I had begun making sketches of the area surrounding my house, but was displeased with how they looked. The watercolor drawings looked tentative and romanticized, as if I were trying to please an art teacher, and the line drawings were dutiful and safe (Figure 4.11). I looked at Partoho's drawing and got a little envious. He was so certain of his lines and (seemingly) so uncaring about the proportions or character of his marks on the page. He drew what he *wanted* to draw, I thought, the *way* he wanted to draw. He saw something clearly in his mind, and he drew it.

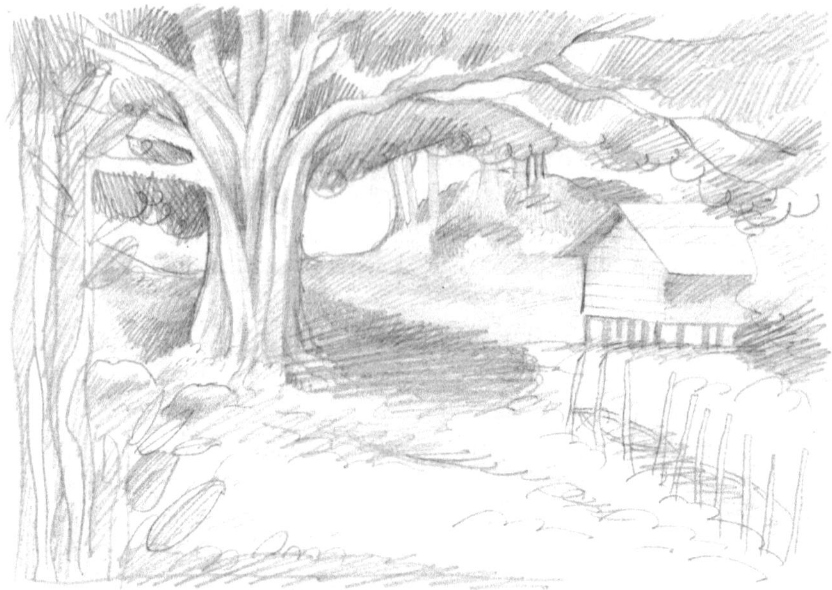

FIGURE 4.11: My line drawing of a landscape.

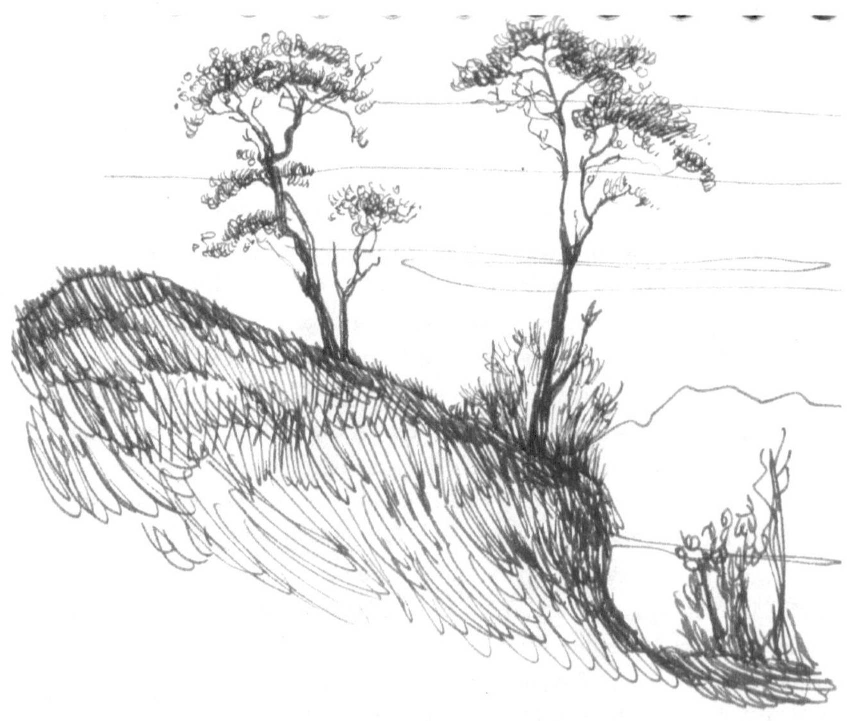

FIGURE 4.12: Pen drawing of the kindling trees.

I decided to follow his lead. I opened my drawing book and looked out the window, not the main room where the "view" was, but out the kitchen, which looked over two work yards, a stone enclosure, and a rugged hill. I was searching for an "honest" or "real" thing, and focused on two tall narrow trees at the crest of the hill. People had been chopping the lower branches of these two trees for years for kindling, giving them a twisted, scrawny look. These two trees told more about life in the village than the more decorative images I had been making, so I drew them. But this time, I tried to make my ink lines reflect something about the character of the trees themselves, so I used short chopping lines, my hand tense as if I were holding an ax rather than a pen (Figure 4.12).

I liked it. To me, the image was truthful. That's when I began to explore using different lines and different kinds of drawing, trying to match the shape and energy of my lines to the character of what I was depicting. Sometimes I used strange, short, controlled lines (Figure 4.13), and sometimes the lines were tight and nervous; some drawings are light and loopy (Figure 4.14), and other times they are slow and determined (Figure 4.15). The reason I experimented with

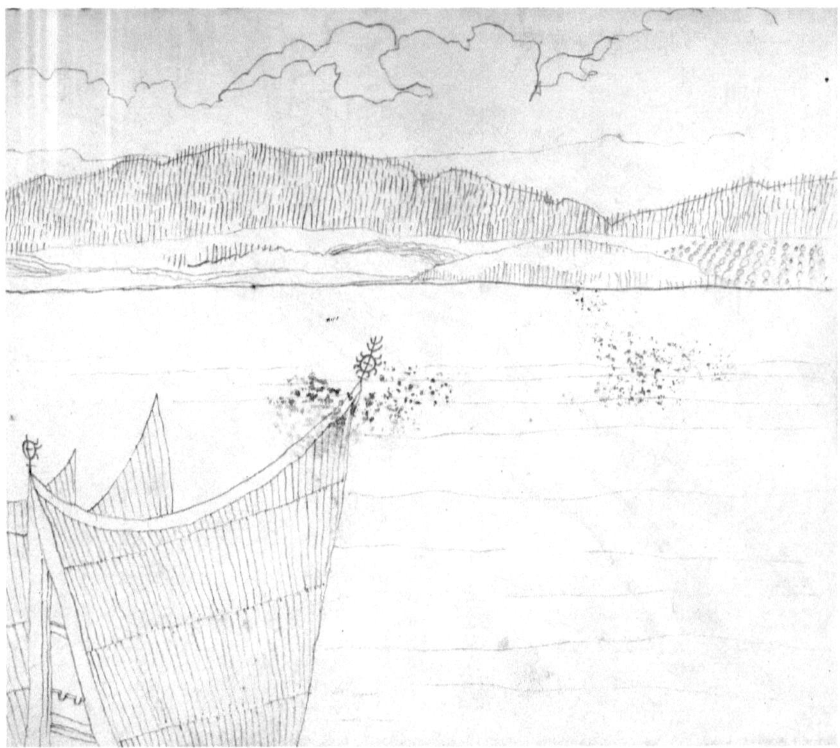

FIGURE 4.13: My drawing with short, controlled lines.

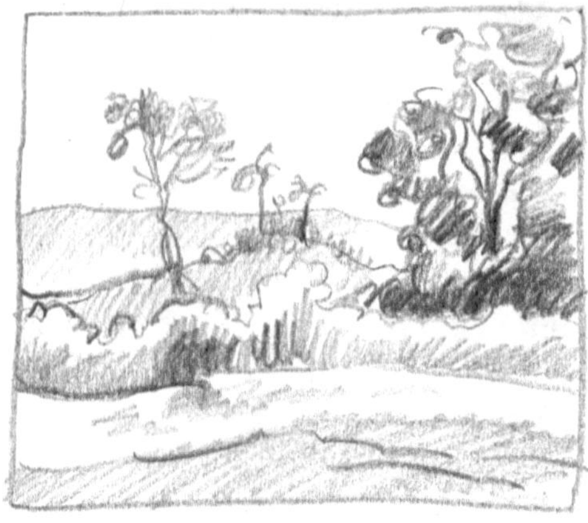

FIGURE 4.14: My drawing with light, loopy lines.

trying to develop a vocabulary of lines was because I wanted them to reveal something about the nature of what I was seeing. I felt mostly unfettered by art conventions now and knew that my drawings were better documents.

Many years later, I found Partoho's drawing again and put it in a small metal frame. I remain inspired by the content of the drawing, but even more by the way the lines communicate, realizing now that the lines *are* the document.

If you've ever needed an excuse to play around with drawing, here it is! Seeing all that your pencil or pen can do when you press hard or light, when you vary the weight of line and experiment with nonsolid lines, will enable you to begin making lines that best represent what you are carefully seeing. Try

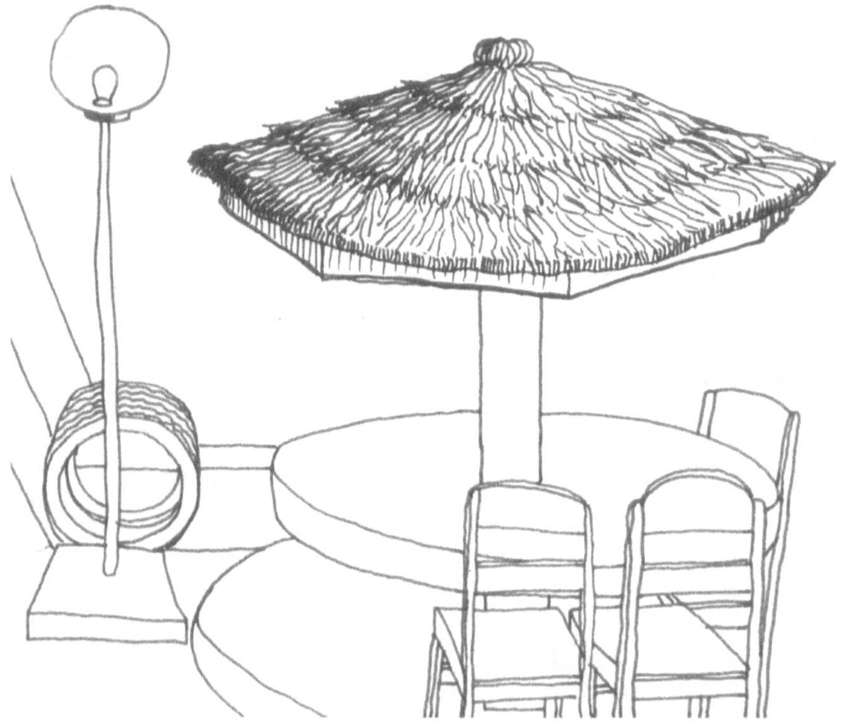

FIGURE 4.15: My drawing with slow, determined lines.

ETUDE TWENTY-ONE, Collecting Lines (ongoing): This Etude, like Etude Thirteen, suggests that you begin collecting a vocabulary of lines (Figure 4.16). To start, I've asked you to draw your lines deliberately and strongly, but now it's time to consider other ways to depict what you experience around you in more varied ways. Like the collection of cartoon "glyphs," this set of lines can be made and saved in a small pocket book you make for yourself. Every time you see a character of line you think might be helpful in your quest to depict your world visually, whether it is from your own doodles or from other artists' work, simply copy it in your book, making note of how you might use it.

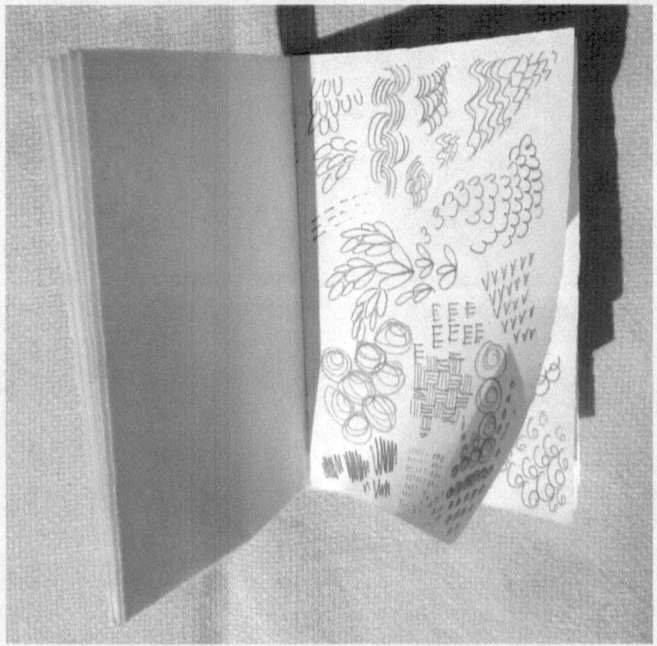

FIGURE 4.16: A collection of diverse kinds of lines.

copying Partoho's drawing, and then consider making a page of broken lines, scribble lines, zigzag lines, and stipple dots; push the pencil up rather than pulling it down, just to see what happens. Try making crosshatched lines and shading lines, to see what they can do for you. If you look at Carol Hendrickson's contour-line drawing documenting a historic building, you'll see she uses a variety of clear, sharp lines to convey the tree, the car, and the structure itself (Figure 4.17). Another excellent source of inspiration for making varied lines is Vincent Van Gogh's pen-and-ink drawings made during his stay in Provence (see Figure 4.18).

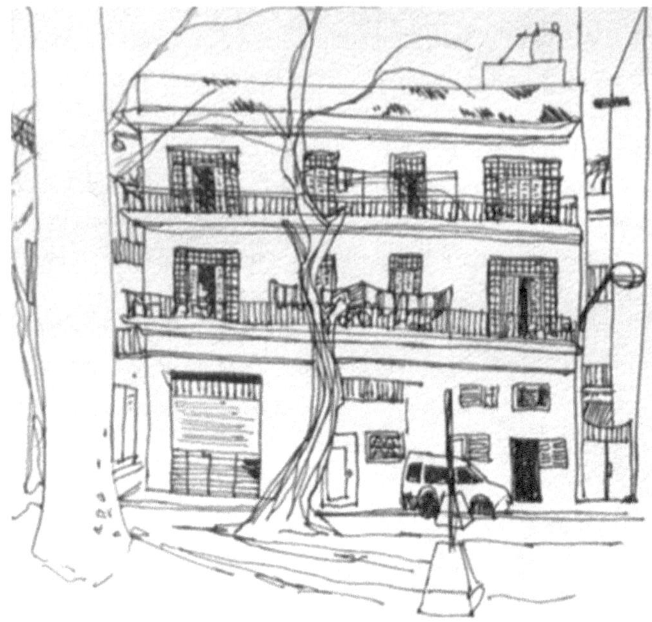

FIGURE 4.17: Carol Hendrickson's contour-line drawing of a historic building (used with permission).

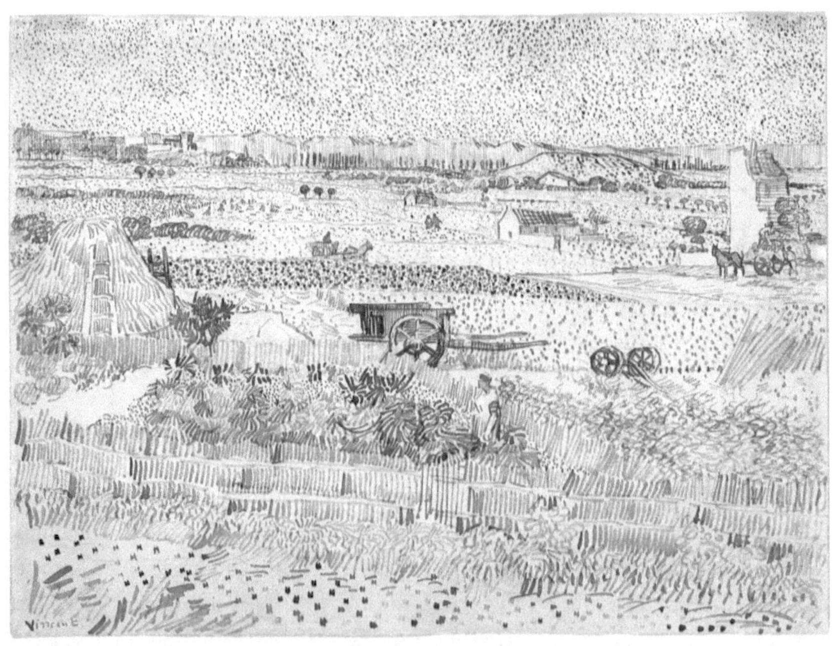

FIGURE 4.18: "Harvest—The Plain of La Crau" (1888), Vincent Van Gogh (Courtesy of National Gallery of Art, Washington).

When you are feeling adventurous, you might think about playing with your lines while riding a bumpy train or bus, or looking away from the paper while your hand moves; you can hold the pencil very close to the lead or very far away from it; you can rotate the pencil with your fingers while you draw, or shudder your wrist and hand when you delineate. Each kind of line will convey something that may be useful to you when depicting what you see in your research.

Last Words

Knowing how to enhance your ethnographic perceptions through drawing is not an insurmountable task, but it does take practice. Understanding what you perceive to be an edge, and recognizing that there are different kinds of edges (here I have focused on defined and indistinct ones) is the first step. Once you accept that edges are really in your mind, you will be better able to delineate them, using whatever kind or character of line you think suits those edges best. Practice is key. As I've mentioned before, none of this is "easy" and not very much of it is "natural." What's needed here is a desire to expand your visual attention and a commitment to practice making marks on paper. The next chapter will help you begin to see what's inside those edges.

CHAPTER 5

SEEING INSIDE EDGES

The Limits to Seeing Edge Lines

I'm happy to have helped you see the variety of edges out there in your world, and to encourage you to try your hand at drawing them; I'm not at all apologetic about telling you, however, that edges are not enough. Attending to edges is just one way to really see your surroundings as an ethnographer and, while it provides a strong foundation for other ways of seeing, it has limits (I think you might have guessed that already). What you need to do now is to start seeing what's *within* the edges: to begin filling in details and features that convey what you perceive more completely. That's what this chapter will help you do.

As I noted in the last chapter, edges represent an ontological assumption about where one thing ends and another begins, or where one slope or plane bends or tips to another angle. We don't have time to pursue the philosophical questions about whether, or how, one thing is separable from another because then we'd get lost down a side road bordered by weedy examples proving we don't exist or that we see only phantoms. (As an example of this kind of fascinating jaunt down that side road, consider this most rudimentary scenario: Think of a pond, lake, or ocean. Where does the "shore" end and the "water" begin?) Rather than wandering in those thought-provoking stalks and stems along the thought path—fascinating though they are—let's just assume that there are boundaries between things, and that (for the most part) we *can* perceive them. The same goes for what we see inside the confining boundary edges: they are there and we can (mostly) know them.[1]

1 Please refer to Gibson (2015) and Willats (1997) for much more detail and explanation about human perception and how we use lines to convey what we see.

Perceiving edges (and trying to draw them) tends to flatten our environs. Even though we may be seeing our world richly when we compose contour lines, we are not documenting the full depth that we experience. So now we will begin to think about representing aspects of the fuller reality of our ethnographic experiences. First, let's try seeing the structure beneath the complexity of the human form.

ETUDE TWENTY-TWO, "Skeletonizing" (3–5 minutes): Like Etudes Two and Fourteen, this one uses an existing photograph from a magazine or newspaper. It's best to find a picture with a variety of subjects in it: people, furniture, buildings, plants, animals. Simply put, you are going to draw in the "skeletons" of the subjects in the form of basic lines. Examine the figures and draw the basic armatures that hold the things up. People might be reduced to four or five lines, while trees might be indicated with two or three. See Figure 5.1.

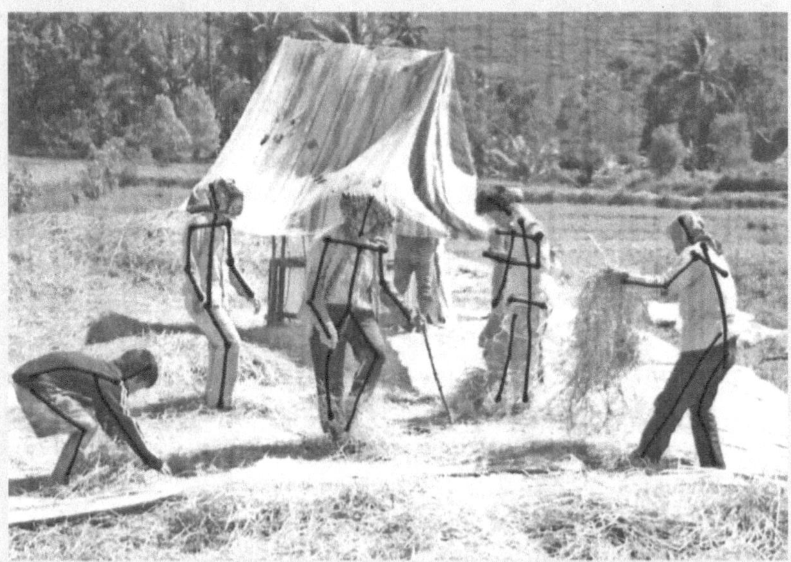

FIGURE 5.1: Example of "skeletonizing" a photograph to see posture and position.

"Skeletonizing" is a simple exercise, but it can teach you a lot about human bodies and how they comport themselves. We'll discuss movement and gesture in the next chapter, but for now, we are trying to look at pose: weight, angle, tension, proportion. Static objects (human-made, such as chairs, buildings, and cars; and natural, such as trees and mountains) are fairly easy to skeletonize because their armatures tend to be visible—or at least stationary. Living things not only are flexible, but often exist in multiple simultaneous planes (forward, upward, twisting, curving). Catching these emergent qualities requires careful, concentrated seeing via drawing.

Because ethnographic research involves so much work with seeing (and responding to) what people are doing, in conjunction with animals and plants as well as with the more static material world, understanding how to observe their behaviors with precision, and then to document them, is vital. Finding the structure, the skeleton beneath, is a first step.

The Silhouette, Positive and Negative

Let's think about lines in a different way for a moment, not as outlines and not as skeleton structures. For now, let's think about the line as the subject. Here we are talking about what is called the "content line" or the "silhouette line" (Willats 1997, 214–19), which can be delineated in both positive and negative form. In the positive form, your drawing tool (pencil or pen) produces the line that is the object on a light surface, and in the negative form, you use an extractive tool (pencil eraser or sharp blade) to subtract the line from a dark surface. There are Etudes for both below.

An example of the positive silhouette line which you may be very familiar with from childhood is the stickman. The typical stickman is actually a composite form: in the body, the lines are the torso and arms, whereas the round head is a contour line. Children create such depictions at around age four or five and do not move to fully outlined drawings showing position and scale to represent what they see until about age seven (Willats 1997, 75, 11). If you look at some ancient cave paintings, you will find some human representations done in this positive silhouette form, and you might also be reminded of certain Asian ink paintings (Figure 5.2), which use the brushstrokes themselves to represent the thing being observed.

Examples of negative silhouette lines are found in woodcuts, where the solid flat plane is methodically cut away to leave raised surfaces that are then inked and pressed onto paper. This extractive method of drawing, where you are taking away everything *but* the line you want to show,[2] is harder for some people to do, so when you try it, concentrate on what you are seeing and try not to get too frustrated.

2 Refer back to Chapter Four, where my carving teacher Partoho told me about the difference between Batak and Minangkabau carving styles.

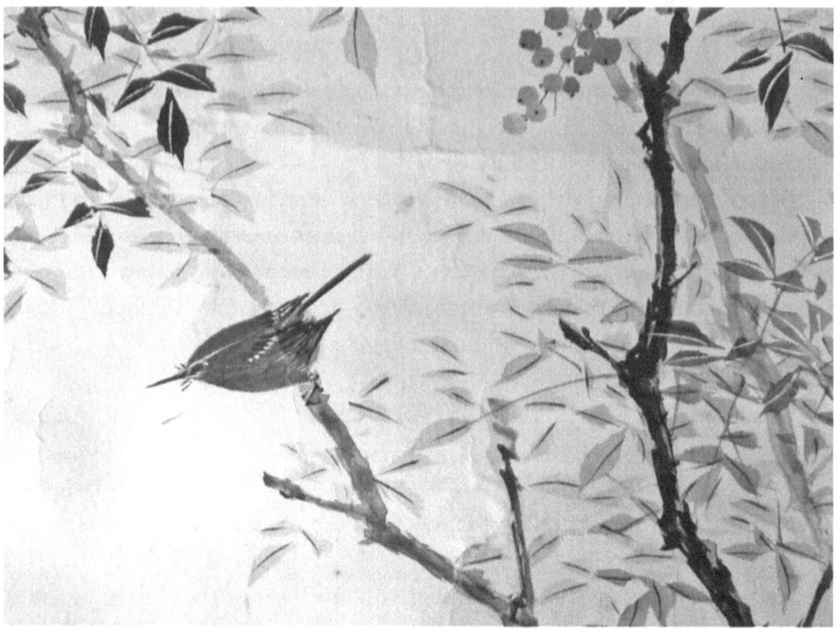

FIGURE 5.2: Detail of a Chinese ink painting.

The two kinds of silhouette line drawings require opposite kinds of seeing. In the positive form, you are perceiving your subject as a solid mass that your line will represent in total. The negative form, however, forces you to see the world in a very different way. Here, you are seeking to represent the subject as a total mass, but you are allowing it to emerge from a dark background. Once you practice this form a little, you may see that it can be used in a more complex way, representing the variety of highlights in a thing, not just the thing-as-whole. Seeing the lightest parts of a thing and representing those by erasing or scraping can open new doors both for perceiving and also for representing what you see.

ETUDE TWENTY-THREE, Positive Silhouette (3–5 minutes): There are at least three ways to make this drawing, so my suggestion is to try all three so you are familiar with them when the need arises.

Part A: (Refer to Etude Seven.) Choose a very absorbent paper (paper napkin, paper towel, facial tissue) and tape the edges to your ordinary paper. Using a new (full of ink) felt-tip pen, focus your seeing on some subject, then touch the pen lightly to the surface, letting the paper soak up the ink to mimic the shape of what you see.

Part B: Using your ordinary paper and your pencil worn down to a broad width, focus your seeing on some subject, then scribble (round and round or zigzagging, but hard) what you see, letting the scribble-line create the edges of the thing.

Part C: On ordinary or absorbent paper, dip your finger into some tinted fluid (ink, paint, even coffee or berry juice) and create a representation of what you see in blobby form; playing with the amount of fluid and finger pressure will help you understand how this kind of drawing works. For examples, please see Figure 5.3.

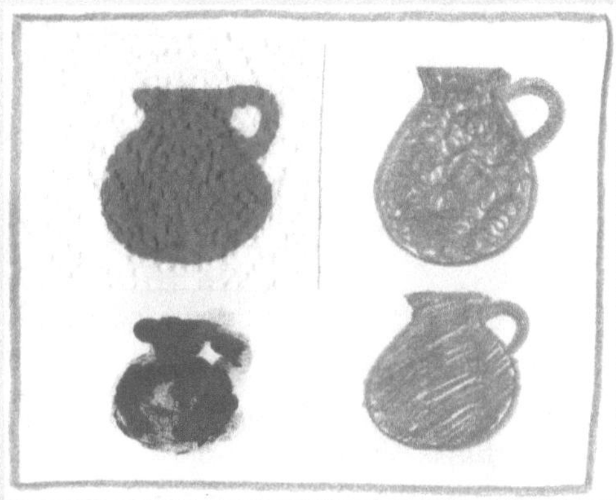

FIGURE 5.3: Examples of positive silhouettes.

ETUDE TWENTY-FOUR, Negative Silhouette (4–5 minutes): Now you are going to experiment with making negative silhouette lines. Start by finding a very saturated and dark picture or advertisement in the newspaper (magazines pictures won't work). Cut out a square of the darkest area and tape down to a sheet of paper. Choose an object (something simple like a mug, for example) and examine it carefully before proceeding. Look carefully where

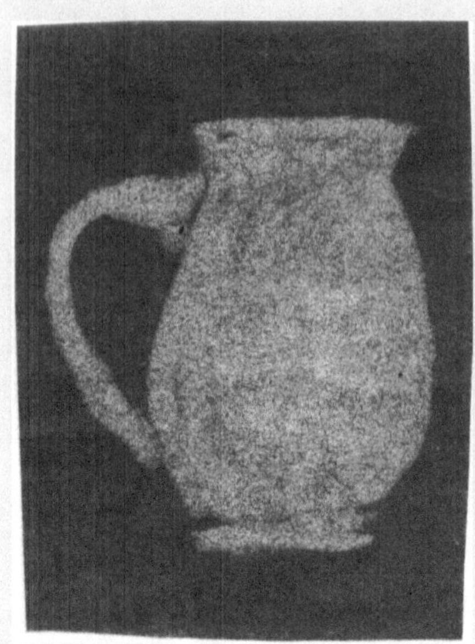

the highlights are, and where the dark areas are. With your pencil eraser, remove the dark ink where you see the light parts of the object. Don't focus on edges now, but rather on the inside of the object, letting the edges reveal themselves as the places where the light is not.[3] For an example of negative silhouette, please see Figure 5.4.

FIGURE 5.4: Example of negative silhouette.

Ethnographic Application: There is a lot to discuss (philosophically or theoretically) about how these kinds of silhouette lines can depict the world around you (consider, for example, what it means to say "the line *is* the object"), but for the purposes of this book, we can simply accept that these kinds of lines are ethnographically useful: lively, descriptive, and engaging. Look at the positive silhouette line drawings made by anthropologist-artist Carol Hendrickson while she was observing surfers in Hawaii (Figure 5.5) and you'll see how much rich information can be recorded in a few strong lines.

And consider Rudi Colloredo-Mansfeld's negative silhouette drawing of a chair in Otavalo, Ecuador, observing how the object pops into view from its background (Figure 5.6). It takes practice, of course, to learn how to put this kind of drawing to use in your ethnographic work, but once you teach yourself to remain calm, to concentrate, and to deeply see, you'll find that silhouette drawings can produce excellent results, not just helping you to perceive entities with energy and vibrancy but also giving you a new tool when you need to make quick, meaningful depictions quickly.

3 If you are more adventurous and have a little money to spend, art stores often have small samples of a product called "scratchboard" you can experiment with. This is a waxy white paper completely covered in black ink that can be scraped with a mat knife to reveal the white paper below.

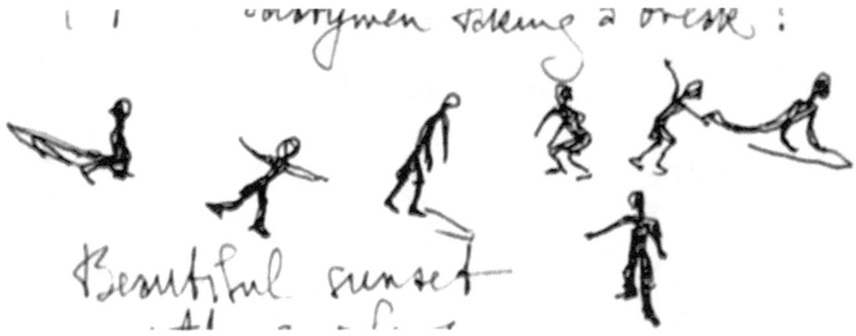

FIGURE 5.5: Carol Hendrickson's positive silhouette drawings (used with permission).

Surfaces: Decorations, Designs, Patterns

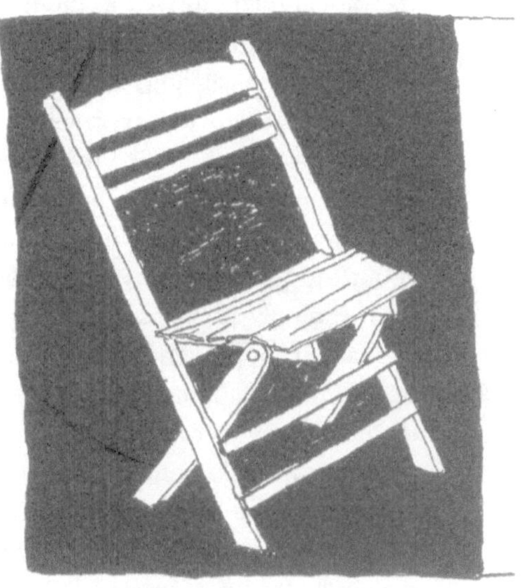

FIGURE 5.6: Rudi Colloredo-Mansfeld's negative silhouette drawing of a chair in Otavalo, Ecuador (1999, 128; used with permission).

We've seen that lines can represent what you see as the outline of a thing (contours) and can also compose the thing itself (silhouettes), so now let's consider how lines can help define the surfaces of a thing. Ethnographers often discover that some aspect of their research—whether their focus is prenatal health practices in Nepal, gang affiliations in south Chicago, or economic exchange networks in Micronesia—will require that they take note of symbolic elements in local costume, art, or architecture. While such decorations, designs, and patterns might seem to be beyond the realm of their research, ethnographers may soon realize that knowledge of such details will assist their understanding of a group in unforeseen ways.

Even those of us whose research topics address what might be termed aesthetic fields discover connections we were unaware of, once we begin to take notice of the details of surfaces. David Guss describes how he worked with the Yekuana people of southeastern Venezuela to transcribe their epic creation story, the *Watunna*, but soon realized that he must first study the complexities of basket weaving before he could begin to understand how the Yekuana view the world, and how they integrated the Watunna into it (1989, 1–4). As he began to study the manufacture and designs of the baskets, he became aware that the baskets intercommunicated with tales and chants, and with rituals and prohibitions, leading him to realize that "the ultimate subject matter of the baskets is culture itself" (1989, 91).

Decorations, designs, and patterns help define who we are. Whether it is to identify our individuality with body modifications or to claim our heritage through the display of emblems, the use of ornamentation has deep meaning and should be documented and studied carefully by ethnographers. My own research, as noted, dealt with Batak wood carvers, which meant that I had to learn as much as I could, not just about how to carve, but about *what* to carve. I learned the proportions and variations of the basic traditional forms as well as the more unusual ones, but my carving teacher Partoho spent much more time trying to teach me the particulars of the surface foliate carving, gorga (Figure 4.1). The curves and tendrils of the gorga work seemed very straightforward to me until I tried to draw them. Partoho would then take his pen to every drawing I made and correct it, telling me that the nodes between leaves was too wide, or that the flow of a line was too stiff. In trying to draw what I saw, I was learning, imperfectly, about the aesthetic sense of the Bataks.

It was only after I had made some progress with the gorga drawings that I was taught about women's most valued work, weaving. Because I was having trouble understanding the proportions of lines in gorga, Partoho reached into the family storage cabinet and brought out a delicately woven shawl, showing me how the edges of this sacred woven fabric, called *ulos*, was finished on each end (see Figure 5.7). I learned that the twined fringe decorations were said to be "carvings" (thus of the masculine world) and were woven by men, not women.[4] Had I not attempted to imperfectly draw the gorga carving designs to document them, I would never have learned about the forms and their proportions, their meanings, and the sexual division of labor of these ritual fabrics.

Ornamental surfaces could simply represent aesthetic expressions and preferences, and color might be purely about personal choice or taste. But in many cultures, what outsiders might see as ornament or decoration actually demonstrates wealth, status, caste, cultural tradition, or family or village identity. The Tukano people of Colombia draw and paint elaborate designs on their houses, but if you think they are merely decorative additions to the architecture, you would miss the fact that each element has a name and

4 Sandra Niessen states that men are often involved with this kind of weaving, but notes that early ethnographic photographs show women also doing the work (2009, 523, 529).

meaning (often associated with incest), and, further, that the elements represent glowing phosphenes (what we in the West might call hallucinations) caused by the narcotic *yaje* ingested by many adult men (Reichel-Dolmatoff 1978). By asking the Tukano men to draw what they saw with colored pencils on white paper, the ethnographer was able to analyze their complex works. Only because he redrew them as isolates was he able to understand the connection between the semiotic and decorative value of the elements (294).

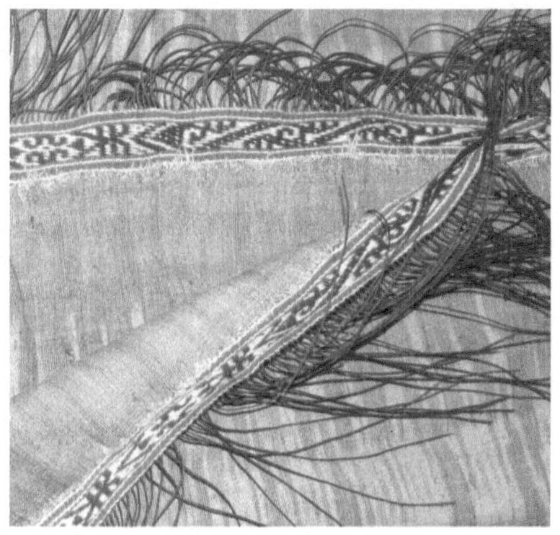

FIGURE 5.7: Fringe weaving on the edge of the traditional Batak *ulos* fabric.

You may not always need to focus on the details of patterns, however. For the various groups of Chiapas, Mexico, and Guatemala, the elaborate woven or embroidered images on their clothing indicate where they are from, sometimes also conveying their marital status and position in the community (Hendrickson 1995). Even so, depicting the specificity of surface decorations on their costumes is not always necessary in ethnographic drawings. Instead, when decorations are not the focus, they can be implied with a few attentively seen lines to give the general character of the clothes, as shown in a drawing by artist-anthropologist Christine Eber (Figure 5.8). Among the Minangkabau people of Central Sumatra, the elaborate geometric supplementary-weft designs woven of silk and metallic-wrapped threads (called *songket*) can represent plants and animals in abstract form, but can also make metaphorical reference to well-known proverbs that recall to viewers' minds such things as valued personal traits or social responsibilities (Summerfield and Sutan Madjo Indo 1999, 171–99). There are times when the researcher

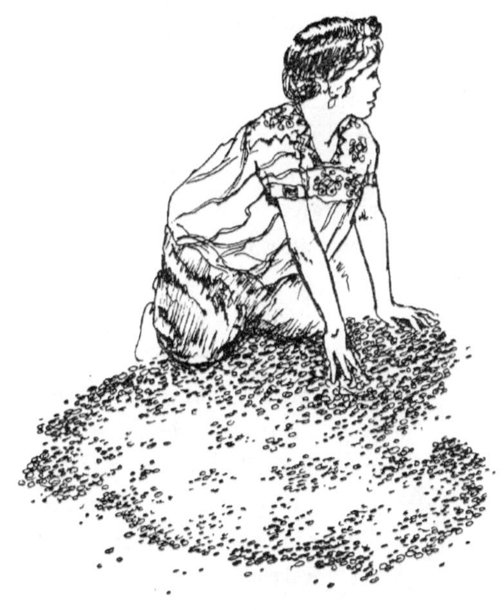

FIGURE 5.8: Christine Eber's drawing of a Maya woman sorting beans (used with permission).

must depict these patterns with care in drawings, but other times they may be sketched as a general form; each situation will indicate how much detail is needed.

Ethnographers must learn to see and then appreciate the semiotic use of all of these kinds of lines if they are to begin to understand the culture being investigated. Documenting the designs, patterns, and decorations through drawing is one of the most direct routes to that kind of deep understanding.

ETUDE TWENTY-FIVE, Center-Out Drawing (7–10 minutes): Find an interestingly dressed person in a public space like a library or café. Now, draw that person from the center moving out, focusing on details of their costume and accessories. For example, if you are drawing the leg, start at the pants' center seam and move out from there; if you are drawing the torso, start with the rows of buttons down the center of the shirt and draw the patterns and designs you see as they move to the edges. Maybe you want to start a face with the nose and move up and out toward the ear and hair, letting the contour of the head be only implied. Use basic shapes (such as letters and numbers) to depict the designs and patterns you see. Remember, it's the process of seeing, not the final product you are attentive to. It doesn't matter what the drawing looks like (although you might be charmed by what you see); it's how you got there.

Ethnographic Application: Most people's inclination is to focus on documenting designs by making a contour line and filling it in. The trouble with this approach is that the design, the pattern, or the decoration is sublimated to the shape drawn. By working the other way around, that is, by carefully seeing-drawing the characteristics and proportions of the elements and defining the outline of the shape later, you will find that your focus will not be on trying to fit the design into a confining space but rather giving these "inside" lines your full attention. This is the vital point of drawing to see: to document your observations, not to "make a drawing."

Surfaces: Textures, Topographies, Features

Sometimes the surfaces you see inside a constraining edge will not have a clear line for you to copy like the designs and patterns discussed above do.

Sometimes, what you see in your ethnographic research is just a plain textured surface, or it will be composed of an undulating exterior, or perhaps covered in features like ridges or bumps. It's easy to gloss over such surfaces, but they may be culturally meaningful. If you see them, then of course you must try to draw them. To simply convey the complex world you experience in your ethnographic research without making note of the surface characteristics might make your drawing look as though everything was composed of smooth plastic, where the skin of a human face would be represented the same as a field of swaying crops or a plaster-covered brick wall. To do that would be to miss the opportunity to document the depth of meaning you see, and so miss the point of seeing-drawing altogether. Just like some of the beauty of music comes from different timbres (tone voices), so a drawing gains depth from its ability to represent different textures, topographies, and features.

Conveying the complex character of surfaces via attentive marks is not as difficult as it might sound. In the last chapter, Etude Twenty-Two asked you to begin paying attention to different kinds of lines to create varied contours, and to collect them in a small book. Now's the time to look back at those marks you made (and to add to them) and start applying them in a slightly different way. The same varying kinds of lines you drew as continuous can now be abbreviated: wide, dark solid lines can become smudged dashes; soft, feathery lines can become broken meanders; and long, clean lines can become a series of short twigs (Figure 5.9).

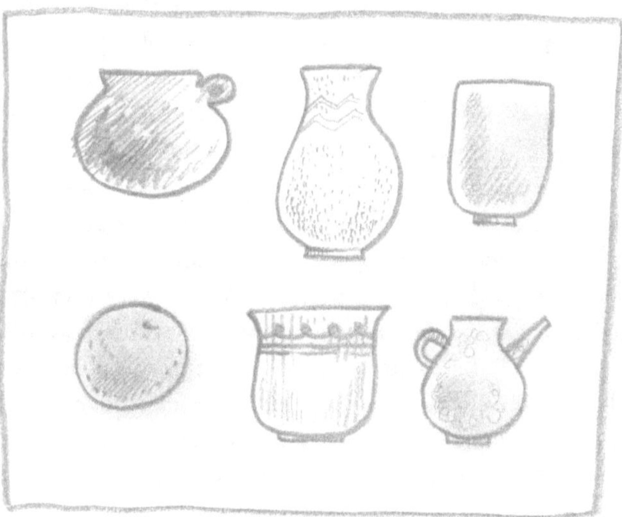

FIGURE 5.9: Varied kinds of broken lines used to convey surface texture and character.

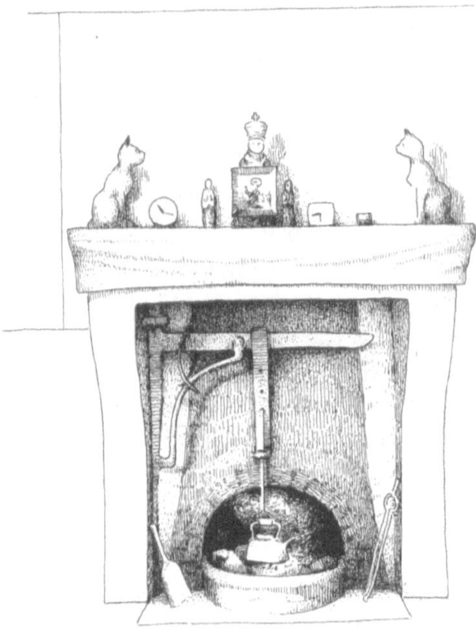

FIGURE 5.10: Henry Glassie's drawing of an Irish hearth, showing texturing lines ("The hearth at the home of Paddy and Mary McBrien. Ballymenone, Fermanagh, Northern Ireland. 1972" in *Vernacular Architecture*, H. Glassie, p. 50. Reprinted with permission of Indiana University Press).

Surface marks can take the form of "coloring in," cross-hatching, or pointillist dotting. The work, and joy, of this kind of documentation is actually seeing what the surface looks like, translating that perception into an image, and then testing your interpretation on paper with the pencil until you are convinced there is a definite link between what you draw and what you see.

Have a look at two drawings to get some ideas of how you might proceed. The first is a drawing by folklorist and ethnographer Henry Glassie. It depicts the McBrien family hearth and possessions in Ballymenone, Northern Ireland (2000, 50). Notice how he has used contour lines to demarcate both the objects and architectural features, and also how he has used a variety of dots and short strokes to convey their varying textured surfaces (Figure 5.10). You can see that with these simple lines, he is able to bring life to his drawing, and to render this focal part of the Irish home in a way that tells much more than an architectural elevation (side view) depiction would.

The second drawing (Figure 5.11), by artist-anthropologist Manuel Joao Ramos, depicts two people illegally crossing a river boundary in Spain, a memory shared by elderly participants in these illicit activities, then drawn by him based on their descriptions because no photographs existed (Afonso and Ramos 2004, 78). Look carefully at how he has used layered, continuously connected U-shapes to depict the lapping water in a very simple way, and also how by using a series of recurring and overlapped curved lines, he effectively communicates the nature of the swimmers' wet hair. These two very different textures, water and hair, are drawn with the most direct kinds of lines.

What can be more difficult to render in simple lines is the difference between textures of atmosphere and those of the material world. Imagine an ethnographic situation where you see something happening in a fire- or

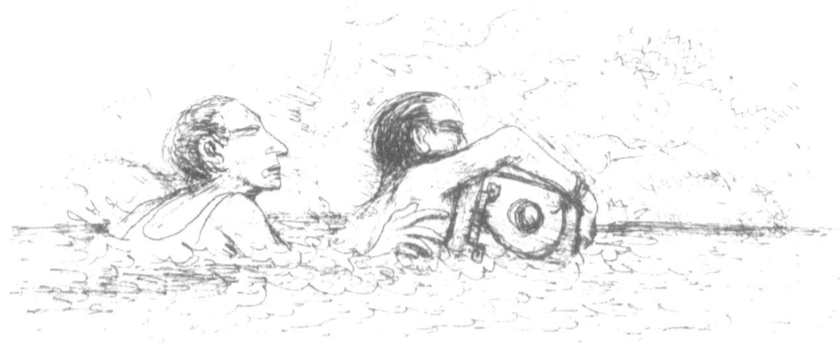

FIGURE 5.11: Manuel Joao Ramos's drawing showing how simple lines can depict water and wet hair (from Afonso and Ramos 2004, 78; used with permission).

candle-lit room that is thick with incense or smoke, and where you see people dressed in intricate clothes interacting with varied implements on both tamped-down earth and a decorated platform. How will you distinguish between the smoke, the fabrics, the leather, paper, or yarns, the hard earth and the ornamented concrete? By practicing now using different line strokes—short, firm, wispy, curving, straight, scribbly, smudgy—you will soon be able to convey varied aspects of any event you experience in the future.

ETUDE TWENTY-SIX, Varied Lines (2-3 minutes): Choose a view (perhaps out a window to help you define the limits of your picture) that has many complex textures and surfaces. Convey the materiality of that scene by using as many varied lines as you can. Don't focus on edges, but rather see objects in the scene from the center—or the inside—out. Let the character of the lines, whether scribbled or zigzagged, dotted or smudged, create the character (texture, weight, depth) of what you see, and allow the edges to be indistinct.

Seeing It All

So far, the Etudes have asked you to perceive your surroundings—and to draw them as a way to help you see—from a fairly predictable position: facing your subjects and depicting their contours and surfaces from that single perspective.

But now that's not enough. Now, we're going to consider what's going on all around and, perhaps, what emanates from within.

As noted in Chapter Two, our efforts to document the 3-D world using a 2-D visual code is imperfect, whether we are using photography or drawing as our method. In drawing, we can attempt to suggest three dimensions by using the varied surface marks discussed above, but we are still limited in our representations by the need to identify edges. Whatever is beyond the slope or curve, or whatever is on the other side of the limiting boundary, cannot be seen by us from our single position and so we cannot render it. But what if we were to leave behind, for the moment, the dominant paradigm that tends to control our notions of what an "accurate" picture looks like? What if we were able to free ourselves for a moment or two and convince ourselves that we can see, and render in drawing, more than one plane at a time?

We won't be the first to experiment with such seeing. As John Willats explains it, the most typical post-Renaissance painting or drawing in the West is done in a system called perspective (where lines of sight converge—which means objects in the distance are depicted as being smaller and smaller—toward a vanishing point), and we believe that it best replicates what we see in the world around us. But there are other systems of denoting the world. In oblique projection, characteristic of some traditional Chinese and Japanese art, distance is shown as tipping back and away from the foreground, but all things are the same size, whether in the background or close up (Willats 1997, 4–15).

In addition to these drawing systems, there are depiction systems from other cultural traditions whose ways of seeing the world might assist us. One fits under the category of "inverted perspective," where lines of sight do not converge, but rather *diverge*. It's as if the world around you could be understood as having a malleability such that on looking from an angle down, the back corners of a table would be the same distance or further apart than the front corners, or where people, animals, objects, and natural features can be spread across the drawing paper in all directions, like the picture of a caribou hunt drawn by Nunamiut Eskimo Simon Paneak (Figure 5.12). (It's what the Cubists were playing with back in the early 20th century, so an investigation into the art of Picasso, Braque, and Leger, as well as artists such as Diego Rivera and Frida Kahlo, will open your eyes to ideas on how to proceed.)

Among the various groups of the Pacific Northwest Coast, it is not uncommon to see animals portrayed in "split representation," where the head of the creature is seen face-on, and each side of its body is portrayed on either side of the head. In addition, interior details of animals, such as their bones and joints, are also pictured in stylized form. These split-open animals are found on flat wooden house panels and also wrapping around

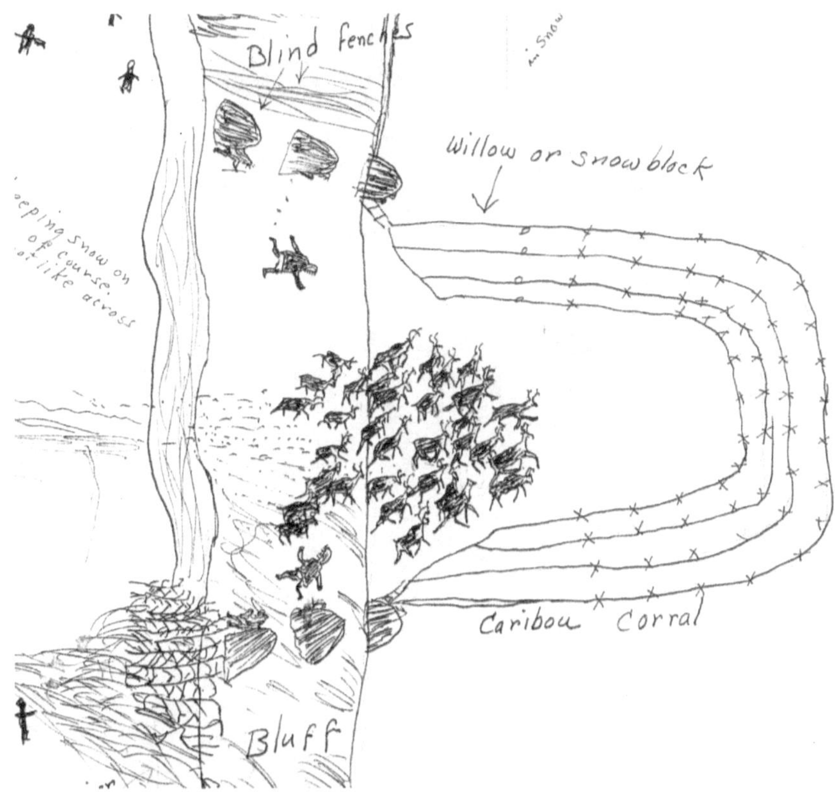

FIGURE 5.12: Simon Paneak's drawing of a caribou hunt showing a kind of "inverted perspective" (Drawing by Simon Paneak, Plate 35 from *North Alaska Chronicle: Notes from the End of Time* by John Martin Campbell. Used with permission of Museum of New Mexico Press, Santa Fe, 1998).

the sides of storage boxes (Malin 1999, 118) (Figure 5.13). Claude Levi-Strauss suggested that this form of portrayal was often done to render the entire animal at one time on a flat surface, saying, "the chests of Northwest Coast art are not merely containers embellished with a painted or carved animal. They are the animal itself, keeping an active watch over the ceremonial ornaments which have been entrusted to its care" (2006, 67). In fact, however, it is not just about the energy of the animal being represented and respect to its form, but it is also about an aesthetic sense of design. Bill Holm has noted that Northwest Coast art traditions often consider content to be equally balanced to form, where elements are added to a figure to give a proper distribution of visual weight to the composition, allowing the design to "move" (1965, 72–83).

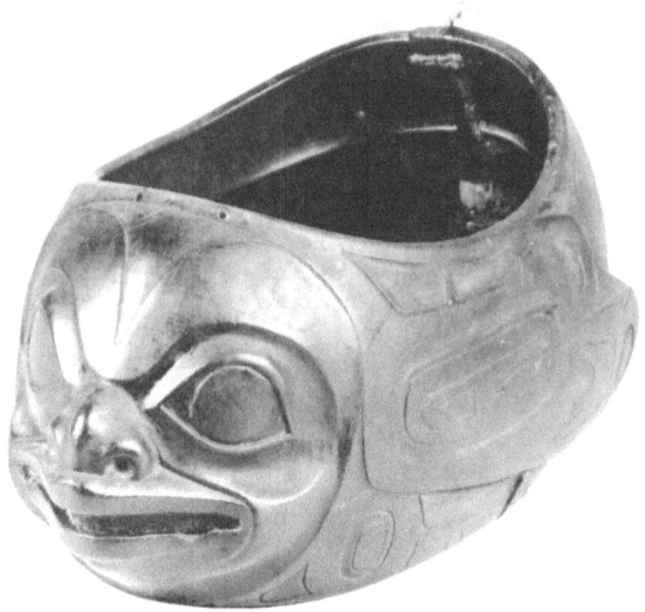

FIGURE 5.13: Illustration of a Haida (Masset, British Columbia) carved bowl decorated with an animal depicted in "split representation" form (from W. Sturtevant, *Boxes and Bowls*, 1974, Smithsonian Institution Press).

ETUDE TWENTY-SEVEN, Seeing in the Round (10–12 minutes): Why always draw on a flat surface? Thinking about what you've read about the Northwest Pacific Coast art traditions, find something unusual to draw on (using either a pencil or a pen) and try to depict on it an object, an animal, a person, or a scene in the round. Try to see the *whole* of your subject, moving around it to see all sides. For a scene, you might use a disposable coffee cup, using the entire surface, inside and out. For an animal or object, look for a chalky rounded rock that has a general resemblance to your subject, and render its totality, using split representation if you need to. (Other possible drawing surfaces: a paint stirring paddle, the shell of a hard-boiled egg or a cardboard egg carton, a ping-pong ball, a pear, or . . . a butternut squash! Be inventive.)

The Curious Surface

Several social theorists have suggested that life in the current era (sometimes referred to as the "postmodern condition") is characterized by a general contentedness with the mere surfaces of our surroundings: we lack much interest in the underlying essences there—the content, the gist, the pith, the substance, the kernel . . . however you want to put it (Sturken and Cartwright 2003, 254–59; Dorst 1989, 104–7). It's as if the surface glimmers and the exterior glosses are enough for us: we are content to read about celebrity antics without a care about their inner lives; we accept brilliant veneers without worrying much about the structure beneath; we choose technology that is fast, new, and cheap without bothering much about the built-in demographic data collection software whose amalgamation of individual characteristics into consumer types subsidizes the affordable prices. We all seem content with surfaces. Me too, apparently, because here I am in this chapter telling you to focus on surfaces, not on the vigorous content below the rough sheaths and shimmering skins.

Is it good enough to look at surfaces, or must we simultaneously see what supports them? The question is: how can you, as an ethnographer interested in seeing an accurate version of what surrounds you (via the act of drawing), do so without succumbing to the postmodern acceptance of simple surfaces? Is there any way to depict the surface but also represent the vibrant entity that pulses beneath? How can you concentrate on, and perceive, both a surface *and* an inner potency . . . and then record that complex totality that you see? In short, how can we be curious about the surfaces of the world we perceive while also seeing, then drawing, a much deeper, energized interpretation?

I don't really have an answer, and I can actually guide you only so far. I can tell you that it is often easier to sense the vigor or radiance of your environment when it takes the form of living things because we are raised to believe that they are "animate." While it may be difficult to actually perceive the animating spirit of something like a tree or a field of grain, at least we *believe* it's there. If we believe these examples are animate and concentrate on seeing-drawing them, perhaps some aspect of our empathy will be reflected onto the marked page.

It is much more difficult, of course, to feel the energy or vibrancy of our world if we believe it to be composed of "inanimate" objects and "natural" features. How can we render what we see with vigorous lines if we believe there is, in fact, no life there? Perhaps it's as easy as adjusting our thinking. What if, as an ethnographer, you accepted as possible the perspective that there is no certain division between the animate and the inanimate, or that the inanimate can be energized and enlivened?[5]

There are examples from all over the world for us to consider (if we are willing to open our minds a little), which provide evidence for our curiosity about this topic. Consider the following few cases: the Maori of New Zealand believe that a pregnant woman weaving a grass and feather cape for her infant imbues it with her own generative energy, and that a greenstone ax owned by a powerful chief likewise absorbs power through his use of it (Weiner 1992, 44–65); in the Japanese Shinto religion, *kami* (sacred spirits) are believed to inhabit a variety of natural places and entities, and the creation of art must be a faithful representation of them in these forms if the kami are to be pleased, thus enhancing human existence (Anderson 2004, 208–12); among many Toba Bataks it is still believed that the enormous lake that is contiguous with their traditional homeland is alive and can directly affect the lives of those who interact with it (Causey 2003, 43–44). Ordinarily, many people would not freely state that spiritual essences can inhabit or animate what are defined as nonliving entities, but when you dig a little deeper during your ethnographic work, you might find that what that person says and what she or he believes are often different. Ask such a person why they refuse to wear an intimate article of clothing from a second-hand store—even when it has been washed in hot water and bleached—and if you can probe deeply enough you may soon discover a firm belief in "spiritual essences"!

So let's assume for the moment that there might be a possibility that objects in our surroundings have agency (the ability to act) and that you can sense that agency through seeing deeply. How might you render that character in your line work? My apologies, but I have very little in the way of help to offer you, for it is something that each of us must discover in our own seeing-drawing explorations during ethnographic work. Nevertheless, I can share two hints from very different depiction traditions that might inspire you.

The Yolngu Aboriginal people of Australia create bark paintings that represent ancestral designs containing spiritual power, some of which that can be seen publicly and others that are hidden from view (Morphy 1994, 186). In creating the work, the artist aims for three goals: "to produce a correct design, to produce an ancestrally powerful design, and to produce a painting which enhances or beautifies the object it is painted on" (188). To create

5 Readers interested in reading more about the possibilities of a world composed of so-called inanimate objects that might possess agency should investigate works that treat affective interactions, such as Robert Plant Armstrong's *The Affecting Presence* (1971) and Timothy Morton's *Realist Magic: Objects, Ontology, Causality* (2013).

the second effect, the artist uses a series of crosshatched lines that are said to give it *bir'yun* (i.e., brilliance), which is likened to such things as glistening or shimmering water and which evokes generally positive responses such as joyfulness or happiness (194). Bir'yun is said to stimulate in the viewer a sense of the original brightness of the ancestral world beings, perhaps evoking the vibrancy of that creative time. The bir'yun lines seem to "enliven" an otherwise "dull" painting.

In an entirely different way, and for an entirely different reason, cartoons also uses lines to communicate the brightness of enlivened beings. Manga drawings, for example, depict cartoon figures in highly energetic poses, which communicate, to viewers who know how to "read" the imagery, that these characters are very much alive and moving. But when the artist wants to show a close-up of one of the figures, depicting only a portion of the face, it is hard to denote the same kind of aliveness while lacking pose or other signs of action. In these cases, the cartoonist will insert over the eyes' irises and corneas a variety of white shapes (ovoids or rectangles) that are intended to mimic the reflection of light on a moist eye. The absence of such marks of "brightness" are, in fact, how death or demonic possession are indicated to readers.

Perhaps thinking about these ways to communicate aspects of the character that vibrates below the surface will give you instructive stimulation to develop and practice your own attempts to show that your observational curiosity is more than skin deep.

Using the "Other" Hand

Another way to explore how you might depict the inner energy below a surface is to use your "other" hand. For a long time now, people have toyed with the notion that we have "right" brains that control our empathetic and artist sides, and "left" brains that control our logical and reasoning aspects. While there may be no definitive results from the research done in this area, there is certainly circumstantial evidence to prod us to seriously consider it (e.g., Edwards 1979). If it's true that our brain lobes differ in their ability to control the character of our actions, whether or not it is a difference between artistic and logical thinking, it is worth considering if the use of the nondominant hand can help us produce line-work that will render a different kind of seeing-drawing. While we would still be using both eyes stereoscopically as we always do, funneling that seeing through the non-normal writing hand might potentially give us access to a different way of depicting what we perceive, perhaps giving us access to that depth, below the surface, that we are seeking.

ETUDE TWENTY-EIGHT, Your Other Hand (10–15 minutes): This can be a very revealing and satisfying drawing to make: put your pencil in your "other" (nondominant) hand, and hold the paper with your ordinary writing hand. Now draw the holding hand. Look very closely, deeply seeing all the hairs, veins, lines, warts, moles, spots, and fingernail oddities. Draw your hand in loving detail, and really SEE what your taken-for-granted hand actually looks like. Please see Figure 5.14.

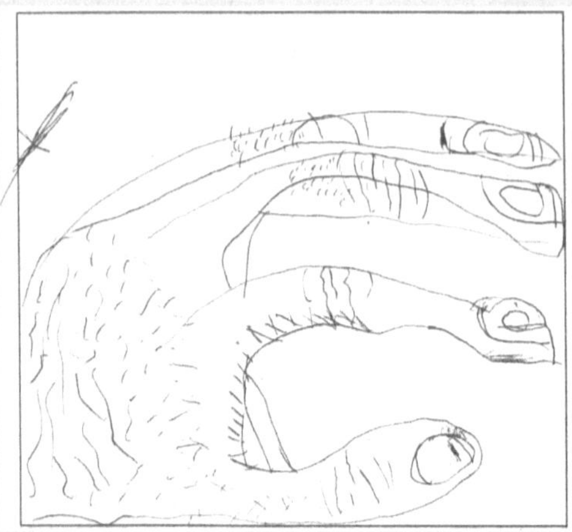

FIGURE 5.14: Student drawing of "The Other Hand" (by Kevin Vekony, used with permission).

Last Words

When we perceive the world around us, whether it is our familiar surroundings or the ethnographic contexts we find ourselves studying, we may accept surface manifestations as being representative of the real. And, in fact, that may be all we *can* see, lacking any other way to dive below and see structures, foundations, inner workings, or motivations. What I have tried to suggest here is that sometimes we can give ourselves the chance to infer what's below if we examine surfaces with attention and curiosity.

Taking the time to see the character of surfaces—their textures and topographies, their designs or decorations—can't always provide us a lens through which to actually see the depth, but it will stimulate our curiosity and let us begin to wonder what new questions we might ask in doing our ethnographic work. That attentive eye, working with the probing drawing hand, will give us the practice we need in seeing deeply, and will surely help us when it comes time to see something even more fleeting and evasive: Movement.

CHAPTER 6

SEEING MOVEMENT

From Static to Emergent

I've never been lithe or athletic, so it still seems strange that I would have agreed to take biweekly lessons in traditional ritual dance with a well-known teacher from Bali. I had gone to East Java to hone my rudimentary Indonesian language skills, not to explore dance, but my friend Chris could not get permission to study this extracurricular subject unless there were at least two people interested. So I agreed. I tried to explain upfront what a poor classmate I would be, so there would be no disappointments or frustrations when I inevitably held up the sessions with my lunging, wavering, and gasping. I entered the first class feeling pre-defeated, and thus was relaxed knowing that I had little to lose.

I was, in fact, terrible, even on the first day. If you can conjure the image of an aged raccoon wobbling upright to reach a table in order to feel around for unripe tomatoes in the dark, you would have a pretty accurate picture of me in a sarong contorting my arms and legs to the ancient poses of the Gabor dance. When I tried to do the energetic *malpal*, which required lifting up my heels to the opposite knee and then stepping forward, I would lose my balance, try to readjust my weight, then clomp my foot down like a drunk off a curb. Chris, on the other hand, was all elegance and suppleness, which was really fine because he took the teacher's attention away from me. Not only was he able to learn how to shift his bones and muscles to make the tensely oblique moves necessary, but he was also able to memorize all the steps. That's what frustrated me.

Traditional Balinese dance is transmitted from master to student strictly by imitation and hands-on positioning, not by explanations or references to books. I was unable to learn this way, and would forget a move as soon as I was taught it. The lessons were happening so fast I was unable to learn both the complex series of gestures and subtle manipulations of foot, knee, hand, and eye at the same time. I was learning what Chris called "body memory," a term I had never even heard uttered before that moment.

I was so terrible, in fact, that even though I had entered the course with no aspirations, I was embarrassing myself by forgetting the moves over and over. I began to preserve, in secret, what I could recall in a book of illustrations to assist these alien maneuvers. After class, I would try to draw the movements and positions, writing down their names phonetically, and taking note in words what was not clear in the drawings. Referring back to the notes in the quiet of my own room, I began to improve! Neither Chris nor the teacher had any idea that I was practicing from my drawn notes before class, and both seemed amazed at my sudden improvements.

By about the fourth week, I was pleased enough with myself that I decided to show them how I had begun to catch up: I triumphantly hauled out my book of drawings. Chris just laughed because the drawn figures were comical, but the teacher just seemed to go limp. He stood there flipping through the book saying things like "This is not how it's done," and "You simply don't understand Balinese dance . . . you must feel it." I tried to explain, but it was clear that I had disappointed him so fundamentally that he was speechless.

I kept on making the drawings after that and he let me continue the lessons, but he rarely pushed me to *feel* the pose, as he had before. When the lessons were finally finished, he wished me good luck, but tried once more to help me see his way, saying something like, "Remember, it's the whole dance, not parts added together . . . it's a single movement, not different words joined."

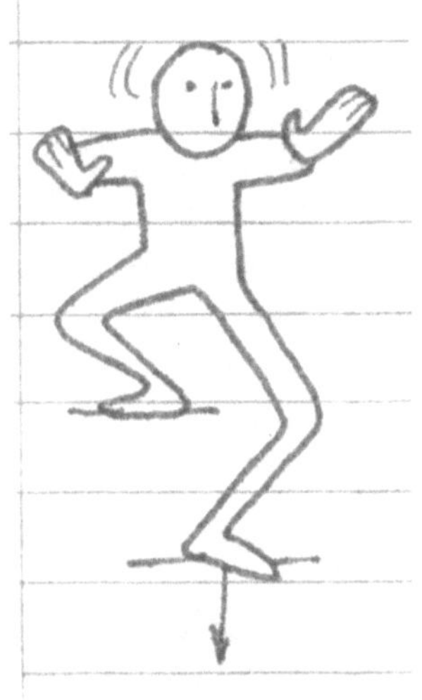

FIGURE 6.1: A Balinese dance drawing showing generalized movement.

When I found the book again recently, I had to laugh. The figures are pretty funny looking and, thinking back on my motivations, I see now that I was clearly desperate to succeed at dancing. Beyond that, however, when I look at the drawings now, I see how hard it is to make a drawing *move*: to create a sense of life and of unfolding gesture . . . to find the emergent action within the static line. In some cases, I used perhaps the most basic cartoon-inspired lines—for example, the ((and))—to show generalized movement, whether it is meant to communicate waving, shaking, shivering, or vibration (Figure 6.1); in others I used schematic lines to indicate direction (Figure 6.2).

Life is action, as you must know by now: all that is alive is perpetually shifting and becoming, and even those things we sense as being inanimate are nevertheless unavoidably part of the flow of time in space. Yet

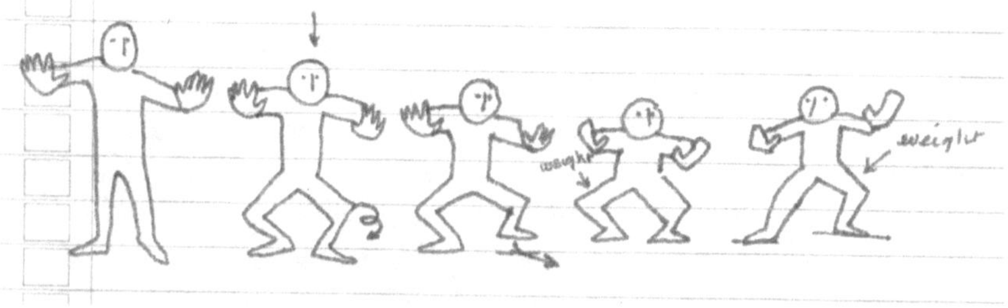

FIGURE 6.2: A Balinese dance drawing showing directional movement.

we are not simply bodies in motion. As Tim Ingold so evocatively puts it, "In life . . . there are no start points and end points. There are only horizons that vanish as you approach them, while further horizons loom ahead. As infants we come into the world moving, and continue on our way, now in pursuit, now in retreat, carried along and in turn carrying, approaching and leaving, or just going around, continually overtaking any destinations to which we might be drawn in the very course of reaching them" (2011, 13). Nothing is inert or unscathed, for we grow up or burst forth, become new, age, fall into entropic states, decay, die, then perhaps become again, still moving and changing. What we sense as static is probably just moving incredibly slowly.

Ethnography itself is perhaps an act of preserving discrete moments, trying to save some of the endlessly advancing behaviors—of which we perceive only a fraction—to say "this is how it is (was)." But, of course, as soon as they are recorded they are no longer representative of the real here-now, but rather are a memory of the "then-was." Nothing wrong with that, is there? The desire to preserve something about another person's present life is, after all, the same one that causes journalists and novelists to record what they experience and perceive in their times, and their works are later valued as "history" and cherished as "literature"! My point in bringing up this topic is not to confuse the purpose of ethnographic research, not to say it's worthless because it's always stale and dated, but rather to ask: Given that life reveals itself in a perpetual onslaught, how can we use line drawing to help document those momentary movements nestled within change and emergence? How can we energize our pencil lines as well as document the complexity of unfolding action? In this chapter, I will examine some of the issues related to recording movement, and will give some ways to help you practice bringing your pictures alive.

ETUDE TWENTY-NINE, Energized Line (2–4 minutes): I'll admit that this is a peculiar exercise, but ask you to give it a try without resisting too much to see what happens. Here I'm asking you to try making an "energized line," and the way you start is by creating the feeling of energy in your own drawing arm and hand. To do that I ask that you concentrate all your might into your arm and press down on your desk or table with just your fingers (like you are playing an intense piano chord with all five fingers). Press down as hard as you can from the shoulder and elbow with the rest of your body untense: feel the energy surging down to the surface and make your digits as hard and intense as you can for 30 seconds. Then stop. Feel the residual buzzing feeling in your hand, then quickly pick up your pencil and draw a very short but invigorated line slowly for about one inch (give yourself another 30 seconds for this), forcing all that same intensity into the pencil without pressing down too hard. The line should be energized, not tearing into the paper. You may want to try this two or three times.

ETUDE THIRTY, Fish Alive! (3–5 minutes): This one's easy. Just draw the image of a simple fish using the energized line. Now, practice making the fish "come alive" using the kinds of communicative lines described above, as shown in Figure 6.3.

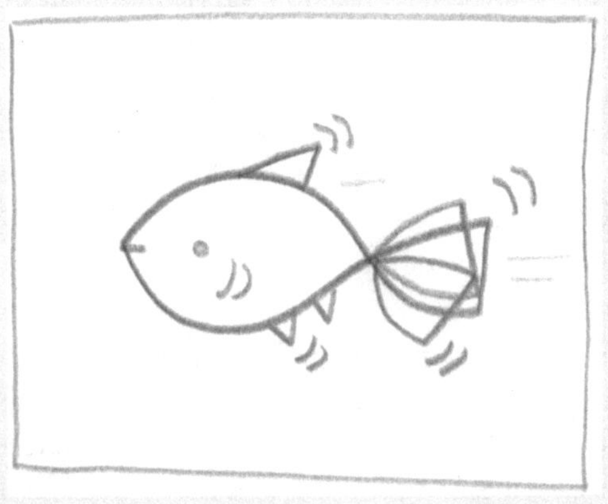

FIGURE 6.3: Drawing showing Fish Alive!

Invigorating Alive-ness

As noted earlier, part of the work of the ethnographer is to record the "data" observed (whether through writing or drawing) while still keeping the events feeling alive. It sounds easier than it is. When one is doing anthropological research, there are times when the easiest way to document experiences is through short, verb-less sentences, fragments of impressions, and disjointed words, phrases, or images, and that's because the action of life is unrelenting and there's little time to stop and compose complete sentences. One way to capture the energy of the vital flow through drawing, as discussed in the previous chapter, is to see and draw varieties of line textures and characters that evoke surfaces that are vibrant and vigorous.

Another way is to try capturing actual movement as it appears to you when you are *seeing* with focus and concentration. Expression of action in line drawing is one of the most difficult things to portray for *professional* artists to do, so of course it is going to be a real challenge for ethnographers still learning to see deeply via drawing. Still . . . we've got nothing to lose in trying, right?

The first step is actually *seeing* movement, and that does not just mean seeing things move. Usually, when we observe the world, we are aware of things moving because they have gone from *here* to *there*. But that does not mean that we've conceptually registered the tiny increments that caused their movement, just that we've noticed that the thing, animal, or human is not stationary. No, observing movement is different. That's when we are taking the time to see what creates the change: the small sequential actions that take place speedily, one after the other, generating the timely progression indicative of movement through space. We ignore this most of our lives, but in doing ethnographic research, where those tiny details are the very stuff of our interest, we should seriously attend to it. Of course it's difficult to observe, because you have to put yourself in a kind of "hyper-aware" state of mind. But once you've practiced it a few times, even though you may not be able to see the details of every action, you will be able to infer such movements, and may even be able to document them in line drawing.

Here are two drawings by artist-anthropologists who have tried to express movement; I offer them as models for your own drawing-seeing. In the first case (Figure 6.4), Carol Hendrickson uses very simple wavy and curving lines to indicate the movements of dancers in Havana, Cuba, and if you look carefully, you'll see that while some of the figures are drawn almost completely, others are only implied by a partial arm or torso. The whole drawing vibrates with energy. The next example (Figure 6.5), by Manuel Joao Ramos, shows a packet of smuggled goods zipping down a rope. Notice how the angle of the pendant rope (along with its slight curve above the knot) and the uncomplicated use of motion lines give the impression of swiftness and action!

Each person will find their own solutions to the problem of showing action, and with a little practice at seeing actual things move coupled with attentive examination of other people's drawings, your ethnographic line-work will begin to have vibrancy and energy.

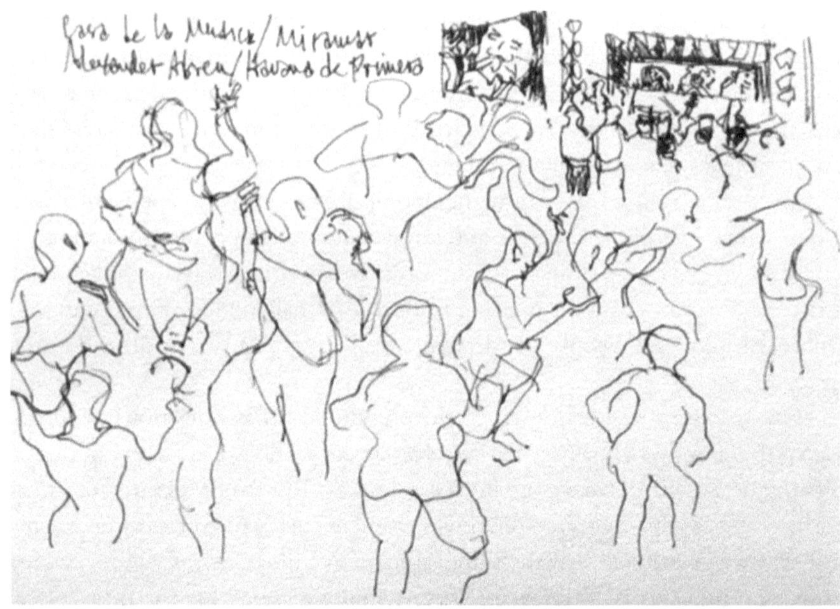

FIGURE 6.4: Carol Hendrickson's drawing of people dancing in Cuba (used with permission).

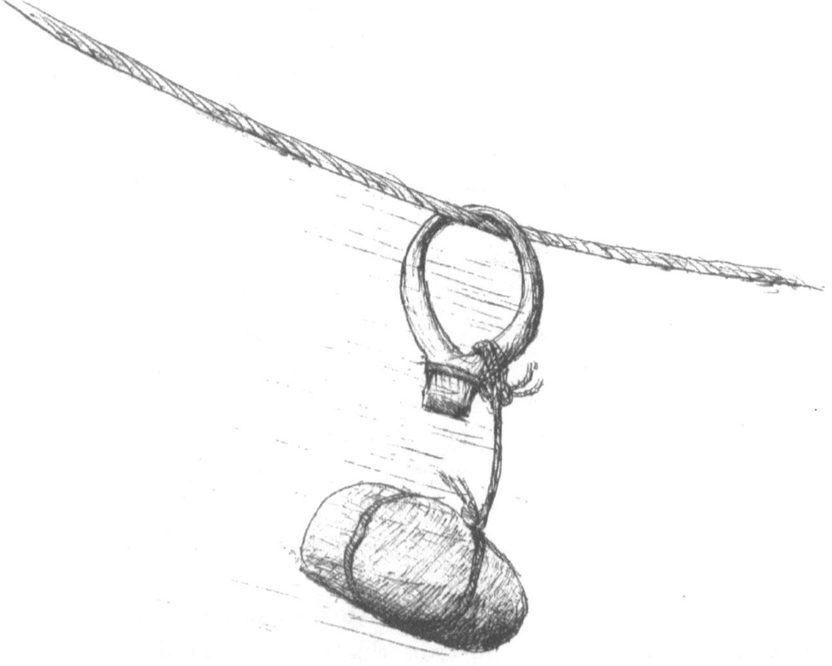

FIGURE 6.5: Manuel Joao Ramos's drawing of a package zipping down a line (from Afonso and Ramos 2004, 84; used with permission).

ETUDE THIRTY-ONE, Fish Alive! (redux) (3–5 minutes): Now that you've tried your own methods to make a drawing that evokes vitality, draw the fish again and refer to Figures 6.6 and 6.7 for ideas on how indicate movement, action, or vigor. The first figure, from

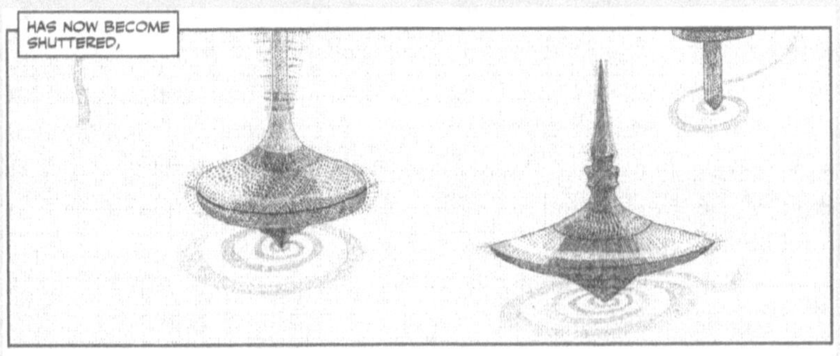

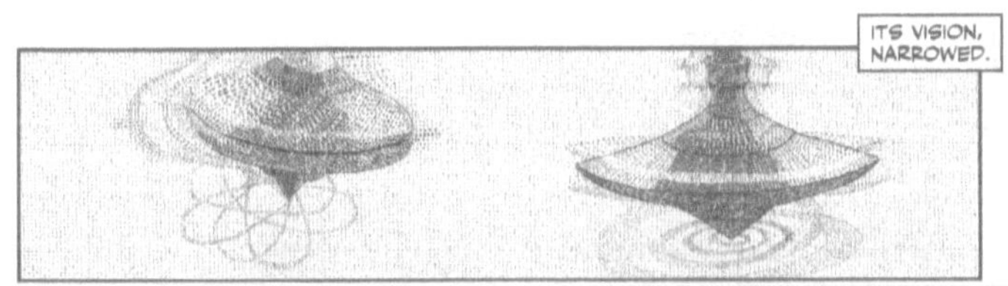

FIGURE 6.6: Nick Sousanis's drawing of spinning tops (from *Unflattening*, by Nick Sousanis, 2015, 16, reprinted with permission of Harvard University Press).

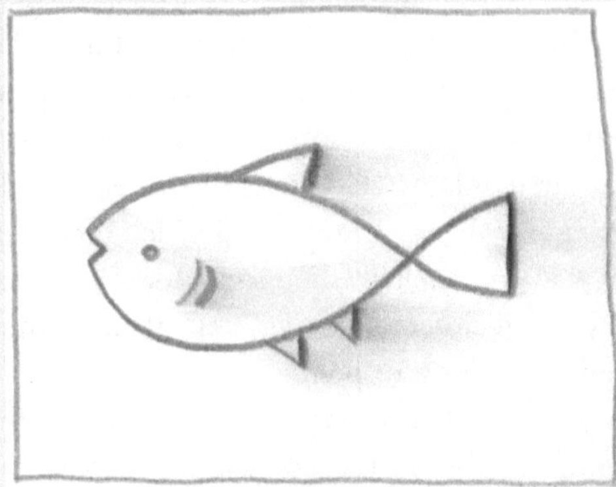

FIGURE 6.7: Example of drawing using smudged lines to show movement.

Nick Sousanis's book *Unflattening* (2015, 16), cleverly uses dots to communicate a top's spinning and shuddering. Try it! The next figure shows you a simple way to indicate something's transit from a static position by smudging the pencil line. Play around with each of them to make your fish *swim*.

Stopping to Make Time for a Telling Line

The funny thing about making such a concerted effort to see and then depict the action of other entities is that you must often sublimate your own action and aliveness to do so. As you may find in your research, your act of seeing-drawing may require you to sit quietly and contentedly, perhaps moving only your eyes (from action to paper and back) and your drawing hand and arm. It's almost as if you are paying for the chance to record the spirit and animation of what you perceive by reducing your own vigor, and that by stopping your attention to your own emergent life you are then able to channel it to the line. How difficult it is to take the time out of your lived life to record life as it is lived! This section is meant to help you ponder what you must leave behind to experience, and then capture, the essence of action and movement with the drawn line. How can this be done?

As I mentioned in Chapter One, there is a potential conflict for researchers when we are trying to both participate and observe the emergent world surrounding us, and this seemingly ironic situation has been a fundamental part of the ethnographic project since its very beginnings. How can one, after all, join in on the dynamism of life while also being in the state of reserve required of careful watching? It's as if one is asked to be engagingly active and intently passive at the same time.

For authors like Tim Ingold (2013), one of the ways to mend the supposed breach between them is twofold: first, accept that they are not, in fact, all that distinct from each other; and second, find a position that engages them both, through active integration with materials in the process of "making." Participating in the making of the world, rather than merely participating with it or simply observing it, allows a person to use all the senses joined, to explore the motivations and challenges of discovering how our surroundings are articulated, how they evolve, how they are shared, how and why they are valued, and how they are used and eventually decay. In short, the making process gives us an opportunity to practice sensually experiencing the world in specific cultural contexts at the same time we are discovering the unfolding characteristics that explain the necessity of its particular formulation. Drawing, as it turns out, is a kind of making.

In trying to understand how pictures can "tell" their story, Ingold suggests that the act of drawing is probably much closer to making music than anything else, proposing that the implement (the pencil or pen) is like a musical instrument in that it creates the line that "tells." He is saying that drawing is in effect "performative," and that we should attend to its process as much as to its final product. He says, "Thus, the drawing is not a visible shadow of a mental event; *it is a process of thinking, not the projection of a thought*" (2013, 128; italics in original).

So, to address the subheading of this section, how can we stop and find time to make the lines that we hope will "tell"? I think it is as simple as *using* our time differently, not really stealing it from our already over-scheduled lives. If drawing is a process of thinking, and if it is a kind of making that can tell a story, then perhaps all we have to do is readjust our notions about what it means to "sit and think." Maybe our acts of thinking could be done with a pencil in hand and with our eyes focused. That way, we could concentrate and ponder while also giving ourselves a tool—the drawing—with which to review how and what we've been thinking. By recognizing our own aliveness in these thinking acts, by feeling it from within, we may be able to successfully merge the "participation" with the "observation" as well as better understand the vitality of those things around us; in this way, we will be better positioned to transmit some of that vigor into our performative line making.

Drawing and Body Memory

Let's move back to the idea of trying to see and draw our surroundings in ways that convey a sense of liveliness. Part of the effort, as mentioned above, is to simply find the time to concentrate and practice this behavior, but another aspect of learning how to render vigorous movement and energy depends on developing a renewed access to the sensual body. Most of us have become so familiar with the way we move through time and space that we scarcely notice our own physicality: how we reckon our balance, how we judge our positions in reference to other bodies, how we calculate weight or distance, how we remain aware of our self's boundaries. Perhaps you have a different sensation of your body simply by reading the previous sentence's list; it's often just a matter of reviving a conscious recognition of your body as you.

I won't delve too deep into specialized studies related to the analysis of the phenomenology of human movement (although ethnographers interested in doing research on martial arts, dance, kinesthetics, trance, or any other performance-based topic will want to dive deep into that), but I will tell you that, for me, to write about movement I must be able to act it. My experience in learning Balinese dance taught me that if I am to know how to *depict* the moves, I must *enact* them, and likewise, if I am to know how to *make* the moves, I must *draw* them. Here, the seeing part of seeing-drawing is perceived from the inside . . . through the sensual body.

Ethnographers interested in how bodies move sometimes refer to our overt perceptions and practices of action as "postural awareness" (Sheets-Johnstone 2011, 116), as the "neuroanthoropology of expertise in movement" (Downey 2011, 77), or as "sophisticated whole-body intelligence" (Farnell and Wood 2011, 97), each term of which might mean something slightly different. But for our purposes here, we can use the more encompassing term "body memory," as mentioned in the opening story. When we talk about body memory, we are referring to the fact that humans across the globe learn to move in certain culturally sanctioned ways and that those learned movements become memorized, embedded in the muscles and sinews, in the active practice of daily life. You might want to think of it this way: each of us learns how to be a member of our culture partly through our persistent experiments of moving in ways that fit our particular social identity as it exists in the social environment. As ethnographers we settle ourselves into a new culture by carefully perceiving those around us, trying to pick up, and copy (when we can), how those people enact their everyday bodily performances as a way to fit in.[1]

Similarly, when we learn new activities, such as playing a musical instrument, practicing a sports move, or performing any other such routine action, we use whichever of our senses will help us generate awareness of how to repeat what we are being taught, whether we are drawing notes (as I did with the Balinese dances), directly mimicking what we see, feeling how someone presses our body parts into correct positions, or self-testing our postures and gestures until we feel that we've "got it."

The conscious awareness of such behavior, the thinking back and "re-sensing" familiar moves not only helps us both reenact the gestures and postures and talk (and write) about movement, but it can also help us *draw* the movement. As Maxine Sheets-Johnstone describes it, because we self-perceive our body's actions as though they are moving in a line, "we draw imaginary lines with various parts of our bodies and our bodies as a whole . . . (thus) imaginatively temporalize a spatial dimension of movement, namely, its direction

ETUDE THIRTY-TWO, Body Memory Drawing (3–5 minutes): Try it! Be intensely conscious as you move your arms as if you are paddling in water. You will notice that you actually see your arms creating certain action patterns in the air, but you'll also feel yourself gesturing and can imagine what another person might see. Now try to translate those sight and body memory impressions into actual lines on paper: simply try to draw the character of lines your arms made (wavy, curving, zigzagging, whatever) and that you saw and felt by using the energized line you practiced in Etude Thirty-One. You may notice that your marks have a dynamic quality that is affective, that is, they have a vital quality that will communicate energy to viewers.

1 Sally Ness (1992) evocatively describes this process in detail as it pertains to doing ethnography of choreography and dance in Cebu City, Philippines.

and changes in direction" (2011, 116–17).[2] Following this line of investigation, we can now think about drawing movement as a sensing ("seeing") of our bodies from within (by imagining what the movement must look like if perceived by another).

Learning to See Emergent Action

One of the hardest things to capture when making drawings during my research in Sumatra was action. From my position sitting at the dinner table inside my fieldwork house, I could often watch one of my neighbors digging up the soil in her dry-land field, which was very hard work. I was particularly intrigued with her because she liked to don a *kebaya* (a lacy, long-sleeved, thigh-length jacket usually worn to parties or church) to do her digging. Somehow, she managed to break up the compacted dirt into enormous clods without ever catching or soiling her fancy jacket, and when she was done for the day, she would stand up straight, fasten the front buttons, and walk back home with a very dignified gait, her hoe on her shoulder. Her movements were at once elegant and brutal, and I wanted to preserve some visual aspects of her actions in a way that was factually documentary and at the same time alive with her great vigor.

I decided to draw her one day, using a technique I had learned in a beginning figure drawing class many years before. Called "gesture drawing," the point of the effort is to capture raw energy in fast and swirling lines that try to imagine action as if it were an electric current coursing throughout the body, swiftly racing from the coiled, compact torso to the arms, flying to the steadying legs and back to the torso, around and around, swerving to every joint and limb that is experiencing action (Figure 6.8).

Kimon Nicolaides describes it like this: "As the people you watch move, you are to draw, letting your pencil swing around the paper almost at will, being impelled by the sense of the action you feel. Draw rapidly and continuously in a ceaseless line . . . *without taking your pencil off the paper.* Let the pencil roam, reporting the gesture" (1969, 14; italics in original). Nicolaides later notes that, "What the eye sees—that is, the various parts of the body in various actions and directions—is but the result of (the model's) inner impulse, and to understand one must use something more than the eyes. *It is necessary to participate in what the model is doing*, to identify yourself with it. Without a sympathetic emotional reaction in the artist there can be no real, no penetrating understanding" (24; italics in original).

2 See also Kantrowitz 2012b, who says in reference to gestures made while speaking that "hands sometimes know what words may not yet be able to articulate" (7).

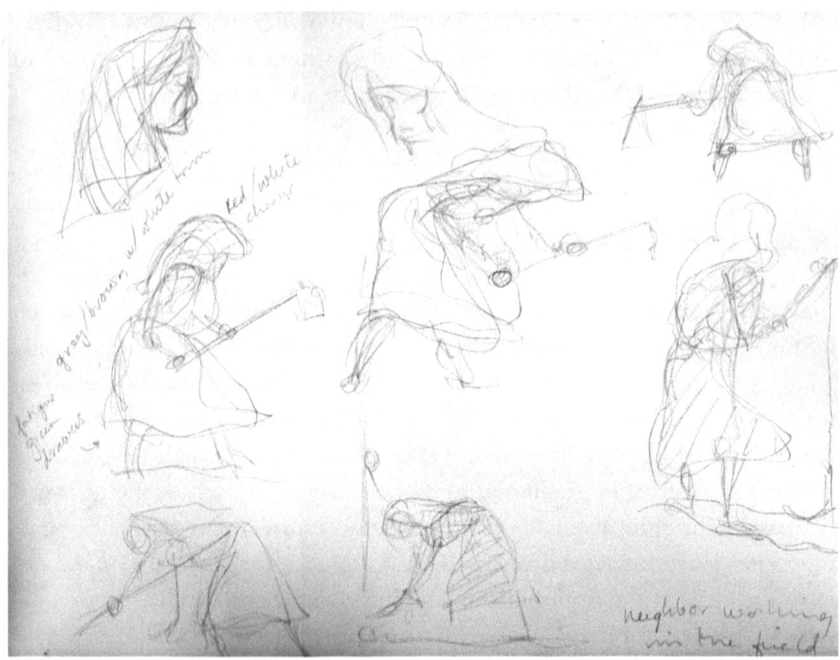

FIGURE 6.8: My gesture drawing of a Toba Batak neighbor working in the field.

Gesture drawings are abstractions of living forms and movements so, really, depicting the realness of the subject is not the point. As the art instructor Scott Foster puts it, when you do gesture drawing "(you) are forced to make quick decisions about abstracting the figure into its essence. Movement and weight distribution must be translated into line . . . details must be subordinated to the integrity of the whole" (2012–13, 7). Your aim, he says, is twofold: "1). To economically suggest the mass, volume, and surface of the body through the use of line . . . ; and 2). To emphasize motion, action, and/or weight through the use of abstraction, and, where appropriate, distortion" (2013, 5). When you relax enough to see the energy of a body, and let your pencil speedily find and depict that energy by trying to feel the whole all at once, you may discover that your picture is nothing but a tangle of scribbled coils. Perhaps that is exactly what the essence of the figure actually looks like.

Ethnographic Application: Gesture drawing in the ethnographic setting can help us capture the culturally specific movements of people at our field site in ways that words may not be able to convey. Translating the "movement-lines" directly into graphic lines using the technique of gesture drawing may be frustrating at first, but in my experience it is well worth the effort. Not only will you create potentially useful documents of action at your field site, but there is a good chance you'll learn something about yourself, too. That's because in the process of trying to make drawings of the series of actions or postures observed, you will develop a better understanding of how those other people move in, around, and through their particular surroundings. That knowledge, in turn, will help you experiment with your own bodily movements in those environments, which will help you better integrate yourself into the world you've chosen to investigate.

ETUDE THIRTY-THREE, Gesture Drawing (6 to 10 fast drawings, 3–5 minutes total): To practice gesture drawing, it is vital that you first free your own body: stand up and move away from your desk or table. Find a public place where people are in action, perhaps a café or a gym. Find a countertop or tall table at about elbow's height at which you can stand and freely move your arm, from shoulder to hand. Loosen tension in your body before drawing by moving around your torso and neck as well as your drawing arm: shoulder, wrist, and hand. Choose a subject who is moving and try to depict their energy as described above: in a fast, swirling, looping but continuous line. Create your drawing movements not from a tense hand but from an active shoulder and elbow; you are not drawing circles from your wrist, but rather gyrating your whole arm as if you are swimming. Give yourself only about 30 seconds to capture the vitality of your subject, then move on to the next drawing. Speed is the focus here, not lingering, thoughtful lines.[3]

Film as a Model for Seeing

Since it is difficult to see (much less draw) the ongoing movement of emergent action, it might help for us to look beyond line drawings and hand-produced pictures. In 1878, when Eadweard Muybridge developed his photographic system showing a horse galloping in separate pictures, he not only proved that a running horse does, in fact, lift all hooves from the ground in mid-stride, but he also provided his contemporaries with a new way of perceiving movement. Until

3 There is a reason for moving so quickly, for as Betty Edwards says, "As for gesture drawing, it does work in the sense that (I believe) it causes a shift to R-mode [that is, right-brain mode] because it is too fast for the left brain to keep up (L-mode is relatively slow, going one step at a time—now we draw the head, next we draw the neck, etc.), and students doing gesture drawing produce 'good' drawings, but they don't exactly know why or how they did it" (July 2015, personal communication). For more directions on how to do gesture drawings, please refer to Chapter 13 in Edwards's *Drawing on the Artist Within* (1986).

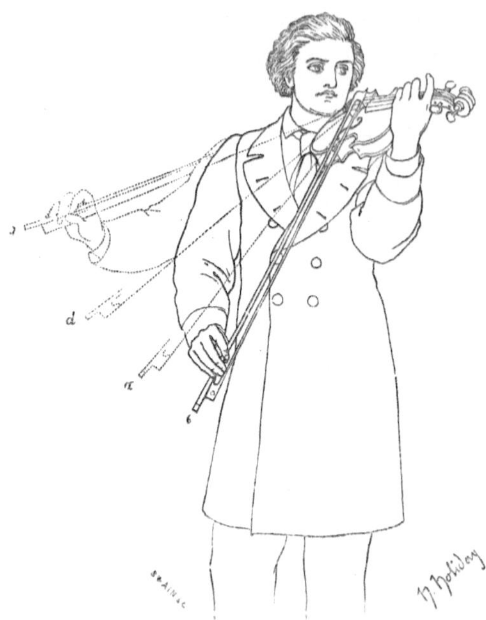

FIGURE 6.9: Drawing of a violinist bowing, showing episodic movement (from Holmes 1878, 176).

that time, most artists showed action as a frozen gesture (usually the peak moment) that tried to imply what had happened before and after. If you were to look at images of the death of the Biblical figure Holofernes, you will see that some artists depict Judith holding his severed head, while others show her as she seduces him; some show her in the very act of cutting his neck. Of course, none can show the whole scene in detail because painted pictures in the Western tradition only show a "snapshot" of action.

While the Zoetrope toy, which presented a series of drawings that appeared to be in movement, had been invented decades before, it is mostly after Muybridge's filmed experiments were popularized that drawn pictures begin to show novel renderings of movement seemingly influenced by aspects of his episodic-motion photographs. Rather than showing a series of pictures of figures with slight changes in their posture or position, however, these pictures show a single composite figure whose moving parts are drawn separately, as depicted in an illustration from *Spohr's Violin School*, edited by Henry Holmes (1878, 16) (Figure 6.9).[4]

ETUDE THIRTY-FOUR, Episodic Motion (3–5 minutes): Find a newspaper photograph of someone with at least one arm free and visible. Cut out the image and tape it down on a sheet of paper. Using Figure 6.9 as your model, imagine where the figure's arm *could go* if furthest extended up and down. Once you have imagined this full range of motion moving in both directions from where it is pictured, try to draw a series of arm positions directly onto the photograph to create the impression of movement.

4 This same idea was later used by cartoon animators to save time and energy: drawing the static part of one figure, they could then draw each of the variations of the moving body part on different cels to be superimposed on the static drawing.

Ethnographers can learn a great deal from this kind of depiction, for it shows us a way to document action with only a few extra lines. It will take practice to learn how to see deeply enough to recognize the character of changes occurring in what appears as a blur of action, but the process is actually straightforward. Follow the directions for Etude Thirty-Four carefully, then try to do the same thing when observing action in your fieldwork setting.

ETUDE THIRTY-FIVE, Stopped Motion (6–10 minutes): To start, it is easiest to observe someone or something making a repetitive movement, one that is expansive enough to see with clarity (you might find some such action on TV, or you might consider finding such action in your daily life, perhaps asking a friend to perform a single movement repeatedly). First, just watch the movement as a whole to get an idea of where the "start" and the "finish" are. Now, concentrate on what you consider to be the first move and try to memorize the figure's position and gesture. Draw that: use a simple, quick gesture drawing to capture the basic shape and energy. Once you have that base, concentrate on seeing what you consider to be the last move (before the repetition starts). Add to your gesture drawing; focus on depicting just that "finish" movement. Finally, concentrate on seeing the action somewhere in the middle, focusing on whatever changes in posture or gesture you see. Add that to your gesture drawing, again capturing the energy of the action. Your single figure will have the same moving part shown in three different stopped-motion aspects (similar to Figure 6.9).

Taking the Responsibility to Represent

I spoke a little about the ethics of drawing in fieldwork situations in Chapter Three. Now that you have tried a variety of different ways to draw what you see, I think it's time to talk a bit more about the responsibilities of representing cultural worlds, and particularly representing any other person. Artists and photographers might not have to worry about the issues of representation, but ethnographers, because we are claiming to document and depict others in accurate, honest, and sensitive ways (and in multiple media), well, we *must* consider what we are doing, carefully.

I learned this the hard way. I was once invited to a very formal party by my carving teacher's wife, Ito. It was the ceremony that celebrates the moment when an aged parent decides she or he can no longer take care of themselves, and so bequeath everything they own to one of their children (usually the youngest son) so that they will be cared for until death. The situation is charged but not somber: it is a party after all, so everyone is dressed up in their best clothes and are waiting for the time when they can visit with old friends and distant relatives. But because the parent is relinquishing autonomy, it is a time for serious reflection, and many of the guests are considering their own futures, wondering what will become of them.

I didn't account for the reflective nature of the party, and because everyone was shifting their positions so slowly as they attended to the Master of Ceremonies discussing the situation, I started to draw, focusing on depicting the energy of constrained movement. I was sitting far to the back of the main room, in the shadows really, and thought that I was essentially unseen. I'd finished a couple of gesture drawings, putting more careful detailing on top of the spinning and circling lines of energy. When the Master of Ceremonies had finished, there was a break in the proceedings, and two older women, beautifully coiffed and elegant in their fanciest kebayas, maneuvered over to me without actually standing up. They had seen me writing or drawing, and wanted to know what I was doing. They knew I was a friend of the parent's daughter, so I had some immunity, but they would not be put off by my shutting my sketchpad. "Show us! Let us look at your work! Is it writing?" they said. I told them I was drawing, but just quickly, to remember the day. "Show us!" they demanded, frowning. I turned to the page I had just finished, a lovely and dignified woman a little older than myself, and tried to shrug the whole thing off as a sort of "playing." (By the way, "shrugging something off" may be a distinctly Western behavior, not something that translates to other traditions, least of all, perhaps, the Bataks'). They took the little book in hand and looked over at the woman, who by now was looking back at us with a little bit of alarm. She also inched her way over, and grabbed the book from them. "This is supposed to be ME?! Well . . . *really*!"[5]

I was embarrassed, of course, because I thought I was just passing the time during a tedious ceremony in formal Toba Batak, which I understood imperfectly. No, they saw it as a strange portrait with many drifting gesture lines beneath, some of which they read as contours and edges (Figure 6.10). I heard a litany of comments and criticisms, which only served to bring more women into the fray. "Her glasses are too big . . . She looks too old . . . Her head is too big . . . It looks like her hair is messy!"—these were the sorts of comments I heard. They insisted that I "fix" it immediately. They weren't

5 My translation does not suffice. What she said in Indonesian was, "Itu gambaran SAYA?! ADUHHHHH!" *Aduh!* is a kind of expletive that shows both frustration and surprise, with a hint of anger.

mad, just concerned that I produce an "honest" picture. I apologized as I tried to change the image, but frankly, I don't know how to make a proper portrait, as I've noted before; my drawings all tend to look like cartoons.

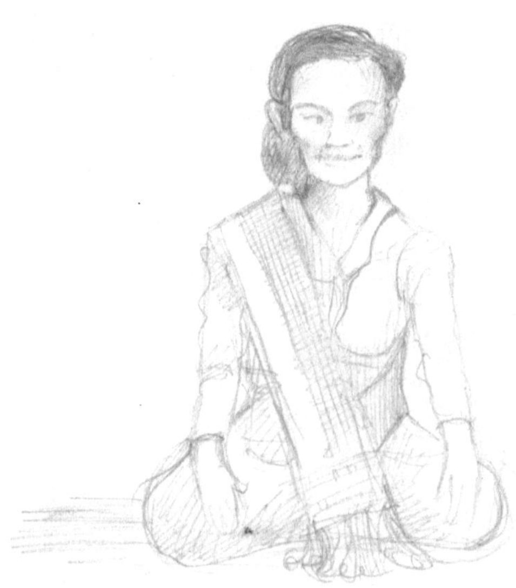

FIGURE 6.10: My drawing of a Toba Batak woman seated at a party.

In the end, they could see that I was nervous and was trying to make the drawing better (to no avail), so once I got to a certain point, they pronounced that the drawing was "good" and complete. Relieved, I closed my book and put it deep in my bag, leaving it there for the rest of the event.

What I hadn't considered until that time was that documenting the Batak world around me could have repercussions. My photographs were a permanent document, sometimes the *only* document, of everyday moments and serious traditional rituals that were seen by the local people as a record that might last forever. They knew my writing would produce a book, but that was much more distant and ephemeral. The photographs (which they rarely saw because I had to have them developed in the city), but even more the drawings (which they could see because they were immediately available), were things they could hold in their hands, comment on, critique, and chastise me about. I saw them as "research," but to the Toba Bataks I lived with, they were documents that verified things that had *happened*, movements that had *occurred*.

Sometimes, as ethnographers, we become so involved in gathering our own "data" that we forget that we are documenting others' real lives. We may see our work as essential to producing our papers, our theses, our dissertations, but the people of our field sites, the ones who are kind and generous enough to spend time with us, may see our actions as extractive: taking away all the small movements and passing moments and preserving them forever, defective and broken as they may be, in *our* files or archives. It is something for every ethnographer to consider seriously and empathetically: are you willing to take on all the responsibilities for representing the world of lives you experienced? Are you willing to take seriously what it means to permanently "represent" people, even in unguarded moments?

Most ethnographers decide the project is worth it in the end: the weight of all the obligations they take on when working with a group of people, publicly representing them in published form to people who will never meet or know them, preserving all these words and images as documents for some future generation. This is, however, an issue that each ethnographer must recognize and reflect on before continuing with the work, for it's not a light burden.

Last Words

I mentioned above the difficulty of depicting motion in ethnographic seeing-drawing, and now that you've tried some of the exercises you may understand what I mean. The task of preserving action and movement in the drawn line while also keeping it vital and alive takes sharp eyes, serious practice, perseverance, and I think, most of all, courage. It takes courage because you are attempting to do a kind of representation that challenges famous artists. That should not deter you from trying. Your project is not the artists' project, for you are simply trying to improve your perception using line drawings to document the world you see around you. Perfect rendering is not your goal, *seeing* is, and that should relieve some of the pressure of thinking that there is something to do "properly" here.

Your job is impossible and simple: you are to condense the emergent unfolding-ness of a changing world that exists in all directions in space and time, reducing all that to a few pencil strokes to conjure up the events and actions you perceive while also keeping your drawings alive and honest. When you allow yourself the chance to draw to see the world ethnographically, you are recognizing that your task is totally unreasonable and insurmountable! And that is what frees you. There is no proper or correct or perfect way to make a picture based on seeing live and unpredictable movements, so anything you produce from your attentive gaze will be a "note,"[6] a small mark to remind you of your experiences ... where you were, how you felt, and what you saw.

6 In some ways, drawings of what we see and interpret are probably much more like musical notes than Theodor Adorno suspected, for the lines are truly "non-intentional" and end up signifying the ideal of the view, not its meaning (cf. Adorno 2006, 4).

CHAPTER 7

SEEING ABSENCE

Memory Eyes

"The picture," says art philosopher Suzanne Langer, ". . . is an apparition. It is there for our eyes but not for our hands, nor does its visible space, however great, have any normal acoustical properties for our ears. The apparent solid volumes in it do not meet our common-sense criteria for the existence of objects; they exist for vision alone. The whole picture is a piece of purely visual space. It is nothing but a vision" (1957, 28). A picture is, of course, more than that, as Langer goes on to explain. She notes that pictures abstract the ordinary and normal world to emphasize what she notes art critic Clive Bell called "significant forms" as a way to "uncouple them from nature" so that we may see their realness with new eyes. The creator of the picture uses illusion to communicate with viewers, but this is not the illusion of make-believe. It is, rather, illusion used to exemplify the real, as is necessary when reducing the three-dimensional world to two while also maintaining the "vital feeling" of the view (35).

I suppose what I've been explaining and showing you through the past chapters are ways to create that vital, real illusion in the name of documenting cultural worlds ethnographically. As I've noted, it's particularly difficult to accomplish this feat of seeing, then drawing, "real illusion" when you are actually observing the emergent, enacted, alive world around you, partly because it is unending in time and space, but also because it's very difficult to see all that is encapsulated in a moment of life (the contours, the surfaces, the details, the movements) and document it with mere lines on paper. In the first chapters, I urged you to concentrate on simplifying the world you see in order to draw it: to discover which of the many actions and objects carefully observed and interpreted are the ones you will record accurately and honestly. What that has meant, so far, is that you must consciously decide—*while observing*—which things must be visually marginalized and which will be engaged with.

In this chapter, I want to continue talking about seeing and drawing the real world, but now focusing on the visual world that is absent, whether that means it's only dimly present, whether it's no longer present (as in a memory), or whether its physical manifestation is temporarily removed. Addressing absent things in the world requires a different kind of "seeing" (thus a different sort of drawing) than I've discussed before, but in some ways the seeing-drawing of things not there is easier because the simplification of the image is performed in the mind through acts of partial forgetting and visual consolidation. Maybe you've already guessed how remembering an event might entail the partial forgetting of a scene for, after all, we can't remember every detail of a complex event we see, even when just a few minutes have passed. Sure, we can recall the peak moment of an important event with clarity, and may even remember most of the people attending, but will we also be able to bring back details about the character of the light in the room, the placement of serving baskets and platters on the side tables, and the particular smell of perfumes or incense? Do you remember events or scenes that happen in dim light or in the shadows as well as you recall those things that happen in bright daylight? How well do you "see" and remember the lightless worlds you've only felt by touch as you grope around trying to make sense of where you are?

Most of us clearly remember aspects of our most happy experiences (and even those fade with the passage of time), but can we depend on our imperfect memories to preserve accurate details of everyday life, of twilight moments, of things lost? I think with practice that we can, and that what it takes is a little bit of training or instruction, some concentrated practice, and a lot of motivation. My own ethnographic experiences tell me that motivation to remember what you see is the most important of these because once you tell yourself that you *want* to recall the cultural worlds you experience—not necessarily because you have a professor or editor demanding it, but rather because you are curious to understand how people live and want to better learn how to interact with them—you will naturally focus and concentrate on the particularities that make up the unfolding day's action.

ETUDE THIRTY-SIX, Dark Peripheral Vision (2 minutes seeing, 2 minutes drawing): This Etude must be done outside during the darkest moments of dusk or dawn. Standing safely on a sidewalk of a mostly dark neighborhood, stare intently straight ahead. Try to see as far into the distance as you can, as if you are looking for the horizon, but don't move your eyes to scan what's before you. Just focus on some far-off light or glimmer. Concentrate on what you see in the distance, in the middle ground, then in the foreground (using peripheral vision). Because it is so dark, you'll only see basic shapes and lights. Once you've memorized what you've seen, try to draw it with your eyes wide open, still standing in place in the dark.

ETUDE THIRTY-SEVEN, Seeing Through Touch (3-5 minutes each): Ask someone to put a small, common household object into a paper bag without telling you what it is (nothing sharp, nothing dangerous!). Seated at your desk or table, put your nondrawing hand into the bag and try to "see" the object through touch while simultaneously drawing what your fingers tell you. The point here is to try making a direct connection between your two hands, the one sensing the shape, density, weight, and texture of the object, the other one registering those sensations via line drawing. Now, do the same exercise but in near darkness so that the drawing you are making is nearly impossible to see. Focus, concentrate: make one hand draw what the other one "sees."

Ethnographic Application: Both of these exercises are trying to help you extend your ability to sense the world, and draw it, under conditions of limited visibility. Ethnographic work rarely happens in perfectly ideal conditions: a storm will knock out the electricity; you'll lose your glasses; something crucial will happen in the shadows; you'll be shown an object at night that cannot be shown under other circumstances. You still need to try observing whatever it is, even under the most difficult circumstances. By practicing now, you will give yourself the opportunity to capture some rendition of your experiences that you can use as a document, even if its purpose is only to prod your memory to conjure up the situation.

Mental "Snapshots"

When working with Toba Bataks, I learned very quickly that direct note taking was a distraction from the work I was trying to do. That's because the Bataks I knew tended to be a very literate and curious group of people, were fascinated by the act of writing (their own as well as mine), and were attentive to the truthful content of words put on paper. No sooner did I bring out one of my notebooks then one of them either slipped it out of my hands to inspect it page by page, or hovered over my shoulder either to help me with word spellings or to comment on the legibility of my handwriting or the quality of my pen. By the time we finished discussing these varied topics, inevitably they'd need to get to work, leaving me with fragmented ideas and fractured grammar rules. I soon learned that I must develop my short-term memory to mentally record events, actions, and details so I could write them once I got home. In fact, I got to the point that I could memorize a full day of events to be typed, specific and complete, into the computer during the evening hours, with drawings added, if necessary, once the sheets had been printed out.

It's not just that note taking can be a distraction. There are times when writing notes is inappropriate in certain ethnographic situations. I am reminded of the time I attended a Batak friend's baby-naming ritual, *Mampe Goar*, in the next village over. The event took place in a large rectangular room covered in decorative mats, and guests were ringed around the periphery of the room, crowded very close to each other. The focus was on the little baby sitting on his father's lap, very close to me, and all eyes were on him, including mine. Because everyone was looking my way, it was very difficult (and rude) for me to be looking anywhere but at the boy, and yet there were many things happening all around me. Two women to my right were bickering in a whisper, people were coming into the room late, and two old gentlemen began reciting the traditional couplet poems called *umpama* back and forth to each other. Because such rituals are fraught with religious and spiritual overtones, and because the naming of a baby is a formal introduction of the child to the community, it is an event of great seriousness. I was invited to participate with the understanding that I would remain silent, that I would take no photographs until the very end, and that I would not take notes while in attendance. The recitation of umpama seemed to go on forever and the room was unbearably hot, but when I heard the final shout of "*I-ma to to*!" I knew it was time for the food to be brought in; the ceremony was over.

The way I learned to capture events such as this was to make a series of mental "snapshots" of what I saw and heard (also called "after drawings" in Chapter Three).[1] By this I mean simply that at various times during the ceremony I concentrated on my surroundings with my most intensely aware sensate self, trying to take in the full character of the place (perceptive to sounds, visuals, smells, people, objects, juxtaposition, poses, lighting, temperature) for a brief moment, as if a camera's flash had gone off and everything was temporarily frozen and memorized. I never had the concentration to do it for more

1 Some anthropologists refer to making written notes of this character (that is, words written down after the fact from memory), sometimes calling them "headnotes" (Ottenberg 1990, 144; Sanjak 1990b, 93).

than a long second at a time, but that was often enough to provide me with the detailed information I could then record at home, in words and drawings. I would use my "memory eyes" to guide my other senses in the memorization, and by making a series of long-second mental snapshots would be able to preserve events and experiences that to this day remain fairly clear to me.

Had I not already registered the entire room based on my previous practice of making 360-degree drawings of my surroundings (Etude Nineteen), I would not have known where to cast my eyes when the ritual was over, and thus would not have better known who was whispering and who was reciting, how the guests were arrayed around the room, and what was served at the ritual's completion, details that I visually memorized and later recorded in the field notes.

ETUDE THIRTY-EIGHT, The Memorized Place (3 minutes Part A, 5–7 minutes Part B): This is a two-part Etude and can be practiced often. First, when you are in a public place, such as a café, memorize everything in the space: people, things, furniture, doorways, windows. Concentrate, and force yourself to remember as much as you can by thoughtfully examining such things as how many tables there are, how many people are seated at each, how close the trash receptacle is to the counter. Remember *anything* you can, and freeze it in your mind as a "snapshot"[2] that you can retrieve later. Second, when you return to your desk, draw a bird's-eye view map of what you saw (contours of edges of everything from above), doing your best to depict proportion and spatial relationships, and putting in as much detail as possible.

Ethnographic Application: This is, I think, one of the most useful exercises in the book, and will become less demanding once you have convinced yourself to be motivated to see and recall such detail and have practiced memorizing it. Coupled with Etude Nineteen, this exercise will help you take stock of your complex surroundings visually, so that when you are unable to take written or drawn field notes you will still be able to store in your short-term memory where you were and what you saw long enough to return home

2 Betty Edwards calls this a "mental photograph," and notes that "Degas, to train his students to recall an image, had the model pose in the basement where they could study the image, but their paints, easels, and canvases were on the sixth floor, where they were to reproduce their perceptions," which, she notes, is extremely difficult. Understanding the difficulty of this kind of exercise, she says, will make you "overwhelmingly grateful to have the image in front of you, but don't think you will remember things. You won't. Still, we can all be trained to take a mental photograph" (personal communication, June 2015).

and make a permanent record, whether it takes the form of written words or inscribed lines. Exercising your mind in this way now (and often) will help build the kind of perceptive mind you will need to depend on when doing your ethnographic fieldwork in the future. While they may not be as detailed as a photograph made at your fieldwork site, your mental snapshots will provide you with images of real-illusion mentioned above that have what Langer (1957) called the "vital feeling" of an experience. If you get good enough at capturing such images, you too will be able to access this visual information in your mind fairly accurately for years to come.

Seeing Loss Ethnographically

Sometimes in ethnographic work, absence takes other forms from that discussed above. Sometimes, it is not the ethnographer who is now absent from an unfolding action or ritual, at home trying to conjure up a recollection of mental snapshot images, but rather the person or object of interest that is gone. In the anthropological literature, loss is often situated in terms of cultural loss (of language, of traditions, of sacred sites) or the death of humans (whether in the form of genocide or of a loved one, a revered elder, or leader). There are also, of course, references to the loss of objects, including heirlooms taken for sale to outsiders (Forshee 2002; Causey 2003), and meaningful objects disbursed through donation and disposal (Miller and Parrott 2009), but these examples tend to address issues such as memory, tradition, and human relationships more than the individual's emotional attachment to the objects themselves, which is what I'd like to talk about here, as a basis for continuing to think about the use of line drawing as an ethnographic method, and as a doorway for thinking about loss.

I want to tell you an extended story to set the foundation for thinking about the parameters of drawing-seeing in terms of absence caused by loss, so please bear with me. My example is about losing *things*, but I think my thoughts and comments are comparable to the loss of people, too.

Presence and Absence

In 2012, I returned to my fieldwork site on Samosir Island, carrying varied papers, pencils, pens, watercolors, and brushes. During my short stay, I made numerous small drawings and paintings of what I saw. Not prolific, I completed about 10 documentary images reflecting my attention to the mundane ethnographic moment. On my return home, my suitcase was delayed, then "lost." When it was finally returned days later, I exuberantly opened it only to find strange flotsam in disarray: a broken brass stanchion, an iron pipe lid, a reeking t-shirt, and dozens of unread newspapers.

The rude shock of the sight dissolved into disbelief and I called the airline to complain, demanding they find my possessions. Weeks passed with no news. Sadly resigned, I realized that all my things, including my artwork, were gone. I spent a long while angrily thinking, and then talking—to whoever would listen—about the things lost, perhaps as a way to regain them, or retain them better in my memory, but the feeling of loss remained. It wasn't grief—that's too strong—but more like an annoyed, sad longing. Yet, while the ethnographic objects and clothes had simply vanished, two years later I decided I could try to reclaim the artwork because I was their creator. They would not be the same images, of course, but when I concentrated, I realized that I could still see many of the lost renditions I had drawn, clear in my mind. I discovered that these were mental snapshots . . . of mental snapshots! What amazed me was that when I focused, I could even "see" *other* potent images I had seen but not drawn.

I didn't know how to explain or seriously consider what I was experiencing, but maybe, in the realm of human relationships with objects, loss and discovery are not so different.

Ethnographic Losses

I'm not the first ethnographer to lose some of his notes, for many researchers have permanently misplaced written, photographic, or drawn documentation at some time or another. In 1942, Sir Edmund Leach lost all his photos, notes, and the draft of his dissertation during World War II as the British moved out of Rangoon, Burma, to escape the invading Japanese army. Once he had walked to Kunming, China, he was airlifted to Calcutta where he began preparing a second draft, entirely from memory, which eventually became the classic monograph *Political Systems of Highland Burma* (Anderson 2007, 13–16). And in 1970, M. N. Srinivas's office at Stanford was torched: he lost all his processed notes for his book on the village of Rampura, Mysore. Although he was able, with the help of others, to recover from the ashes some slips of paper with written notes, and later had his original field notes microfilmed and sent to him, in truth he wrote his work, *The Remembered Village* (1976), from memory.[3]

In both cases, the authors were challenged by their circumstances, but both also grappled with their reconstructions confidently, assured that their memories were as clear as their notes. Srinivas went so far as to prefer his memory to the lost drafts, even acknowledging the arsonists' part in the creation of his book.

These two authors' responses to the disaster of loss have served as the model for my own experimental work with line drawing to recuperate accidental absences like these. Like Leach and Srinivas, I decided to try to recreate my research after it was taken from me.

3 For additional harrowing tales of the loss of ethnographic field notes, see Sanjak 1990a.

Disbelief of Loss

When I returned to Samosir Island in 2012, I had solid questions in mind about line drawing as an ethnographic method: Which visual observations are best suited to line drawing? What's the best drawing technique to capture an observation? What kinds of information can be encoded into a line drawing, and to what extent must the process remain objective? What do I expect the drawings to *do*?

In making the sketches and drawings, I was attentive to the fact that I was documenting but not preoccupied with making "factual" renditions of what I saw. I wanted to work at incorporating playfulness into the works, too. I made a couple of landscapes, two genre scenes, a still life, and a few images of whatever appeared before my eyes as I sat at tourist coffee shops. I saw these both as permanent documents for later reference and also the basis for telling a different kind of story.

As noted, I lost the precise content of my drawings, but I also lost actual objects. In Figure 7.1, you'll see that I had drawn a picture of a glossy beetle I had found and for which I had created a tiny box lined with cotton and tied with sewing thread. This recreation drawing includes more textual detail than

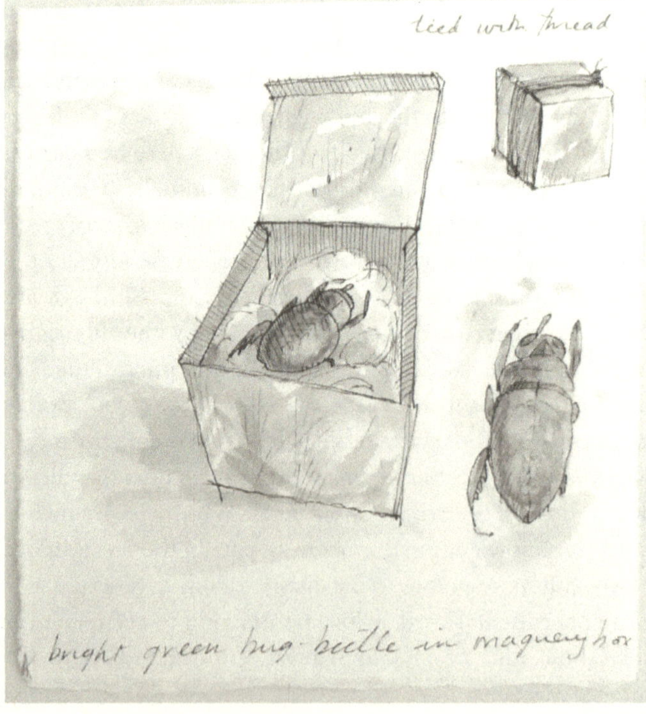

FIGURE 7.1: My drawing of the green beetle I lost.

the original drawing and speaks to the need to compensate for the lost material objects (the real bug and box) that might have been used for comparison and investigation.

In the reconstituted image seen in Figure 7.2—very close to what I remember drawing originally—I was trying to capture my sense of astonishment and disbelief that the ancient axis mundi tree[4] that stood in the center of Siallagan village for generations had fallen. All that was left of it was its huge, sad stump and enormous slices of wood, wheels of lumber stacked, leaned, discarded. What I recalled upon redrawing this image is that my standing there drew the attention of a young man (a boy, when I had done my fieldwork) who recognized me. I had written about this incident in my notes, but in the drawing, I was taken back to the moment: he told me his grandmother, one of the central characters in my book, was dying.

Drawing the tree again fired my memory, and I could see with utmost clarity the sequence of events leading to my meeting with a person of great importance

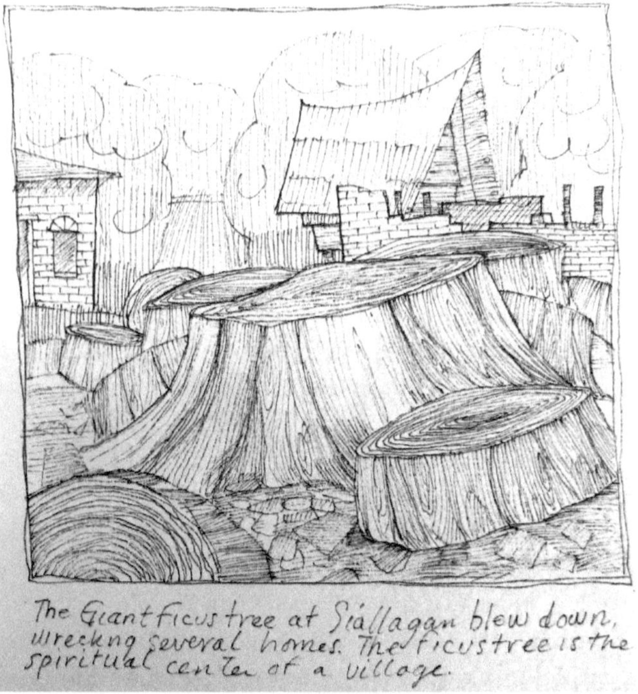

FIGURE 7.2: My drawing of the downed axis mundi tree at Siallagan.

4 Toba Bataks often plant a ficus tree in the center of their villages to represent the mythical "origin tree" that connects the lower, middle, and upper worlds.

to my original fieldwork, the old vendor I referred to as "Ibu Sirih"[5]: walking into her unkempt home, entering her and her husband's gloomy bedroom tinted in various shades of jaundice, greeting her again briefly before she collapsed in weariness, and lightly grasping the hand of her husband who lay near her, the two of them slowly expiring before me as I stood in shadows and golden afternoon light.

Redrawing the grand tree, already dead and dismantled, helped me try to recapture what I re-experienced in that moment, and I pushed the memory of the tree aside in a rush to draw what I now mentally saw. I raced to try capturing the newly remembered image of the old folks, trying again and again to correctly capture the mental snapshot I now "saw" in my mind. Some of the drawings didn't capture the sadness of the room, and others were inadequate at depicting the sapped energy of the old folks, or too cartoonish in their rendering. What I learned is that my mental-visual "snapshot" was fleeting, and that trying to depict it ended up—as Michael Taussig says—"pushing reality off the page" (2011, 16). No one of these images captured the moment for me, but together they did.

Resignation and Hyper-Awareness

As suggested, loss of a thing eventually results in a moment of clarity: it's gone.

Like many other incidents of facing truth, sad questioning soon shifts to calm resolve in a flicker. The sense of resignation to the condition of loss[6] might linger a little, but a sense of hyper-awareness about the character of the thing lost takes over very quickly. This happens, I think, because when we know loss is certain, we spend all of our psychic energy trying to remember what we can about the thing before it gets any further away from us. The clarity of that instant of awareness is experienced as a "flood" of memories, and in this state we often allow our minds to replay every encounter with the thing, every detail of its composition, letting our present bodily circumstances lapse and dissolve.

The point is this: the process of rendering in such circumstances is the focus of the drawing, and the product is only a mnemonic artifact of the process. In the case of redrawing an image, the original scene or object conflates with the original drawing: the redelineated image is an interpretation based on the real (the material) *and* the replica (the visual rendition, the drawing), where the memories of both are allowed to *arise* in the mind, rather than being rummaged for, an effort that may in fact drive them away.

One of the drawings I made in 2012 was of a field near two intersecting roads near my fieldwork site. I always enjoyed the view of low rolling hills foregrounding the looming mountains, so made a point of returning to the

5 The name I invented for her, for privacy's sake, translates to "Mrs. Betel-nut," a reference to the fact that she was always chewing betel, which makes a person's lips turn bright crimson.

6 Contra Susan Stewart (1993, 23) who, when discussing "longing," is talking about a nostalgia for something not there, rather than a sadness for actual loss.

spot to see it again to make a sketch of it. When I tried to redraw that lost picture from my mental snapshot, the composition didn't seem right. In truth, even though I had stood in that field near the road for several minutes making the sketch, now that I wanted to recreate the scene I realized I was drawing a romanticized version of what I *wanted* to see (Figure 7.3).

As soon as I saw my finished drawing, I recognized that it was not accurate or honest: it did not represent to me what I saw. The view was too tidy and perfect, so I started over. As I drew the mental image the second time, using a very different paper and a pen rather than a brush, I began putting far too many structures in the scene, thinking that if this were to be a romantic vision, then I should truly idealize it, including all the different types of tombs I could recall (Figure 7.4). Suddenly, the clarity of my situation standing there in 2012 returned to me, and I remembered that I'd had to cross a broken concrete ditch, passing over a deep gully of eroded clay and rocks. The structures in the first drawing are more honest, but the context of the tombs

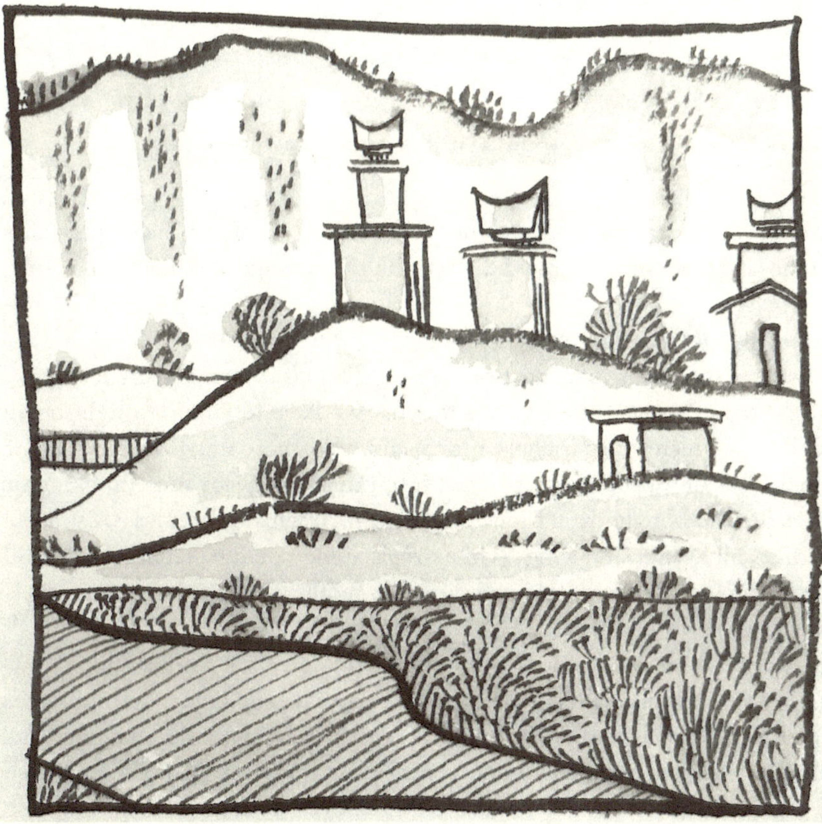

FIGURE 7.3: My first rendition of a remembered view.

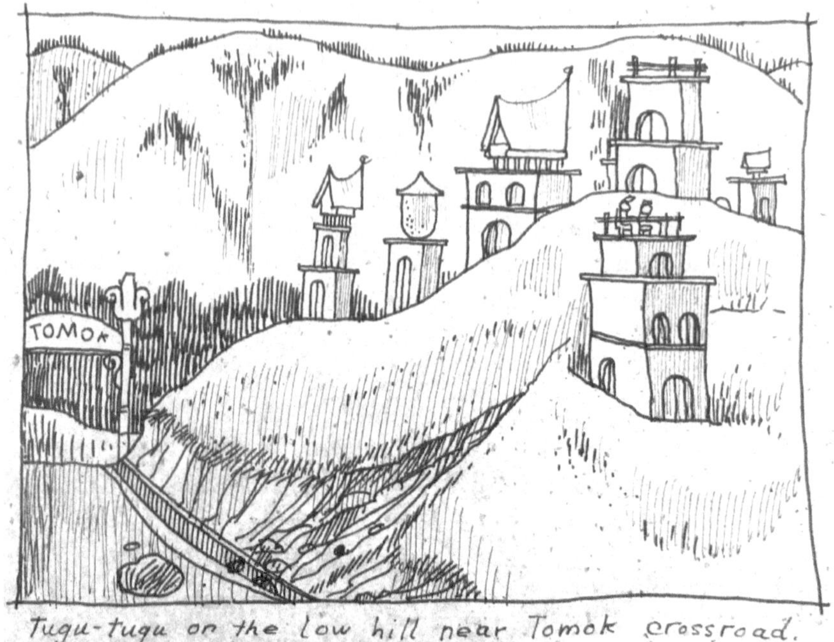

FIGURE 7.4: My second rendition of the same remembered view.

in the second drawing is for me more accurate. Again, it was the combination of the two that communicated the breadth of my original sensual experience.

Drawing All Over Again

The final surrender to a situation of loss of things can take many forms. We might try to replace and rejuvenate what we have lost, or we might try to replicate or recreate, in the exact form and style, those things that are absent. There was no possible way to substitute other things for the ethnographic objects I had bought from friends and craftsmen while on Samosir Island, but perhaps my original drawings, while irreplaceable, could be replicable. When I decided to proceed with this experiment in recall and recreation, it was simply to see what would happen.

As you've seen, my experimental project (admittedly at the margins of legitimate and traditional ethnographic methodology) required me to reconsider the experience of object loss, to rekindle memories of drawn interpretations, and to allow the possibility that other memories, sharp distinct images, could also find their way to paper, even when so far removed from the original moment. Once complete, my task convinced me that recall of visual memory can work just like that of narrative memory—such as used by Leach and Srinivas—when we admit that the ethnographic project is really about telling a compelling story of our honest experiences. Viewers of the visual ethnographic story will create their own meanings since the multi-vocalic system of drawing is simply not didactic in the way that verbal systems can be. Rather than try to compare them or judge them against each other, perhaps we can understand that such story-images are about as literal as a poem is.

The last two images shown here are "flash" images mentally stimulated and illuminated by the act of redrawing the landscape with tombs mentioned above. For reasons unknown, while recreating that picture, I suddenly saw my friend Ito sitting at her kitchen table, wracked by arthritic pain, talking to one after another of her nine children as I tried to get a word in. The more I worked on drawing this new mental image (Figure 7.5), the more I recalled of

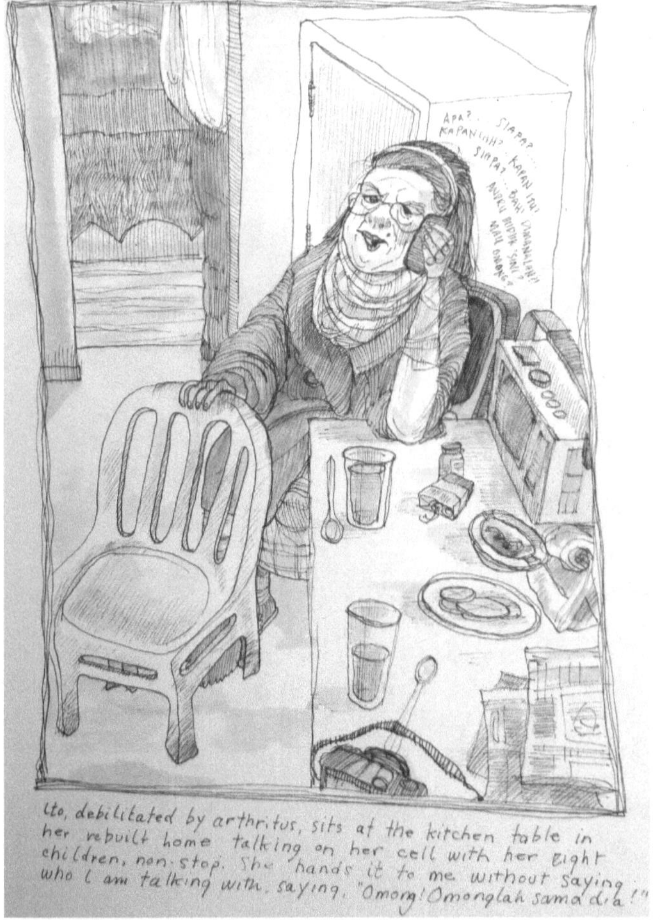

FIGURE 7.5: My drawing of a newly remembered image of Ito.

the moment, as if my mind's eyes were scanning the room to see the objects on the table, her husband Partoho standing outside smoking, and then her face as she handed me her cell phone without telling me who was on the line, saying, "*Omong! Omonglah!*" ("Go ahead and talk! Just talk!).

Immediately linked to this memory, I then saw in my mind an image of us eating lunch, knowing that Ito was sitting at the table separated from the rest of us since she could no longer manage to get down on the fancy floor mat because of her arthritis. I saw the faces of the others sitting around the mat as they attended to her brother-in-law as he smoked and intoned "*Gini Pak Guru . . . Inilah . . .*" ("Here's the way it is, Pak Guru, it's like this . . ."), his idiosyncratic way of introducing listeners to a narration of his skewed view of the world (Figure 7.6).

I present this extended ethnographic example to you here in this book because, interestingly, the ethnographic clarity of these recalled moments, prompted by creating a redrawing of a seemingly distant image, gave me reason to later write about my much richer "observations" in words, adding parenthetical details to my original fieldnotes about these encounters already factually outlined there, but not composed to evoke vibrancy and vitality. The fascinating circuit of

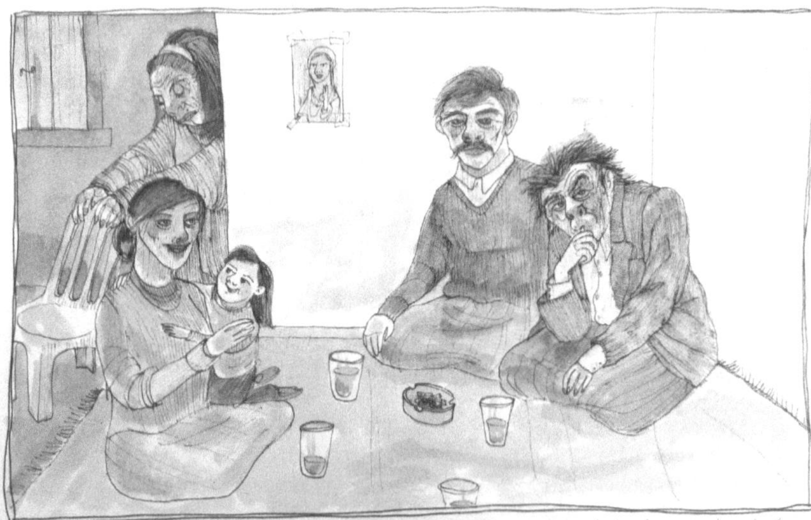

FIGURE 7.6: My drawing of a linked remembered image of eating lunch on the fancy mat.

experiencing, seeing, drawing, losing, redrawing, re-remembering, and finally rewriting suggests to me that there is no single way to "observe" and "participate in" emergent cultural worlds and, more importantly, that there is no single way to document and preserve its incredible complexity.

ETUDE THIRTY-NINE, The Absent Object (5–7 minutes): This last Etude is very simple, but you must be relaxed to do it correctly. Choose an object and place it on the table in front of you. Concentrate your vision on the object, examining it with great care (as you did in Etude Fifteen, Contour Drawing). For about two minutes (yes, that long!), examine its edges, its surfaces, its sense of being and of weight, its textures, and its character and "gesture" calmly but with deep focus. Try to memorize everything about it, and after you have concentrated on the object, remove it so that you can no longer see it. Now draw it in with as much accuracy and detail as you can. (See Figure 7.7 for an example of this exercise: an Indonesian knife handle examined for one minute, then drawn by one of my students from memory.)

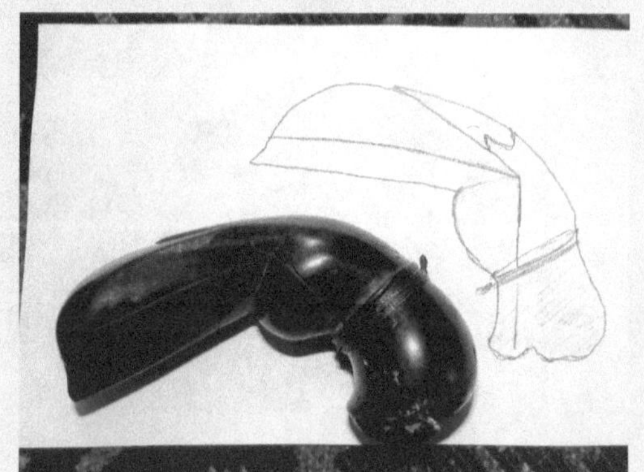

FIGURE 7.7: Student drawing using the memorization technique described in Etude Thirty-Nine (drawing by Steven Santoyo, used with permission).

"Not-there-ness"

There are other kinds of absence (or, if you are willing, "not-there-ness") to see and draw, too. In ethnographic work, insights can come from a variety of other responses to the unseen world. You might try to draw a mythic tale, a spiritual encounter, or someone else's memories based on verbal descriptions given to you by the people you are working with, as did artist-anthropologist Zoe Bray while listening to a story being told about experiences in the Basque countryside during World War II (Figure 7.8). Or you might try depicting

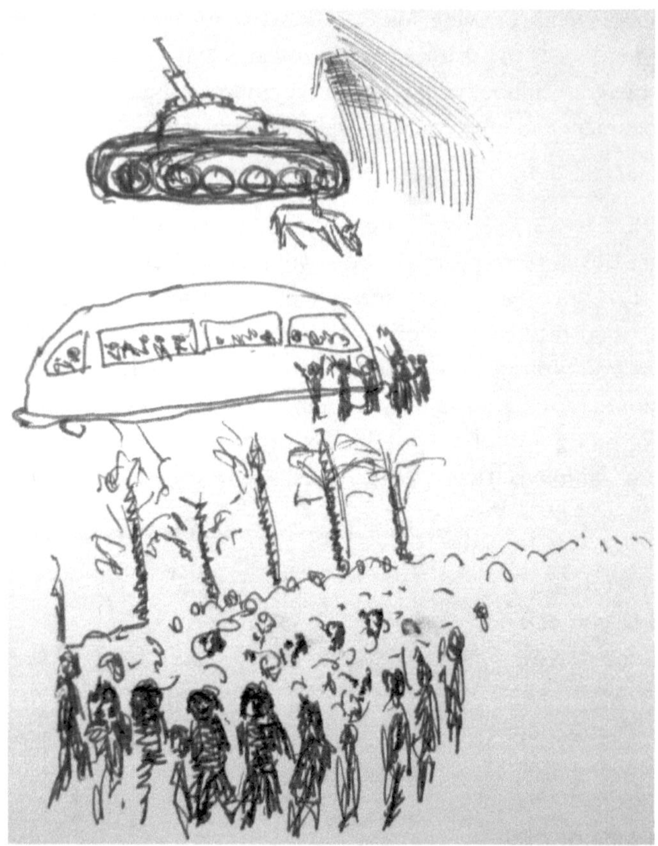

FIGURE 7.8: Zoe Bray's drawing inspired by another's story of memories (http://365days365drawings365dosh.blogspot.com/search?updated-max=2011-10-04T15:01:00-07:00&max-results=20&start=40&by-date=false; used with permission).

images seen in your fieldwork dreams to help you process your sensual and emotional experiences. The value of a deeply experienced event is not always derived from physical perception with the eyes, and a truly enthusiastic ethnographer will recognize that expanding the notion of what "seeing" means, to include other aspects of the sensed world that can be interpreted through line drawing, may open crucial doors for understanding unfamiliar cultural worlds.

Steven Feld, working with the Kaluli people of Papua New Guinea, listened to the songs they sang, songs that created a mental map of a deceased person's life in terms of the local places and landmarks they frequented. In trying to understand the character of these emotion-packed and place-based songs, he drew the maps they created in words, an act that helped him understand the complex relationships they had to their homeland (Feld 1990, 150–56, 193; personal communication).

It's very hard to know how much dreams may inform our ethnographic understandings of cultural worlds, but current research is promising. Iain Edgar's research among dream-work groups in the United Kingdom suggests that group analysis of dream interpretations can increase participants' self-understanding, but more importantly can help form the basis for a group's construction of meaningful ontologies (1999, 41). Arianna Cecconi's work with peasants in the Ayacucho region of the Peruvian Andes, on the other hand, shows that narrating dreams about disappeared relatives could provide a door into an individual's personal and political life story (2011). Dreams are, of course, "seen" in the sense that the events experienced leave a visual trace in the mind of the dreamer, but to what extent can that visual image have self-accuracy when drawn, and consequently, what use will that drawing be to the ethnographer?

In my case, dream drawing was very productive. During my original fieldwork research, I had a strange and very real dream, and when I awoke was confused and rattled. What I remembered was being surrounded by large heads on willowy bodies trying to talk to me. I drew what I could remember but, as is often the case, dream images are fleeting. The picture I made looked like a humorous cartoon, even though I had intended it to be as serious and as slightly ominous as it felt. The important thing for me, however, was that by drawing a fraction of the dream, I was able to fix it in my memory—to give it an anchor. Later, when the topic of the unseen worlds of spirits came up in conversation with my carving teacher Partoho, I asked him what my dream might mean. His answer, whether representative of shared cultural values or idiosyncratic, opened yet another door for me in my ethnographic research, allowing me to explore the broader world of dreams, ghosts, and phantoms and to write about it creatively (Causey 2002). To draw the dream I saw was to save it, then use it as a springboard for continued research.

Last Words

When the world we see and know goes missing or is absent, we need to make sure we don't lose it completely. Leaving behind a vibrant event or ritual is not so devastating if we can feel certain that we can reconstruct it in words and drawings, and losing sight of something in the dark is not so traumatic if we've taught ourselves how to recapture a vision of it in a pencil sketch. In losing objects, however, we are not simply losing the meaning of them; we are not merely losing a metaphorical relationship. We have lost material connection to objects that impact our real lives, and our research. What I've tried to show here is that loss of materiality can be intimately connected to rediscovery of it: of a different materiality, or of a reconstituted access to it through memory and recreation.

CHAPTER 8

FINAL WORDS

The aim of this book has been to introduce you to the simple idea that line drawing can be an effective way to engage in ethnographic research. I've suggested that many of us don't perceive as clearly or deeply as is necessary to gather the quality of data that we want to have, and I've told you that I'm convinced one way to see better is to use the act of drawing to focus your attention. This is not a new idea. But just saying it is not enough. I have tried to show you *how* to do it.

Along the way, I've encouraged you to allow yourself to draw, sometimes by giving you lists that help you get yourself in the right frame of mind (telling you to relax, focus, concentrate, slow down, be accepting, be curious, just *see*, lose your ego temporarily, and practice), and sometimes by reminding you of things you probably already know, like "Drawing is not easy" and "Allow yourself to be mindless," as well as things you might not know, like "Reduce complexity to see" and "Abandon caution." Mostly, what I've tried to prod you to understand is that if you draw in *order* to see, you'll end up being *drawn to see*. Once you've begun to recognize how much more there is to perceive in the world that surrounds you (your own cultural world, and those of others, too), you'll find yourself becoming more curious to investigate its intricacies.

Seeing-drawing can be a transgressive act (you are claiming, after all, to make an accurate visual rendition of the visual world), and that means you must take charge of the work you produce. That doesn't necessarily imply that you can't find some fun in making your drawings, but it does mean that the risks you might decide to take must be based on thoughtful and ethical decisions about the timing and subject matter of your efforts. Whether you are depicting edges, surfaces, motion, or memories, all that you record in your drawings must be respectful and understanding of the lives and traditions of those you interact with. This is no different from the other ethnographic work you do during your research, of course, but drawings can be more direct and more easily "readable" to people you engage with, so perhaps more care is needed in producing these kinds of documents. As long as you remain true to your ethical purpose in gathering ethnographic information visually, your drawings are free to take whatever form you allow.

Whether you decide to use your seeing-drawings merely as a momentary tool to perceive (thus write) more precisely, or as vehicles to get other people talking, as illustrations for your work, or as a kind of playful release, I hope the book, and its Etudes, has been able to help you strengthen your memory and exercise your perceptions.

APPENDIX

Links between ethnographic method and Etude number:

METHOD	ETUDE NUMBER(S)
Participant Observation	15, 17, 19, 20, 25, 33, 38
Artifact Analysis	2, 10, 11, 14, 25, 27, 37, 39
Visual Documentation	2, 6, 7, 9, 18, 19, 20, 22, 33
Focus Group	28, 33, 37, 38
Semistructured Interview (drawings to elicit data)	37, 38, 39
Participatory (collaborative or group drawings)	5, 11, 13, 19, 28, 33, 37
Narrative Creation (using drawing to start)	1, 6, 10, 27, 37, 39
Drawing as Way In (letting locals teach with drawings)	5, 7, 12, 37, 38

REFERENCES

Abel, J., and Madden, M. 2008. *Drawing Words and Writing Pictures: A Definitive Course from Concept to Comic in 15 Lessons*. New York: First Second.

Abel, J., and Madden, M. 2012. *Mastering Comics: Drawing Words and Writing Pictures Continued*. New York: First Second.

Adorno, T.W. 2006. *Towards a Theory of Musical Reproduction* (H. Lonitz, Ed.; W. Hoban, Trans.). Cambridge: Polity Press.

Afonso, A.I., and Ramos, M.J. 2004. New Graphics of Old Stories: Representation of Local Memories through Drawings. In S. Pink, L. Kurti, and A.I. Afonso (Eds.), *Working Images: Visual Research and Representation in Ethnography*, 72–89. London: Routledge.

Anderson, R. 2004. *Calliope's Sisters: A Comparative Study of Philosophies of Art* (2nd ed.). Upper Saddle River: Pearson Prentice Hall.

Anderson, R. 2007. The Biographical Origins of *Political Systems of Highland Burma*. In F. Robinne and M. Sadan (Eds.), *Social Dynamics in the Highlands of Southeast Asia: Reconsidering 'Political Systems of Highland Burma,' by E.R. Leach*, 1–30. Leiden: Koninklijke Brill. http://dx.doi.org/10.1163/ej.9789004160347.i-331.7.

Armstrong, A. 2007. "Visual Literacy/Literary Vision." *American Arts Quarterly*, Summer, 23–28.

Armstrong, R.P. 1971. *The Affecting Presence: An Essay in Humanistic Anthropology*. Urbana: University of Illinois Press.

Arnheim, R. 1969. *Visual Thinking*. London: Faber and Faber Limited.

Asma, S.T. 2001. *Stuffed Animals and Pickled Heads: The Culture and Evolution of Natural History Museums*. Oxford: Oxford University Press.

Bakhtin, M. 1990. In M. Holquist (Ed.), *The Dialogic Imagination: Four Essays by M.M. Bakhtin* (C. Emerson and M. Holquist, Trans.), 259–422. Austin: University of Texas Press.

Bakhtin, M. 1994. In C. Emerson and M. Holquist (Eds.), *Speech Genres and Other Late Essays* (V.W. McGee, Trans.), 60–102. Austin: University of Texas Press.

Ballard, C. 2013. The Return of the Past: On Drawing and Dialogic History. *Asia Pacific Journal of Anthropology*, 14(2), 136–48. http://dx.doi.org/10.1080/14442213.2013.769119

Banks, M., and Morphy, H. 1999. *Rethinking Visual Anthropology*. New Haven, CT: Yale University Press.

Barry, L. 2014. *Syllabus: Notes from an Accidental Professor*. Montreal: Drawn and Quarterly Press.

Barsalou, L.W. 1999. Perceptual Symbol Systems. *Behavioral and Brain Sciences, 22*, 577–660.

Berger, J. 1977. *Ways of Seeing*. London: Penguin Books.

Bonnell, V.E., and Hunt, L. 1999. Introduction. In V.E. Bonnell and L. Hunt (Eds.), *Beyond the Cultural Turn*, 1–34. Berkeley: University of California Press.

Bouquet, M. 2012. *Museums: A Visual Anthropology*. London: Berg.

Bray, Z. 2015. Anthropology with a Paintbrush: Naturalist-Realist Painting as "Thick Description." *Visual Anthropology Review, 31*(2), 119–33. http://dx.doi.org/10.1111/var.12076

Bruhn, M., and Dunkel, V. 2008. The Image as Cultural Technology. In J. Elkins (Ed.), *Visual Literacy*, 165–78. New York: Routledge.

Brunetti, I. 2011. *Cartooning: Philosophy and Practice*. New Haven, CT: Yale University Press.

Campbell, J.M. 1998. *North Alaska Chronicle: Notes from the End of Time. The Simon Paneak Drawings*. Santa Fe: Museum of New Mexico Press.

Causey, A. 2002. Samosir's Dark Rains. In R. Emoff and D. Henderson (Eds.), *Mementos, Artifacts, and Hallucinations from the Ethnographer's Tent*, 17–30. New York: Routledge.

Causey, A. 2003. *Hard Bargaining in Sumatra: Western Tourists and Toba Bataks in the Marketplace of Souvenirs*. Honolulu: University of Hawai'i Press.

Causey, A. 2012. Drawing Flies: Artwork in the Field. *Critical Arts: South-North Cultural and Media Studies, 26*(2), 162–74. http://dx.doi.org/10.1080/02560046.2012.684437

Causey, A. 2015. "You've Got to Draw It If You Want to See It": Drawing as an Ethnographic Method. *Teaching Culture Blog*, February 20. http://utpteachingculture.com/youve-got-to-draw-it-if-you-want-to-see-it-drawing-as-an-ethnographic-method/

Cecconi, A. 2011. Dreams, Memory, and War: An Ethnography of Night in the Peruvian Andes. *Journal of Latin American and Caribbean Anthropology, 16*(2), 401–24. http://dx.doi.org/10.1111/j.1935-4940.2011.01164.x

Chomsky, N. 1968. *Language and the Mind*. New York: Harcourt, Brace, Jovanovich. http://dx.doi.org/10.1037/e400082009-004

Clifford, J. 1988. *The Predicament of Culture: Twentieth-Century Ethnography, Literature, and Art*. Cambridge, MA: Harvard University Press.

Clifford, J., and Marcus, G.E. 1986. *Writing Culture: The Poetics and Politics of Ethnography*. Berkeley: University of California Press.

Collier, J., Jr., and Collier, M. 1986. *Visual Anthropology: Photography as a Research Method*. Albuquerque: University of New Mexico Press.

Colloredo-Mansfeld, R. 1993. The Value of Sketching in Field Research. In *Anthropology UCLA: Special Issue: Partial Knowledges: Theories, Ethics, and Methods of Cultural Research in the 1990s, 20*, 89–103.

Colloredo-Mansfeld, R. 1999. *The Native Leisure Class: Consumption and Cultural Creativity in the Andes*. Chicago: University of Chicago Press.

Colloredo-Mansfeld, R. 2011. Space, Line, and Story in the Invention of an Andean Aesthetic. *Journal of Material Culture, 16*(1), 3–23. http://dx.doi.org/10.1177/1359183510394945

Colwell-Chanthaphonh, C. 2011. Sketching Knowledge: Quandaries in the Mimetic Reproduction of Pueblo Ritual. *American Ethnologist, 38*(3), 451–67. http://dx.doi.org/10.1111/j.1548-1425.2011.01316.x

Cox, R., and Wright, C. 2012. Blurred Visions: Reflecting Visual Anthropology. In R. Fardon, O. Harris, T.H.J. Marchand, M. Nuttall, C. Shore, V. Strang, and R.A. Wilson (Eds.), *The Sage Handbook of Social Anthropology*, Vol. 2, 84–129. Los Angeles: Sage. http://dx.doi.org/10.4135/9781446201077.n41

Crowther, G. 1990. Fieldwork Cartoons. *Cambridge Anthropology, 14*(2), 57–68.

Curtis, G. 2007. *The Cave Painters: Probing the Mysteries of the World's First Artists*. New York: Knopf.

Czerwiec, M.K., Williams, I., Merrill Squier, S., Green, M.J., Myers, K.R., and Smith, S.T. 2015. *Graphic Medicine Manifesto*. University Park: Pennsylvania State University Press.

Dallow, P. 2008. The Visual Complex: Mapping Some Interdisciplinary Dimensions of Visual Literacy. In J. Elkins (Ed.), *Visual Literacy*, 91–104. New York: Routledge.

Dark, P.J.C. 2011. *Craftsmanship and Art: An Anthropological Enquiry into the Conditions for Art*. Shropshire, UK: YouCaxton Publications.

De Brigard, E. 1995. The History of Ethnographic Film. In P. Hockings (Ed.), *Principles of Visual Anthropology*, 13–44. Berlin: Mouton de Gruyter. http://dx.doi.org/10.1515/9783110290691.13

Dicks, A. 2015. Stories from Below: Subject-generated Comics. *Visual Anthropology, 28*(2), 137–54. http://dx.doi.org/10.1080/08949468.2015.973332

Dissanayake, E. 1988. *What Is Art for?* Seattle: University of Washington Press.

Dorst, J.D. 1989. *The Written Suburb: An American Site, an Ethnographic Dilemma*. Philadelphia: University of Pennsylvania Press. http://dx.doi.org/10.9783/9780812208443

Downey, G. 2011. Learning the "Banana-Tree": Self Modification through Movement. In T. Ingold (Ed.), *Redrawing Anthropology: Materials, Movements, Lines*, 77–90. Farnham, UK: Ashgate Publishing.

Durkheim, E. 1982. *The Rules of Sociological Method* (S. Lukes, Ed.; W.D. Halls, Trans.). New York: The Free Press. http://dx.doi.org/10.1007/978-1-349-16939-9

Edgar, L. 1999. Dream Fact and Real Fiction: The Realization of the Imagined Self. *Anthropology of Consciousness, 10*(1), 28–42. http://dx.doi.org/10.1525/ac.1999.10.1.28

Edwards, B. 1979. *Drawing on the Right Side of the Brain: A Course in Enhancing Creativity and Artistic Confidence*. Los Angeles: Tarcher.

Edwards, B. 1986. *Drawing on the Artist Within: An Inspirational and Practical Guide to Increasing Your Creative Powers*. New York: Fireside.

El Guindi, F. 2004. *Visual Anthropology: Essential Method and Theory*. Walnut Creek, CA: Alta Mira Press.

Elkins, J. 1996. *The Object Stares Back: On the Nature of Seeing*. New York: Harvest Books.

Elkins, J. 2008. *Visual Literacy*. New York: Routledge.

Errington, S. 2014. Just Desserts: Basic Food Groups, American Industrial. *Gastronomica: The Journal of Critical Food Studies, 14*(3), 70. doi:10.1525/gfc.2014.14.3.70

Farnell, B., and Wood, R.N. 2001. Performing Precision and Limits of Observation. In T. Ingold (Ed.), *Redrawing Anthropology: Materials, Movements, Lines*, 91–113. Farnham, UK: Ashgate Publishing.

Feld, S. 1990. *Sound and Sentiment: Birds, Weeping, Poetics, and Song in Kaluli Expression* (2nd ed.). Philadelphia: University of Pennsylvania Press.

Forshee, J. 2002. Tracing Troubled Times: Objects of Value and Narratives of Loss from Sumba and Timor Islands. *Indonesia, 74*, 65–77. http://dx.doi.org/10.2307/3351526

Foster, S.N. 2012–13. From Structure to Expression: Rethinking gesture drawing within foundations life drawing. *Foundations in Art: Theory and Education, 34*, 3–10.

Galman, S.C. 2013. *The Good, the Bad, and the Data: Shane the Lone Ethnographer's Basic Guide to Qualitative Data Analysis.* Walnut Creek, CA: Left Coast Press.

Geertz, Clifford. 1973. Thick Description: Toward an Interpretive Theory of Culture. In *The Interpretation of Cultures: Selected Essays*, 3–32. New York: Basic Books.

Geismar, H. 2014. Drawing It Out. *Visual Anthropology Review, 30*(2), 97–113. http://dx.doi.org/10.1111/var.12041

Gell, A. 1999. *The Art of Anthropology: Essays and Diagrams.* London: Athlone Press.

Gibson, J.J. 2015 (1979). *An Ecological Approach to Visual Perception* (2nd ed.). New York: Psychology Press.

Glassie, H. 1999. *Material Culture.* Bloomington: University of Indiana Press.

Glassie, H. 2000. *Vernacular Architecture.* Bloomington: University of Indiana Press.

Grant, J., and Dicks, A. 2014. Perceived Benefits of Freirean and Grassroots Comics Workshops within Three Bushmen Communities. *Communitas, 19*, 116–35.

Griffiths, A. 1996. Knowledge and Visuality in Turn of the Century Anthropology: The Early Ethnographic Cinema of Alfred Cort Haddon and Walter Baldwin Spencer. *Visual Anthropology Review, 12*(2), 18–43. http://dx.doi.org/10.1525/var.1996.12.2.18

Grimshaw, A. 2001. *The Ethnographer's Eye: Ways of Seeing in Modern Anthropology.* Cambridge: Cambridge University Press.

Grimshaw, A. 2005. Reconfiguring the Ground: Art and the Visualization of Anthropology. In M. Mestermann (Ed.), *Anthropologies of Art*, 195–220. Williamstown: Clark Art Institute.

Grimshaw, A., and Ravetz, A. 2005. Introduction. In A. Grimshaw and A. Ravetz (Eds.), *Visualizing Anthropology*, 1–16. Bristol: Intellect.

Guss, D.M. 1989. *To Weave and Sing: Art, Symbol, and Narrative in the South American Rain Forest.* Berkeley: University of California Press.

Hallam, E., and Ingold, T. 2007. *Creativity and Cultural Improvisation.* Oxford: Berg.

Hasse, C. 2015. *An Anthropology of Learning: On Nested Frictions in Cultural Ecologies.* New York: Springer. http://dx.doi.org/10.1007/978-94-017-9606-4

Heinz, C.B. 2006. Documenting the Image in Mithila Art. *Visual Anthropology Review, 22*(2), 5–33.

Hendrickson, C. 1995. *Weaving Identities: Construction of Dress and Self in a Highland Guatemalan Town.* Austin: University of Texas Press.

Hendrickson, C. 2008. Visual Field Notes: Drawing Insights in the Yucatan. *Visual Anthropology Review, 24*(2), 117–32. http://dx.doi.org/10.1111/j.1548-7458.2008.00009.x

Henry, K. 2012. *Drawing for Product Designers.* London: Laurence King Publishing.

Holm, B. 1965. *Northwest Coast Indian Art: An Analysis of Form.* Seattle: University of Washington Press.

Holmes, H. 1878. *Spohr's Violin School, Revised and Edited.* London: Boosey and Company.

Hunter, W.C. 2012. The Drawing Methodology in Tourism Research. In T. Rakic and D. Chambers (Eds.), *An Introduction to Visual Research Methods in Tourism*, 126–49. London: Routledge.

Ingold, T. 2007. *Lines: A Brief History*. London: Routledge.

Ingold, T. (Ed.). 2011. *Redrawing Anthropology: Materials, Movements, Lines*. Farnham, UK: Ashgate Publishing.

Ingold, T. 2013. *Making: Anthropology, Archaeology, Art and Architecture*. London: Routledge.

Jahoda, G. 1999. *Images of Savages: Ancient Roots of Modern Prejudice in Western Culture*. London: Routledge.

Jay, M. 1999. Must Justice Be Blind? The Challenge of Images to the Law. In C. Douzinas and L. Nead (Eds.), *Law and the Image: The Authority of Art and the Aesthetics of Law*, 19–35. Chicago: University of Chicago Press.

Jenny, P. 2012. *The Artist's Eye*. New York: Princeton Architectural Press.

John-Steiner, V. 1985. *Notebooks of the Mind: Explorations of Thinking*. Albuquerque: University of New Mexico Press.

Kantrowitz, A. 2012a. Drawn to Discover: A Cognitive Perspective. *Tracey/Journal: Drawing Knowledge*, May, 1–13. https://www.academia.edu/1593263/Drawn_to_Discover_a_cognitive_perspective.

Kantrowitz, A. 2012b. The Man Behind the Curtain: What Cognitive Science Reveals about Drawing. *Journal of Aesthetic Education*, *46*(1), 1–14. http://dx.doi.org/10.5406/jaesteduc.46.1.0001

Kleon, A. 2012. *Steal Like an Artist: 10 Things Nobody Told You about Being Creative*. New York: Workman Publishing.

Kuschnir, K. 2014. Teaching Anthropologists to Draw: A Didactic Research Experience. *Cadernos de Arte e Antropologia*, *3*(2), 23–46. http://dx.doi.org/10.4000/cadernosaa.506

Lakoff, G., and Johnson, M. 2003. *Metaphors We Live By*. Chicago: University of Chicago Press.

Langer, S.K. 1957. *Problems of Art*. New York: Charles Scribner's Sons.

Lavata, T. 2005. Talking Dog Archeology. *Archaeological Reports*, 5(5), 22–26.

Lavata, T. 2007. Hoax at Piltdown. In *Inauthentic Archaeologies: Public Uses and Abuses of the Past*, 31–48. Walnut Creek, CA: Left Coast Press.

Levi-Strauss, C. 2006. Split Representation in the Art of Asia and America. In H. Morphy and M. Perkins (Eds.), *The Anthropology of Art: A Reader*, 56–73. Malden, MA: Blackwell Publishing.

Lewis-Williams, D. 2003. *The Mind in the Cave*. London: Thames and Hudson.

London, P. 1989. *No More Secondhand Art: Awakening the Artist Within*. Boston: Shambala.

Lutz, C.A., and Collins, J.L. 1993. *Reading National Geographic*. Chicago: University of Chicago Press.

MacDougall, D. 2006. *Film, Ethnography, and the Senses: The Corporeal Image*. Princeton, NJ: Princeton University Press.

Malafouris, L. 2013. *How Things Shape the Mind: A Theory of Material Engagement*. Cambridge, MA: MIT Press.

Malin, E. 1999. *Northwest Coast Indian Painting: House Fronts and Interior Screens*. Portland, OR: Timber Press.

Manghani, S. 2013. *Image Studies: Theory and Practice*. London: Routledge.
Maslen, M., and Southern, J. 2011. *Drawing Projects: An Exploration of the Language of Drawing*. London: Black Dog Publishing.
Mavers, D. 2011. *Children's Drawing and Writing: The Remarkable in the Unremarkable*. New York: Routledge.
Maxwell, A. 1999. *Colonial Photography and Exhibitions: Representations of the Native and the Making of European Identities*. Leicester: Leicester University Press.
McNiff, S. 2000. *Art-based Research*. London: Jessica Kingsley Publishers.
Mead, M. 1995. Visual Anthropology in a Discipline of Words. In P. Hockings (Ed.), *Principles of Visual Anthropology*, 3–12. Berlin: Mouton de Gruyter. (Original work published 1975). http://dx.doi.org/10.1515/9783110290691.3
Menke, C. 1998. *The Sovereignty of Art: Aesthetic Negativity in Adorno and Derrida* (N. Solomon, Trans.). Cambridge, MA: MIT Press.
Messenger, J.C. 1975. The Carver in Anang Society. In Warren L. d'Azevedo (Ed.), *The Traditional Artist in African Societies*, 101–27. Bloomington: Indiana University Press.
Miller, D., and Parrott, F. 2009. Loss and Material Culture in South London. *Journal of the Royal Anthropological Institute*, *15*(3), 502–19. http://dx.doi.org/10.1111/j.1467-9655.2009.01570.x
Mitchell, W.J.T. 1987. *Iconology: Image, Text, Ideology*. Chicago: University of Chicago Press.
Mitchell, W.J.T. 1994. *Picture Theory*. Chicago: University of Chicago Press.
Morphy, H. 1994. From Dull to Brilliant: The Aesthetics of Spiritual Power among the Yolngu. In J. Coote and A. Shelton (Eds.), *Anthropology, Art, and Aesthetics*, 21–40. Oxford: Clarendon Press.
Morton, T. 2013. *Realist Magic: Objects, Ontology, Causality*. Ann Arbor, MI: Open Humanities Press. http://dx.doi.org/10.3998/ohp.13106496.0001.001
Mueller, P.A., and Oppenheimer, D.M. 2014. The Pen Is Mightier than the Keyboard: Advantages of Longhand over Laptop Note Taking. *Psychological Science*, *25*(6), 1159–68. http://dx.doi.org/10.1177/0956797614524581
Murray, J.A.H. (Ed.). 1971. *The Compact Edition of the Oxford Dictionary English Language*. Oxford: Oxford University Press.
Narayan, K. 2012. *Alive in the Writing: Crafting Ethnography in the Company of Chekhov*. Chicago: University of Chicago Press. http://dx.doi.org/10.7208/chicago/9780226567921.001.0001
Ness, S. 1992. *Body, Movement, and Culture: Kinesthetic and Visaul Symbolism in a Philippine Community*. Philadelphia: University of Pennsylvania Press.
Niessen, S. 2009. *Legacy in Cloth: Batak Textiles of Indonesia*. Leiden: KITLV Press.
Nicolaides, K. 1969. *The Natural Way to Draw*. Boston: Houghton Mifflin Co.
Ottenberg, S. 1990. Thirty Years of Fieldnotes: Changing Relationships to the Text. In R. Sanjak (Ed.), *Fieldnotes: The Makings of Anthropology*, 139–60. Ithaca, NY: Cornell University Press.
Peirce, C.S. 1998. *The Essential Peirce: Selected Philosophical Writings, Volume 2 (1893–1913)*, edited by The Peirce Edition Project. Bloomington: Indiana University Press.
Price, R., and Price, S. 1992. *Equitoria (with Sketches by Sally Price)*. New York: Routledge.
Rakic, T., and Chambers, D. 2012. *An Introduction to Visual Research Methods in Tourism*. London: Routledge.

Ramamurthy, A. 2003. *Imperial Persuaders: Images of Africa and Asia in British Advertising.* Manchester: Manchester University Press.

Reichel-Dolmatoff, G. 1978. Drug-induced Optical Sensations and Their Relationship to Applied Art among Some Colombian Indians. In M. Greenhalgh and V. Megaw (Eds.), *Art in Society: Studies in Style, Culture, and Aesthetics*, 289–304. New York: St. Martin's Press.

Rohde, M. 2013. *The Sketchnote Handbook: The Illustrated Guide to Visual Note Taking.* San Francisco: Peachpit Publishers.

Rosenberg, T. 2008. New Beginnings and Monstrous Births: Notes Towards an Appreciation of Ideational Drawing. In S. Garner (Ed.), *Writing on Drawing: Essays on Drawing Practice and Research*, 109–24. Bristol: Intellect.

Ruby, J. 2000. *Picturing Culture: Explorations of Film and Anthropology*. Chicago: University of Chicago Press.

Rumsfeld, D. 2011. *Known and Unknown: A Memoir.* New York: Penguin.

Sanjak, R. 1990a. Fire, Loss, and the Sorcerer's Apprentice. In R. Sanjak (Ed.), *Fieldnotes: The Makings of Anthropology*, 34–44. Ithaca, NY: Cornell University Press.

Sanjak, R. 1990b. A Vocabulary for Fieldnotes. In R. Sanjak (Ed.), *Fieldnotes: The Makings of Anthropology*, 92–121. Ithaca, NY: Cornell University Press.

Schiffer, M.B. (with A.R. Miller). 2009. *The Material Life of Human Beings: Artifacts, Behavior, and Communication.* London: Routledge.

Schifrin, S. 2008. Visual Literacy in North American Secondary Schools: Arts-centered Learning, the Classroom, and Visual Literacy. In J. Elkins (Ed.), *Visual Literacy*, 105–28. New York: Routledge.

Schmandt-Besserat, D. 2007. *When Writing Met Art: From Symbol to Story.* Austin: University of Texas Press.

Schneider, A., and Wright, C. (Eds.). 2010. *Between Art and Anthropology: Contemporary Ethnographic Practice.* Oxford: Berg.

Schneider, A., and Wright, C. 2013. *Anthropology and Art Practice.* London: Bloomsbury Academic Press.

Sheets-Johnstone, M. 2011. The Imaginative Consciousness of Movement: Linear Quality, Kinaesthesia, Language, and Life. In T. Ingold (Ed.), *Redrawing Anthropology: Materials, Movements, Lines*, 115–28. Farnham, UK: Ashgate Publishing.

Silver, L. 2006. *Peasant Scenes and Landscapes: The Rise of Pictorial Genres in the Antwerp Art Market.* Philadelphia: University of Pennsylvania Press. http://dx.doi.org/10.9783/9780812207439

Slemmons, R. 1989. *Shadowy Evidence: The Photography of Edward S. Curtis and His Contemporaries.* Seattle: Seattle Art Museum Press.

Smith, J. 2006. *Charles Darwin and Victorian Visual Culture.* Cambridge: Cambridge University Press.

Smith, K.A. 1992. *Structure of the Visual Book (Book 95), the Revised and Expanded Edition.* Fairport: Sigma Foundation.

Sousanis, N. 2015. *Unflattening.* Cambridge, MA: Harvard University Press.

Spivey, N. 2005. *How Art Made the World: A Journey to the Origins of Human Creativity.* New York: Basic Books.

Srinivas, M.N. 1976. *The Remembered Village.* Berkeley: University of California Press.

Stafford, B.M. 2001. *Visual Analogy: Consciousness as the Art of Connecting*. Cambridge, MA: MIT Press.

Stafford, B.M. 2007. *Echo Objects: The Cognitive Work of Images*. Chicago: University of Chicago Press.

Stafford, B.M. 2008. The Remaining 10 Percent: The Role of Sensory Knowledge in the Age of the Self-organizing Brain. In J. Elkins (Ed.), *Visual Literacy*, 31–58. New York: Routledge.

Steiner, C. 1995. Travel Engravings and the Construction of the Primitive. In E. Barkan and R. Bush (Eds.), *Prehistories of the Future: The Primitivist Project and the Culture of Modernism*, 202–25. Stanford, CA: Stanford University Press.

Stewart, K. 1996. *A Space on the Side of the Road: Cultural Poetics in an "Other" America*. Princeton, NJ: Princeton University Press.

Stewart, K. 2010. Atmospheric Attunements. *Rubric*, 1, 14.

Stewart, S. 1993. *On Longing: Narratives of the Miniature, the Gigantic, the Souvenir, the Collection*. Durham, NC: Duke University Press.

Sturken, M., and Cartwright, L. 2003. *Practices of Looking: An Introduction to Visual Culture*. Oxford: Oxford University Press.

Sturtevant, W. 1974. *Boxes and Bowls: Decorated Containers by Nineteenth-Century Haida, Tlingit, Bella Bella, and Tsimshian Indian Artists*. Washington, DC: Smithsonian Institution Press.

Suhrbier, M. 2004. *To Be Made and To Be Drawn* (Vol. 21). Indiana: The Twofold Existence of Objects.

Summerfield, A., and Sutan Madjo Indo, H.A. 1999. Motifs and Their Meanings. In A. Summerfield and J. Summerfield (Eds.), *Walking in Splendor: Ceremonial Dress and the Minangkabau*, 171–99. Los Angeles: UCLA Fowler Museum of Cultural History Textile Series, No. 4.

Taleb, N.N. 2007. *The Black Swan: The Impact of the Highly Improbable*. New York: Random House.

Taussig, M. 2011. *I Swear I Saw This: Drawings in Fieldwork Notebooks, Namely My Own*. Chicago: University of Chicago Press. http://dx.doi.org/10.7208/chicago/9780226789842.001.0001

Taylor, L. 1996. Iconophobia: How Anthropology Lost It at the Movies. *Transition*, *69*(69), 64–88. http://dx.doi.org/10.2307/2935240

Theron, L., Mitchell, C., Smith, A., and Stuart, J. (Eds.). 2011. *Picturing Research: Drawing as Visual Methodology*. Rotterdam: Sense Publishers. http://dx.doi.org/10.1007/978-94-6091-596-3

Tomaselli, K. 1996. *Appropriating Images: The Semiotics of Visual Representation*. Holbjerg: Intervention Press.

Topper, D. 1996. Towards an Epistemology of Scientific Illustration. In B.S. Baigrie (Ed.), *Picturing Knowledge: Historical and Philosophical Problems Concerning the Use of Art in Science*, 215–49. Toronto: University of Toronto Press.

Vannini, P. 2015. *Non-Representational Methodologies: Re-envisioning Research*. New York: Routledge.

Wade, N., and Swanston, M. 2001. *Visual Perception: An Introduction* (2nd ed.). Hove: Psychology Press.

Walker, M. 2000. *The Lexicon of Comicana*. Lincoln: iUniverse.

Washabaugh, W. 2008. Philosophical Bases for Visual Multiculturalism at the College Level. In J. Elkins (Ed.), *Visual Literacy*, 129–44. New York: Routledge.

Webb, V.-L. 1995. Photographs of Papua New Guinea: American Expeditions 1928–29. *Pacific Arts, 11/12* (July): 72–81.

Weber, M. 1969. *The Theory of Social and Economic Behavior.* New York: The Free Press.

Weiner, A.B. 1992. *Inalienable Possessions: The Paradox of Keeping-while-giving.* Berkeley: University of California Press. http://dx.doi.org/10.1525/california/9780520076037.001.0001

Weir, R. 1998. *Leonardo's Ink Bottle: The Artist's Way of Seeing.* Berkeley, CA: Celestial Arts.

Werker, J.F., and Gervain, J. 2010. Speech Perception and Language Acquisition in the First Year of Life. *Annual Review of Psychology*, *61*, 191–218. http://dx.doi.org/10.1146/annurev.psych.093008.100408

Willats, J. 1997. *Art and Representation: New Principles in the Analysis of Pictures.* Princeton, NJ: Princeton University Press.

Williams, H.C. 2002. *Drawing as a Sacred Activity: Simple Steps to Explore Your Feelings and Heal Your Consciousness.* Novato: New World Library.

Williams, I. 2015. *The Bad Doctor: The Troubled Life and Times of Dr. Iwan James.* University Park: Pennsylvania State University Press.

Wilson, M. 2002. Six Views of Embodied Cognition. *Psychonomic Bulletin & Review*, *9*(4), 625–36. http://dx.doi.org/10.3758/BF03196322

Wolcott, H.F. 1995. *The Art of Fieldwork.* Walnut Creek, CA: Alta Mira.

Wolfegg, C.W. 1998. *Venus and Mars: The World of the Medieval Housebook.* Munich: Prestel.

Wood, R.J.G. c.1880. *The Natural History of Man.* New York: Home Book Company.

INDEX

Figures indicated by page numbers in italics

www.ingramcontent.com/pod-product-compliance
Lightning Source LLC
LaVergne TN
LVHW090808070826
844660LV00022B/1122

* 9 7 8 1 4 4 2 6 3 6 6 5 1 *